PIE CAMP

PIE CAMP

The Skills You Need to Make Any Pie You Want

Kate McDermott

THE COUNTRYMAN PRESS

A Division of W. W. Norton & Company

Independent Publishers Since 1923

For my sister Helen

For information about permission to reproduce selections
from this book, write to Permissions, The Countryman Press,
500 Fifth Avenue, New York, NY 10110

For information about special discounts for bulk purchases,
please contact W. W. Norton Special Sales at
specialsales@wwnorton.com or 800-233-4830

Manufacturing by RR Donnelley Asia Printing Solutions Limited
Book design by Nick Caruso Design
Production manager: Devon Zahn

The Countryman Press
www.countrymanpress.com

A division of W. W. Norton & Company, Inc.
500 Fifth Avenue, New York, NY 10110

www.wwnorton.com
978-1-68268-413-9

10 9 8 7 6 5 4 3 2 1

"Find something you're passionate about
and keep tremendously interested in it." —Julia Child

"Damn good pie!" —Dale Cooper, *Twin Peaks*, 1990

Contents

Welcome to Pie Camp! I am so happy you are here.

You've probably heard the phrase, "Easy as pie," and wondered, can that be true? Well, I can tell you from my own experience as a lifelong home baker, that yes, these words really are true. There's no secret to pie making except one, and I'm going to share that with you right now. You don't need to know all that much to make a darn good pie! Once you learn the basic techniques of dough and filling, you are on your way to making whatever pie you can imagine. My goal is to give you the confidence and knowledge to do just that—to make any pie you want.

In these pages, I will show you how to make roll-out doughs using all-purpose or gluten-free flour, how to adapt them for those who are vegetarian or vegan, and how to make super simple press-in cookie crumb crusts. Fruits of every kind will go into our fillings, and I will show you a simple-to-learn formula for any fruit pie that can be finished off with a top crust, latticed, topped with pre-baked designs using cookie cutters, or baked open faced. I will share with you how I make a lofty meringue, light and billowy flavored whipped cream, and crumble toppings. You'll learn to make cool and luscious cream pies, refreshing chiffons perfect for hot summer days, and old-time custard pies that can be made from the most basic ingredients likely on hand in your cupboard and icebox right now. Then, you'll see how easy it is to put your own flavor spin in a filling by using the seasonings that you like. It's your pie, right?

All of these can be made in pie pans of all different sizes—some big, some small, and sometimes without any at all. But let's not stop there. For special celebrations when multiple pies might be needed, I'll break down the steps and stages so you won't have to do everything at the last minute. And for those times when a full-size pie might be more than you need, I'll show you how to size down your dough and filling to make a pie-let for just one or two. Plus, you'll find recipes for homemade ice cream, too, so you can place the à la mode on a slice, a crisp or crumble, or an old-fashioned pan-dowdy, which is a baked fruit dessert you may not know about that is topped with a pie dough.

After decades of making, baking, teaching, and writing about pie, I still can say that I am absolutely enamored with it. It has become my vocation, and like the lattice strips that top a seasonal fruit filling, my life and work have intersected. I have taught over 4,000 pie campers, from beginners of all ages making their very first pie to well-practiced professionals.

As I write these words, our world is upended in the middle of the COVID-19 pandemic. We shelter in place, protecting our world, communities, and loved ones, as just about everything that we once took for granted has been put on hold. Activities of self-reliance and centering have come into the spotlight. Pie making is one of them. It can bring calm to the most stressful of times, as it did when my grandmother Geeg suffered a stroke. As I described in *Art of the Pie*, at that moment I quickly handed her a bowl and ingredients and she began to make pie—a skill that she taught me and that I, in turn, taught my son and her great-grandson, Duncan.

Now, it's your turn to join the unbroken line of the generations of pie makers who have come before us. No matter what your age or skill level, whether it's your first or thousandth pie, put on your apron, get out your rolling pin, and come join me at the Pie Camp baking counter.

A Very Brief History of Pie

In the simplest of terms, pie is dough encasing a filling, which is then baked. It may be the ultimate international food, as it is enjoyed in almost every cuisine. To quote from *The Oxford Companion to Sugar and Sweets*, "Wrapping food in dough before cooking is a very ancient and widespread practice," and one "the ancient Greeks and Romans enjoyed." The first mentions of pie in the English-speaking world show up around the turn of the 14th century. I can imagine my funeral director father chuckling to learn that in 15th-century medieval Europe, "fair little [baked] coffyns" were used to preserve and store food—think the original Tupperware here.

As fascinating and long a history as pie in Europe has, let us jump over the pond to North America in the 17th century, when the first permanent English settlement was established. Along with their hopes and dreams, they brought their recipes for pies, both sweet and savory. Sweet apple pies were among those recipes, but the "receipts," as they were called then, were quickly adapted to make use of new world foods such as squash and cranberries.

Leapfrogging again nearly 200 years to the late 1800s, we arrive at one of pie's less than happy moments, when Wilbur O. Atwater sought to demonize the "wasteful" food traditions of working class immigrants to America with his venture called the New England Kitchen. Sarah Tyson Rorer, the influential food editor of *Ladies' Home Journal*, championed his ideas and went so far as to say, "All forms of so-called pie are to be condemned." Thank goodness the movement lost favor, as pie for breakfast, pie for lunch, and pie for dinner provided standard fare for farming families who made up the backbone of America.

All across America, there are regional favorites and "official" state pies. But as apples originated in Central Asia, and wheat was first cultivated in northern Iran and sugar in Asia, and spices came from Indonesia, the phrase, "as American as apple pie," is truly representative of the international melting pot of our country. As centuries old as the history of pie is, it is with the continued making and sharing of home-baked pie set upon our table that we keep this craft alive for future generations.

A Few Thoughts about Clean and Tidy

You might glance around your kitchen, after a particularly creative pie-making session, to find every counter covered with ingredients, spills, a sink full of bowls and utensils, and a floor sporting the latest in fillings and dough trimmings. When all you want to do is sit down, this can feel overwhelming. Sixty plus years of baking has brought me to the realization that no magic fairy is going to come in to put things back in order with the wave of a wand. I've found that multiple small cleanups take just about the same amount of time when added together as one great big cleanup at the end. I try—and let me emphasize the word *try* because I'm not always successful—to clean and tidy up a few times while making a pie.

- The first is after a dough-making session. I put ingredients away, give a quick wipe down of the counter, and sweep the floor.

- The second is after the filling is made. Once again, ingredients are put away, pots, pans, bowls, and utensils are rinsed, washed, and put away, followed by a second counter wipe.

- The final tidy is after I've rolled out the dough and constructed the pie. If I have done the first two tidy-ups, there are just a few things left needing my attention—bowl, rolling pin, a utensil or two, a final wipe of the counters, and a sweep of the floor.

Now I can sit down and enjoy a cup of tea, catch up on emails, or read a book while I wait for my pie to bake.

I keep my basic pie-making equipment in one place, so I don't have to hunt through drawers for measuring spoons and my lattice strip cutter. After each baking session, I wash and put them back in a basket, cover with a cloth, and stow it away underneath my baking counter. When I do this, I know that everything is right where it should be when I start a new baking session.

Pie
Ingred

Tools &
ients

Kate's Seven Essential Pie Tools

1.
Hands

2.
Bowl

3.
Spoon

4.
Flat surface

5.
Cylinder for rolling dough

6.
Pan

7.
Reliable oven

Pie Tools

Our hands are our most basic tools, and their sensitivity lets us check texture and temperature. But there are other tools that we will use to make our pies, the most basic of which are a bowl, a spoon, a flat surface, a cylinder for rolling out dough, a pie pan, and a reliable oven.

Invest in the best equipment you can and treat it with care so you can pass it on. I still have a few mixing spoons that my grandmother and my mom used, and they bring to mind many happy memories when I use them.

My Basics

Very fine pies can be made with just clean hands, a bowl for mixing, and a cylinder for rolling. But over the years I've added a few more items to my pie-maker's tool kit. Here's what you'll find in mine:

SPOON: The spoon is probably the most basic and versatile tool ever created. I have spoons of all sizes and shapes. Some have long handles. Others have round, oval, deep, or shallow cups. I use a spoon on a daily basis for stirring custards, mixing fillings, and taking tastes. Handmade wooden spoons make wonderful gifts for a pie maker, or anyone for that matter.

BOWL: Use a bowl that you can easily fit both your hands in. I find a 6-quart size great for many baking tasks.

MEASURING: When I was a little girl, I learned to measure with a coffee cup from the shelf, and with spoons—both tea and table—from the cutlery drawer. After making thousands of pies, I can gauge what a pinch of salt looks and feels like in the palm of my hand; feel if a dough may need a bit more water; and when, by sight, smell, and sound, a pie is baked and ready to come out of the oven. In time, I think you will, too. For our recipes here, though, we'll use some standard equipment. Measurements are in both US standard and metric and easily readable.

With Cups:

- For dry ingredients like flour and sugar, use stainless steel nesting cups in ¼-, ⅓-, ½-, and 1-cup sizes. Use the back of a knife to sweep off extra dry ingredients so that they are level with the top of a stainless steel cup. This is called the dip and sweep method.
- For liquid ingredients like water, milk, half-and-half, and cream, use glass measuring cups with a spout in 1-, 2-, and 4-cup sizes. Read a glass cup from the side.

With Spoons: Use a stainless steel set in sizes ⅛, ¼, ½, 1 teaspoon, and 1 tablespoon. The handle should be engraved with both US standard and metric measurements and easily readable. If a recipe calls for both a teaspoon of cinnamon and a teaspoon of vanilla extract, you might want to have two sets so you can easily switch between dry and wet ingredients.

With a Digital Scale: I wasn't raised to be a precise measurer, but I do like using a battery-operated digital scale more than I ever thought I would because of its accuracy. I also have fewer dishes to wash up when using a digital scale because I can add ingredients directly into the bowl I've placed on top of the scale instead of using measuring cups and spoons. Look for a scale that weighs in ounces, pounds, grams, and milliliters, and has a tare option that allows you to zero out the weight of the vessels for all those ingredients as they are added.

PASTRY FORK: Large with wide tines. Nice for mixing and fluffing dough.

RUBBER SPATULA: In *The Fannie Farmer Cookbook* (1979), Marion Cunningham says, "Almost better than the human hand, a rubber spatula scrapes absolutely clean so there's no waste." I have at least four, from mini to large.

KNIVES: Good-quality knives are indispensable to the pie maker. There are three that I reach for regularly:

- A small paring knife
- A 6- to 8-inch utility knife
- A serrated knife for slicing citrus

A sharp knife is a safer knife, as it can slice through fruit more easily. A dull knife requires more force and may be harder to control when cutting sturdy fruit like an apple. Keep a sharp edge on your knives with a steel or knife sharpener. Hand wash and store safely.

MEZZALUNA: Instead of a pastry blender with all those tines that dough can get stuck in-between, I use this single-bladed tool that's shaped like a half-moon. With only one blade, nothing gets stuck.

CUTTING MAT OR BOARD: I use lightweight plastic cutting mats that can pop in the dishwasher for cleanup.

CANNING JAR: One of the first things I do when making dough is fill a canning jar with ice water. (After I've measured out the water I need for my dough, I add a squeeze of lemon and a teaspoon of sugar for a sip of pie maker's lemonade.) We'll use the canning jar lids when we make Canning Lid Pies (page 131).

SIEVE STRAINERS: I use a small 3-inch (8 cm) strainer to keep out any stray ice chips when

cooling rack

sugar shaker

cookie cutters

vegetable peeler

silicone brush

wooden spoon

spatula

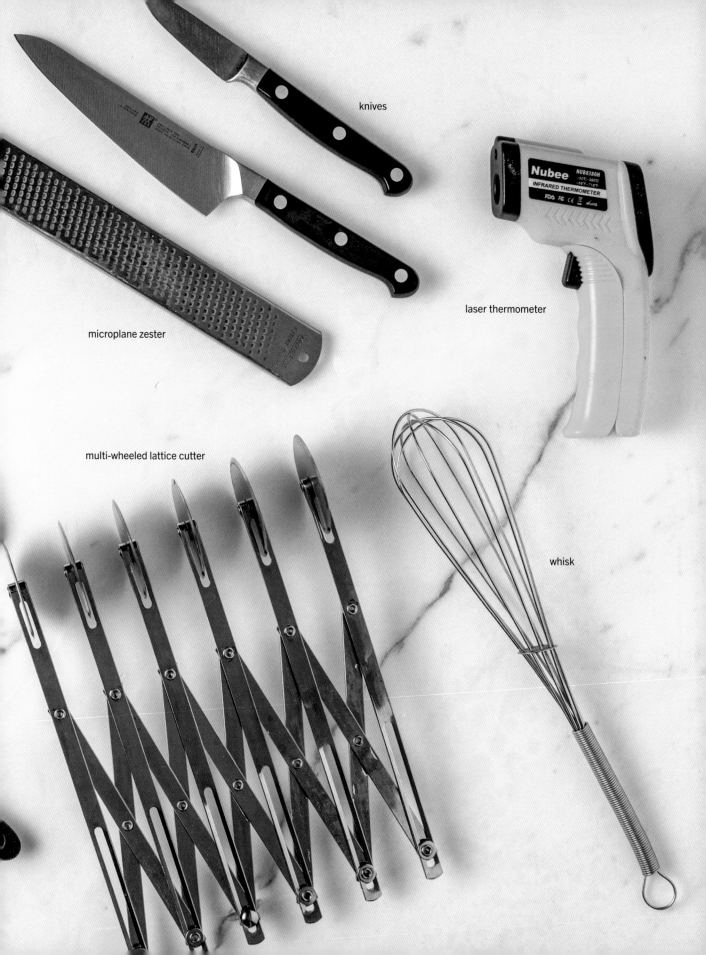

knives

laser thermometer

microplane zester

multi-wheeled lattice cutter

whisk

mezzaluna

rolling pins

towel

pastry fork

measuring cups and spoons

pastry cutter

digital scale

sieve strainer

canning jar for water

pastry cloth

bench scraper

pastry brush

adding ice water to pie dough. A large 8-inch (20 cm) strainer is useful in catching any solids that may have formed when cooking custard.

ROLLING PIN: Rolling pin choices include the classic two-handled pin, or a dowel pin that can be straight or tapered. Rolling pins can be made from wood, marble, stainless steel, nylon, or silicone. All will work. Choosing your pin can feel a bit like receiving a wand in Harry Potter. After picking up and holding a wide variety of pins at a kitchen store one afternoon, a wooden French-tapered dowel pin is the one that chose me. It fits the size of my hand perfectly, and I like the control I get with it when I roll out a dough made with all-purpose flour, although I do use a classic two-handled straight pin for gluten-free dough. And, yes, in a pinch you can use a wine bottle.

PASTRY CLOTH: It is easy to roll out dough on a pastry cloth, and extra flour filters down into the weave. They can be made of heavy cotton, denim, or canvas. I've met pie bakers who have told me that they use a pillowcase, tablecloth, or smooth kitchen towel. After scraping off leftover dough bits and flour, I place mine in a plastic bag and store in the freezer. When soiled with fruit or filling, machine or hand wash in cold water without soap, and rinse several times. If the edges roll up, unfold them while still moist as best you can. Air dry.

PIE PAN: Standard for most recipes is a 9-inch (23 cm) deep or shallow pie pan. Mini-pie pans can serve one or two.

- Glass transfers heat quickly and evenly and lets you see the sides and bottom, which is helpful in gauging if the dough is baked. I use these regularly with very good results. When removing a hot pie from the oven,

be sure to place the pan on a towel or pot holder to avoid the pan possibly shattering. I know that shattering sounds dramatic, but it has happened to me.

- If using metal, look for a dark pan, as it will brown crusts best; shiny pans will deflect heat and crusts may not brown as well.

- Ceramic pans take longer to heat up but hold heat longer so your pie will continue to bake for a time after it comes out of the oven. You will have your choice of many lovely colors, too.

- Disposable aluminum pie tins are nice to have if you like to give pies away or take part in competitions where your favorite pie pan may not be returned. I suggest setting this pan on a preheated sheet pan to help get that bottom crust baked.

BENCH SCRAPER: You'll find this tool very helpful for removing bits of dough and flour from the counter or rolling mat. They are great for lifting and turning dough, and they can be used to divide dough into smaller pieces, too.

LATTICE CUTTER: You can use a knife to cut strips for a lattice, or you can try a wheel cutter. Some have wavy edges, some have straight edges, and some have both. A pizza cutter works, too. For serious stripping, there are adjustable multi-wheel pastry cutters, some with up to 12 wheels that can make precise and even cuts with just one pass. When using a multi-wheel pastry cutter, flour the dough well and start 1 inch (2.5 cm) from the edge so the dough won't come up as you roll across it. Push down firmly for a clean cut.

RULER: For strips with a uniform width or placed an equal distance apart on top of a filling, try a metal straight edge or transparent acrylic quilting ruler.

BRUSHES: These range in size from ½ to 4 inches (1.27 to 10.16 cm).

- Dry: I use brushes with bristles to brush off extra flour from dough. Boar bristle brushes are very nice, but I have also been known to use brushes from the hardware store. Be sure to keep dry the area under the ferrule (the metal ring that secures the bristles) so nothing can breed under it. Hand wash just the tip, and let dry.
- Wet: Silicone brushes are great for applying an egg or milk wash to dough, and these brushes can be washed in the dishwasher. At Pie Camp, we call this the "sloshy brush."

MICROPLANE ZESTER: Great for zesting citrus and grating fresh nutmeg. As for the tiny metal nutmeg graters that I have picked up at yard sales, along with my collection of pie birds, those have ended up on my pie tchotchke shelf. I like a microplane zester best.

VEGETABLE PEELER: Great for peeling fruit and fresh ginger, and for removing thin strips of zest from citrus.

WIRE WHISK: Buy a heavy-duty stainless steel wire whisk. You will use it for many things including adding air and loft to eggs. When making strawberry shortcake for 80 without an electric hand mixer, I successfully whipped up heavy cream with just a sturdy wire whisk and large metal bowl, although my arm did feel like it was going to drop off toward the end.

ELECTRIC HANDHELD BEATER: An electric hand mixer is great for whipping heavy cream and making meringues.

COOKIE CUTTERS: Great for cutting out dough decorations or fancy vents on top of a pie. Sets can be purchased in graduated sizes and shapes. I have animals, fruits, letters, seasonal cutters, numbers, stars, circles, and shapes in all sorts of sizes. Look for vintage metal ones, without rust, at estate and yard sales.

COOLING RACKS OR CANNING RACKS: A wire rack used for cooling pies. While I love my photographer Andrew's vintage round one that fits only one pie, look for one that can hold more than one pie. I also use round canning racks, with handles and rim that will safely hold a pie when moving it from place to place. The windowsill, a deck rail, and the latticed metal bistro table on my deck all do double duty as cooling racks, too.

SUGAR SHAKER OR DUSTING WAND: This is really a little indulgence, but I was given a dusting wand for shaking sugar evenly over a pie top, and it brings a smile to my face every time I use it. Mine is in the shape of a sphere, with one solid side and one sifter side that opens and closes with a twist handle. A snap ball tea strainer works, too.

WORK AREA AND SURFACE: You want some elbow room when making pie, and especially when rolling out dough. Clear enough space on your counter so you won't feel squashed. Before rolling out dough, I place a pastry cloth on top of the surface, or plastic wrap if rolling gluten-free dough. The surface itself can be marble, metal, plastic, or wood. Marble stays cooler, but if any surface feels warm, put bags of frozen peas, or ice cubes in zip-lock bags, on top of it for 10 minutes to chill it down.

HANDHELD LASER THERMOMETER: You can test the temperature of just about everything with this nifty gizmo, including dough, oven, filling, and hands. Just point the laser at the object. The temperature of your hands range between mid-80s to high 90s°F (28 to 37°C). When making dough by hand, even chilly hands at 80°F (26°C) can be too warm to handle butter for any length of time, as butter begins to soften at 59°F (15°C). A laser thermometer will help you know when to cool them off, which you can do by holding ice cubes or placing your hands in an ice water bath, and when to place your dough in the fridge or freezer.

REFRACTOMETER: If you are fanatical about knowing the sugar content in your fruit, this tool, which looks like a 6-inch spy glass, is for you. When a drop of juice from a piece of fruit is placed on its lens, you can hold the tool up to the light, and peer through it to see little lines and numbers showing how high a percentage of sucrose is in the fruit. This is called a Brix reading, named after the German mathematician and engineer who worked with the specific gravity of liquids. Winemakers use this little gizmo all the time, and it can help you to get an idea of how much sugar to add to a filling. Of course, you can also just taste the fruit to figure that out, too.

TIMER: An hourglass, a mechanical or digital timer, or a voice-activated timer on a phone or watch—all work just fine.

POTHOLDERS, OVEN MITTS, OR INSULATED KITCHEN GLOVES: It is mandatory to protect your hands when moving hot pies in and out of an oven. As sizes of hands and fingers are all different, you may need to try out a few options until you find what works best for you.

- I looked a long time to find a pair of insulated oven gloves that were just the right fit for my hands and fingers. You'll want ones that are easy to get on and off but that aren't so big and sloppy that it is difficult get a secure grip on a hot pie pan.
- Oven mitts can bump and break the fragile fluted edge of a just-baked pie, so take care if you are using them.
- When I find a set of potholders I do like, I use them until they become tattered and stained, and then I replace them.

Two Cautions: When moving a hot pie pan, please never ever use a damp or wet towel, as it will quickly transfer heat to your hands, which can cause a painful burn.

Always remember to prepare a place for your just-baked creation to land. Trying to clear off a space while balancing a hot and heavy pie with one hand may find that pie landing upside down on the floor.

REFRIGERATOR: Something we take for granted is the icebox, as my mom and grandmother called it, which is used to chill our dough, cool our custards, set up our chiffon and cream pies, and freeze our ice cream. When its door is opened too often, the temperature inside can raise so that it becomes merely a room temperature storage box. On a day when I know I will be opening and closing the fridge a lot, I adjust the temperature control to the coldest setting possible.

A RELIABLE OVEN: An oven is the most important baking tool of all. Whether gas, electric, convection, or wood-fired, make friends with your oven. Learn its quirks, where its hot and cool spots are, and when and if you need to rotate or move a pie to a lower or upper rack during a bake for the best result. Place an oven thermometer inside to see if it matches the temperature at which you have set it. Plan on a once-a-year maintenance by an oven-tech who will have the training and tools to make sure that your oven is calibrated correctly.

Last but not least . . .

APRON: Aprons have stories attached to their strings. They can be used for carrying fruit from the orchard, wiping flour and dough from hands, and, on more occasions than I can remember, drying tears. When buying or sewing your apron, make sure that pockets are included. I've worn an apron daily for decades and feel underdressed without one.

HEADBAND, SCARF, OR BUFF: Very helpful for keeping stray hairs out of dough and filling.

MUSIC: Essential in my life, as is the silence that punctuates it. From classics to pop, my favorite baking music runs the gamut from Hildegard von Bingen, J. S. Bach, and Gustav Mahler, to Joni Mitchell, Aretha, and Adele.

PIE BASKET OR CARRIER: I have and use stackable wooden pie boxes, but I love best my old-fashioned woven two-tier pie baskets from the Peterboro Basket Company in New Hampshire.

CLOCK: Permanently set to 3:14.

Ingredients

Flour

ALL-PURPOSE FLOUR: I use unbleached all-purpose flour, and Bob's Red Mill or King Arthur Flour when possible. Store flour in a cool, dry place. I keep a 5-pound bag in my freezer at all times for making pie dough.

GLUTEN-FREE FLOUR: Gluten-Free flour mixes, once a rarity, are now widely available. My favorites are Bob's Red Mill Gluten Free 1 to 1 Baking Flour and King Arthur Flour Gluten Free Measure for Measure. Gluten-free flour mixes may weigh differently, so you will want to check the package for weight and volume. If you prefer to make your own flour mix, or one that has no xanthan gum in it, I suggest that you use the recipe for Gluten-Free, Gum-Free Dough in a Food Processor (page 54).

NUT MEAL AND FLOUR: Hazelnut and almond meal (also known as almond flour) are two nut meals I use for crust. Once opened, secure the top well and store in the fridge or freezer. Check the expiration date.

COOKIES AND GRAHAM CRACKERS: For crumb crusts, I use gluten-free and gluten-full graham crackers, gingersnaps, and cookies, including sandwich cookies with filling.

OLD-FASHIONED ROLLED OATS: Oats may be used in dough and as a topping. I bake with gluten-free oats from Bob's Red Mill.

Fat

BUTTER: With slightly higher fat content and less moisture than paper-wrapped butter, I bake with bricks of European-style butter (wrapped in aluminum foil) whenever possible, and use both salted and unsalted, interchangeably, in recipes. Use paper-wrapped butter if that is what is available in your area. Butter can take on other flavors, so store it tightly wrapped in plastic wrap in the fridge, and use within one month. Butter can be frozen for up to eight months. (See Resources, page 330.)

RENDERED LEAF LARD: Leaf lard is enjoying a resurgence of interest in artisan home baking.

The pure rendered fat comes from around the kidneys of the pig and has very little to no pork flavor. It can be substituted for vegetable shortening. Store for six months in the fridge and one year in the freezer. Available by mail order, at some farmers' markets, and at butcher shops. (See Resources, page 330.)

VEGETABLE SHORTENING: Vegetable shortenings are not made from animal products and can replace any fat in recipes, which is especially nice for vegans and vegetarians. (See Resources, page 330.)

Sweetener

SUGARS:

- Granulated sugar, also known as table or white sugar, can be used in most recipes.
- Light brown turbinado sugar is less refined and has a bit of a molasses flavor, and it can be substituted for granulated sugar.
- Superfine sugar (caster sugar) is used for meringues, although my grandmother taught me to make meringue with granulated sugar. (See Hints for Making Meringue, page 198.)
- Confectioners' sugar (powdered sugar) works best when whipping cream, although granulated sugar stabilized with a bit of cornstarch works well, too. (See Master Recipe: Whipped Cream, page 182.)
- Brown sugar, both light and dark, is used for crumble, crisp, and pie toppings, or to add a bit of molasses flavor to fillings.
- Sanding sugar has large crystals that are nice on top of a pie, and they don't melt with oven heat.
- Demerara sugar is another option to sprinkle on a pie top.

MAPLE SYRUP: I use organic amber or dark color Grade A maple syrup. Once open, store in the fridge and use within one year. On one occasion, my former neighbor, a smoke jumper in Alaska, surprised me with a special bottle of Alaskan birch syrup, which is not quite as sweet as maple syrup. It can be substituted in all recipes calling for maple syrup. Pancake syrup is simply not the same.

MOLASSES: I prefer the lighter taste of unsulfured molasses to that of blackstrap molasses.

CORN SYRUP: I generally use light corn syrup, but if I only have a bottle of the stronger-flavored dark corn syrup on the shelf, and I don't want to head out to the store for just one thing, I have been known to substitute the dark corn syrup in a recipe.

LYLE'S GOLDEN SYRUP: Made from sugar and can be substituted for light corn syrup.

Dairy

MILK: I use organic, rBST-free (a growth hormone), whole milk whenever possible.

HALF-AND-HALF: A mixture of half milk and half cream. It makes wonderful custards but cannot be whipped.

WHIPPING CREAM: Heavy whipping cream contains between 36 and 40 percent milk fat.

MASCARPONE CHEESE: A thick and luscious cheese that makes a wonderful layer in filling. Often sweetened.

SOUR CREAM: Thick and slightly sour. Adds a nice tang to fillings.

BUTTERMILK: I use fresh whole cultured buttermilk from the dairy section, and organic when possible.

SWEETENED CONDENSED MILK: A combination of whole milk and sugar that is condensed and thick. Store in the fridge after opening, and use within five days.

EVAPORATED MILK: A condensed milk without sugar. Evaporated milk cannot be substituted for sweetened condensed milk. Store in the fridge after opening, and use within five days.

COCONUT MILK (NONDAIRY): There is a difference between the coconut milk used for cooking and baking that comes in a can, and the coconut milk in a box that is for drinking. I use canned Thai Kitchen Organic Coconut Milk. Before using, place the unopened can in a bowl of warm water. It's ready to use when you can hear the ingredients slosh around inside when you shake the can.

Eggs

Use large eggs and, whenever possible, ones that are organic and free-range. I trade my neighbor pies for freshly laid eggs from her hens.

Ice Cream

For à la mode and ice cream pies, make your own (see Master Recipe: Ice Cream, page 300) or buy a good-quality ready-made ice cream.

Thickeners, Stabilizers, and Leaveners

CORNSTARCH: Used as a thickener for fillings and as a stabilizer for whipped cream. Also used in gluten-free flour mixes.

TAPIOCA: Tapioca comes from the manioc root. It is gluten-free, and can be used as a thickener in fruit pies and also an ingredient in some gluten-free doughs.

- Tapioca flour or starch: Finely ground and can be used as a thickener or in dough.
- Quick-cooking tapioca: Small grains of tapioca used as a thickener.
- Small tapioca pearls: If using these as a thickener, you will want to process them down to the smaller grain size of quick-cooking tapioca, or finely grind into a flour.

CREAM OF TARTAR: Although my grandmother didn't use cream of tartar, it is very helpful for stabilizing whipped egg whites when making meringues.

GELATIN: Like my mom and grandmom, I use Knox gelatin, which is animal based. I have not used or tested these recipes with unflavored vegan or vegetarian gelatin substitutes, although they are available at some markets and by mail order.

BAKING POWDER: A leavener made of a mix of baking soda, an acid, and some cornstarch. The heat of the oven releases bubbles of carbon dioxide that expand and lighten cobbler dough. It can be used in pie dough also. I use aluminum-free baking powder to avoid an aluminum flavor in my baked goods.

BAKING SODA: Another leavener that creates bubbles when moistened. I use this in Shoofly Pie (page 269).

Flavor

SALT: I bake with kosher salt, which has no chemical additives.

SPICES: Buying in bulk is more affordable. And bulk spices stay fresher than the spices found in the small bottles on the grocery store shelf. I buy small amounts of an ounce or less, and replace once or twice a year. Buy from a dedicated spice store that has a good turnover of spices, or a mail-order company such as Penzeys Spices. Check your spices out with the sniff test. If there is little to no fragrance, it's time to replace. Invest in a set of spice bottles, or pick up some at yard sales and save them from the landfill.

PURE VANILLA EXTRACT: Buy the best you can. Imitation vanilla extract is not the same. Pure vanilla extract will last for years when capped tightly and stored at room temperature in a cool dark place.

CHOCOLATE: I think many will agree that Theobroma cacao, the seed from which chocolate comes, and translated from the Greek as "food of the gods," is an accurate description for this well-loved food. Chocolate authority Simran Sethi says, "Quality chocolates only come from quality beans, handled with care." Whenever possible, buy Fair Trade, Rainforest Alliance, single bean bars that are 70 percent chocolate or higher. Store in a cool dry place.

COFFEE: A shot of espresso, a cup of strong dark coffee, a tablespoon of good-quality freeze-dried coffee, or a coffee extract will provide coffee flavor for pie and ice cream.

VINEGAR: In my cupboard, I have organic apple cider vinegar, wine vinegars, and a large selection of flavored vinegars for use with recipes. I occasionally use white vinegar as a substitute for lemon juice.

FLOWER WATER: Orange blossom, rose, and chamomile are a few flower waters that add flavor to fillings and toppings. I use flower waters made by Starwest Botanicals. Store at room temperature for up to one year.

LIQUEURS, LIBATIONS, AND FRUIT WINES FOR PIE: Here are a few ideas to flavor fillings, pastry creams, and whipped cream.

- Orange: Cointreau, Grand Marnier, triple sec
- Raspberry: Chambord
- Apple: calvados, eau-de-vie
- Black Currant: crème de cassis
- Chocolate: crème de cacao
- Coffee and chocolate: Kahlúa
- Elderflower: St-Germain
- Lemon: limoncello
- Hazelnut and herbs: Frangelico
- Walnut: Nocello
- Bitter almond: amaretto
- Rum, both white and dark
- Irish whiskey
- Bourbon
- Cordial-style fruit wines fortified with apple brandy

Nuts and Extras

NUTS: Use almonds, macadamias, walnuts, pecans, and hazelnuts that are whole, chopped, roasted, or raw. Buy fresh, and store in glass jars if possible; six months in the fridge, one year in the freezer. Replace if they smell rancid.

COCONUT: Buy bags of shredded, flaked, sweetened, and unsweetened from the grocery store baking section. Store in an airtight container in a cool dry location.

Dough

Kate's Three Rules of Pie Making and Life

1.

Keep everything chilled, especially yourself.

2.

Keep your boundaries.

3.

Vent.

Basics: Crusts

There are basically two kinds of crusts—those made with dough that we roll out, and those that we press in. Both roll-out and press-in crusts can be made by hand or in a food processor. They can be made gluten-free, too.

Roll-Out Dough

Roll-out dough is known as pastry dough. It's the kind of dough my grandmother showed me how to roll out with her red handled rolling pin. It is used for single- or double-crusted oven-baked pies, like a golden brown apple pie with steam coming out of its vents (see Classic Apple Pie, page 102), or a bubbling lattice-topped berry pie (see Classic Blackberry Pie, page 104). Roll-out dough uses four basic ingredients—flour, salt, fat, and water. Variations can be made with additions of granulated sugar, egg, milk, vinegar, or cream cheese. Roll-out dough can be made vegan, vegetarian, and gluten-free, too (see Master Recipe: Gluten-Free Dough, page 50).

Blind Baked or Par-Baked

A single roll-out dough can also be completely pre-baked or partially baked. An unfilled pie shell can be baked, cooled, and then filled with a filling that doesn't need to go into the oven. This is called a blind-baked crust (see How to Blind Bake a Crust, page 69). For a filling that needs a shorter bake time than the crust that holds it, a single roll-out dough can be partially baked before it is filled. This is called a par-baked crust. This crust is used in Pineapple-Coconut Sweet Potato Pie, page 254.

Press-In Crumb Crust

Press-in crusts are the easiest of all. Ingredients are mixed together, pressed into a pie pan, given a short bake, and then cooled. Now it is ready for a filling that needs no additional bake time. The basic ingredients, cookie crumbs and butter, can be varied with gingersnaps, graham crackers, nut meal, chopped nuts, coconut, oats, melted butter, sugar, and spices like cinnamon or ginger. This is a great crust to make when you are in a hurry, too (see Hurry Up Pie, page 257).

Roll-Out Dough: A Craft of Practice and Patience

Pie makers are passionate about dough, the making of which is a craft of practice and patience. Each time we make and roll dough, it may feel slightly different. One day, a recipe will come together and roll easily, and on the next it can feel like a complete stranger. Don't let this deter you, because every long-time pie maker I have met has had an occasional day like this, too. The temperature of flour and fat, humidity, age of flour and how it is stored, ratios of ingredients, and whether made by hand or machine may affect the outcome. Pie makers love to debate these things, and they are very generous and open in sharing tips learned along the way. There is no one right way to make dough. There is only a difference in the length of time we have been practicing.

Flaky or Tender?

Dough is either flaky or tender, also known as short. We'll be making flaky pastry for our pies, but as both doughs use the same basic ingredients—flour, salt, fat, and water—it's important to know what sets each apart. The difference is that a flaky dough is made of layers of dough that steam apart, leaving flaky pockets where the fat has melted, and a tender short pastry dough has more of a crumbly texture. Flake pastry holds its shape better than tender pastry, too. To better understand how to make dough, here are a few things to know.

Temperature

Keep in mind how the melting point of fats can factor into dough making. Different fats melt at different temperatures. When butter comes right out of my fridge, it is cold and solid, but by the time it has warmed to 59°F (15°C), it has begun to soften. Lard softens at an even lower temperature. Shortening is more stable, which is one of the reasons why many pie makers use it. Whatever fat we use, when it begins to melt and coat the flour, it can change our dough from cold and flaky to warm and short. All of this can happen quickly due to the normal temperature of our hands and kitchens, especially when the oven is on. You can always take a break in the dough-making process and chill the fats back up in the fridge or freezer. Just remember Rule #1: Keep Everything Chilled, Especially Yourself.

How to Smoosh Fat

smoosh | smo͞oSH | verb

Quickly rub and flatten cold fat into cold flour with cold hands when making dough by hand. Our goal is that the fat will be a variety of sizes—ranging in size from cracker crumbs to peas, almonds, and maybe a walnut meat or two, some flat and some not. The entire mess should look incompletely mixed and still feel cold when we are done, so work quickly. There should be some white floury places and it should not look too homogenous.

"Don't think about it. Just smoosh the fat into the flour as fast as you can."

Fats

When making dough, the kind of fat used, its temperature, size of pieces, and how they are handled are all important parts of the process. The higher the fat content, the flakier a dough can be. Lard and shortening are 100 percent fat and make very flaky pastry. The fat content of butter can range anywhere from 80 to 86 percent, and even higher for local artisan butters. The addition of butter gives a delicious flavor to pastry, but the end result may not be a flaky one.

There are two main ways of working with fat:

- For a flaky crust, we add pieces of cold fat to the flour, and then smoosh it to make flat. We want to take care not to coat all the flour in the bowl. The dry flour will mix with water, and when the pie is baking, layers of dough will steam apart, leaving flaky pockets where the fat has melted.

- For a tender short pastry crust, the fat should coat all the flour, until it looks like coarse meal or cookie crumbs. This dough will take less water. Nancy Baggett describes this perfectly in *The All-American Dessert Book* where she writes that fat "cut into flour also reduces gluten development, because it works like a raincoat, coating and protecting the flour particles from becoming wet."

All of this leads us to the G word: GLUTEN.

Flour + Water = Gluten

It is true that too much "worrying" of a traditional pie dough (fussing, handling, or overworking) can create too much gluten, resulting in a tough crust. Some gluten is needed to hold a traditional dough (made with all-purpose flour) together. Without gluten, dough can be a crumbly mess. We want just enough gluten strands, created by combining water and flour, and mixing, but no more. The amount depends on the type of dough: flaky or tender and short. One flaky dough technique, developed by J. Kenji López-Alt, reserves some of the flour. After the remaining flour and fat have been thoroughly combined, the reserved flour is added to coat it, and water gradually folded in. In this way, most of gluten is made from that last bit of added flour. You will find a version of this technique in this chapter (see One Cup Out Dough, page 42).

For gluten-free dough, skip ahead to Master Recipe: Gluten-Free Dough starting on page 50.

Finishing

In a flaky dough, flattened layers of smooshed fat are suspended between layers of moistened flour. Shirley Corriher in *Bake Wise* calls this fat layer a spacer. When we slice the dough in half, we should be able to see these layers. I wrap and place this dough into the fridge for a minimum of 20 to 30 minutes to allow the water in the dough to distribute evenly, the gluten strands to relax, and the fats to chill back down. Two hours is fine, and it can even stay in the fridge for up to three days. When we place the pie into a hot oven, the cold fat won't melt immediately, and the water in the dough will steam the layers apart, giving us a flaky crust.

Our tender short dough should also be placed into the fridge so that the water in the dough can distribute evenly, fats chill back down, and gluten strands relax, before proceeding to rolling. Because there is less moisture and more fat in this dough, rolling it out can be a bit more challenging, so a little patching, either on the rolling surface or after it is placed in the pie pan, may be needed.

Whether made with flaky or tender short dough, once the dough has been rolled out, laid into the pie pan, and the pie is constructed, ideally it should go back into the fridge to chill for an additional 20 to 30 minutes before baking.

What Else Can Go in Dough?

Vinegar, sugar, cream cheese, eggs, and vodka are other ingredients that dough can include. Here's what they all do:

- Vinegar: An acid that helps to weaken gluten strands in dough.
- Sugar: If you like your dough a bit sweeter, add an optional tablespoon or two. Sugar also adds some color to dough. This is especially useful when making gluten-free dough, which doesn't brown as readily. Sugar also weakens gluten formation.
- Cream cheese: Makes a short tender crust that is easy to work.
- Eggs: Provide moisture, color, flavor, and structure in dough.
- Vodka: Adds moisture to the dough without making gluten.

How to Keep Everything Chilled

In *Art of the Pie*, I write that Rule #1 in pie making is "Keep everything chilled, especially yourself." I still feel that this is the most important rule. Butter starts to soften at 59°F (15°C), and melted fat can make for a more difficult dough making and rolling experience. Here are a few tips to help you keep your chill:

- Keep lights off in the kitchen if it is a hot day. Turn them on when you need them, or if it is dark.

- Preheat the oven after the dough has been made, and keep the kitchen cool while you're rolling out dough or making lattice, edges, flutes, and crimps.

- If you have air conditioning, turn it down as low it as it can go. Put a vest on if you are cold. Your dough will thank you.

- Dip your hands in an ice water bath, or hold ice cubes or a glass of ice water to cool down your hands.

- Keep a bag of flour in the freezer.

- Freeze butter and grate it—especially helpful on hot days.

- Solid shortening can be kept in the freezer.

- Measure and chop fats, then place them in the fridge to chill.

- Place an ice-filled bowl beneath your dough bowl to keep it chilly.

- Toss frozen flour over fats when added to the bowl. They will like the chill.

- Use a mezzaluna or pastry blender to cut the fat into the flour.

- Handle your dough as little as possible.

- Stop before you think you are done. Overworking and worrying the dough makes for melted fats.

- Chill down the rolling surface with gel packs or ice bags before you begin to roll out dough. Be sure to dry off the surface before placing anything on it.

- Marble stays cool and will help your dough stay cooler longer if rolled out on it.

- Stop at any time and place your dough in the fridge or freezer for a few minutes if the fats are melting.

- Chill your pie pan in the fridge or freezer before and after filling with dough. Chill your unbaked pie for 20 to 30 minutes in the fridge before placing in the oven.

How to Measure Ingredients

There is no one right way to measure, so I have given both volume and weight measurements in all the recipes to follow. Some will prefer to use a scale, and others will prefer measuring cups. Both are fine but please read over this "how to" list so we all measure the same amounts.

Weight: By Digital Scale

Ingredients, both wet and dry, can be weighed on a scale.

Place a plate, bowl, piece of parchment, wax paper, or plastic wrap on top of the flat scale surface.

Zero the scale out.

Make sure it is measuring in grams, ounces, or whatever unit is called for in the recipe.

If more ingredients are to be added, zero out the scale before proceeding.

Volume: By Measuring Cups and Spoons

Dry Ingredients

- For flour: Dip a measuring cup into the flour bag or container. Level the top with the flat side of a knife.
- For salt, baking powder, baking soda, and spices: Scoop the dry ingredient out of the container. Level the top with the flat side of a knife.
- For granulated sugar: Dip a measuring cup into the sugar. Level the top with the flat side of a knife.

- For brown sugar: Firmly pack brown sugar into a measuring cup. Level the top with the flat side of a knife.

Liquid Ingredients

- For amounts of ¼ cup (60 ml) or more: Set a liquid measuring cup on a flat surface and fill to the mark the recipe calls for. Be sure to check at eye level, too.
- For small amounts: Pour liquid into measuring spoons. From experience, I suggest pouring away from the mixing bowl lest you spill extra into it.

Fats

- For shortening and lard: Spoon into a measuring cup and pack down. Level the top with the flat side of a knife.
- For butter and cream cheese: Cut the amount needed using the marks on the wrapper, or use a scale, measuring cups or spoons.

Master Recipe: Roll-Out Dough

Makes two dough discs; halve amounts for one dough disc

This recipe is the tried and true flaky pie dough that I have taught at Pie Camps since 2008. It can be made either by hand or in a food processor and is generously sized for one 9-inch (23 cm) deep-dish double-crust pie. It uses a total of 1 cup (224 g) fat, the choices of which are: butter, which gives a crust flaky layers and wonderful flavor; leaf lard, which adds flake and crispness; and vegetable shortening, which makes a very tender crust with a greasy flavor and mouthfeel. My favorite dough uses a combination of half butter, half leaf lard. This combination gives both crisp, flaky layers, along with the flavor of butter. If making by hand, we will smoosh the fat into the flour with our fingers. In a food processor, we will combine the flour and fat using a metal blade and quick pulses. Choose the fat(s) and technique that you like, and then follow the directions below.

2½ cups (363 g) all-purpose flour, unbleached, plus more for rolling out dough

1 cup (224 g) chilled fat of your choice, cut into tablespoon-size pieces

1 tablespoon granulated sugar (optional)

½ teaspoon salt

½ cup (120 ml) ice water plus 1 to 2 tablespoons (15 to 30 ml) more as needed

TO MAKE BY HAND

1. Make sure all the ingredients are chilled.

2. Put all the ingredients but the ice water in a large bowl.

3. With clean hands, quickly smoosh the mixture together, or use a single blade mezzaluna or pastry blender with an up and down motion, until the ingredients look like cracker crumbs with lumps the size of peas and almonds. These lumps will make your crust flaky. Don't coat

all the flour with fat. You should still see some white floury places in the bowl when you are finished. Work quickly so that the dough still feels chilly when you are done.

4. Sprinkle 5 to 6 tablespoons of the ice water over the mixture, fluffing and tossing lightly with a fork as you do.

5. Sprinkle over more water as needed, a tablespoon at a time, and fluff with a fork after each addition until it holds together. When the dough looks shaggy in the bowl, you are getting close. Give some of your dough a firm handshake and see if it holds together. If it does, go on to Step 6. If it doesn't, add a bit more water if needed for the dough to come together. The dough should feel moist without feeling tacky.

6. Form and pat the dough into a big ball. If it feels a little dry on the outside, dip your fingers into some ice water and pat them on the outside of the dough in a few places. Don't get it so wet that it is sticky. The dough should feel like cool clay and firm yet pliable as when patting a baby's bottom.

7. Divide the dough in half and make two chubby discs about 5 inches (12 cm) across.

8. Wrap the discs separately in plastic wrap and chill for a minimum of 20 minutes and up to three days. Before rolling the dough, please read How to Roll Out Dough on page 45. To freeze dough, please read How to Freeze and Defrost Dough on page 56.

TO MAKE IN A FOOD PROCESSOR

1. Make sure all the ingredients are chilled.

2. In the bowl of a food processor fit with the metal blade, add all the ingredients but the ice water.

3. Pulse 15 times to combine. Use short pulses.

4. Add 3 tablespoons of the water. Pulse 10 times.

5. Add 3 more tablespoons of the water. Pulse five times.

6. Turn the dough into a medium bowl, add the remaining water 1 tablespoon at a time, and finish by hand as in Steps 5 to 8 above.

VARIATIONS

Art of the Pie Dough

For your fat, use:

8 tablespoons (1 stick; 112 g) salted or unsalted butter, cut into tablespoon-size pieces

½ cup (112 g) rendered leaf lard, cut into tablespoon-size pieces

All-Butter Dough

For your fat, use:

½ pound (2 sticks; 224 g) salted or unsalted butter, cut into small pieces and chilled

Vegan Pie Dough

For your fat, use:

8 tablespoons (1 stick; 112 g) Earth Balance Vegan Buttery Sticks

½ cup (112 g) vegetable shortening

A Pictorial Guide to Making Art of the Pie Dough

1. Measure the flour into the bowl.

4. You can also use grated frozen butter.

5. Chop or blend to the size of cracker crumbs with pea and almond size lumps.

8. Form and pat the dough into a big ball.

9. Divide the dough in half.

2. Add the cold leaf lard cut in pieces.

3. Add the cold butter chopped in pieces.

6. Or smoosh the lard and butter into the flour with your fingers.

7. Add water and fluff the dough with a fork.

10. You should see pieces of fat and layers.

11. Form into two chubby discs.

One Cup Out Dough

Makes two dough discs

As I've mentioned, the combination of flour and water makes gluten. Gluten has its place—in bread, and kneading bread dough until I can see those wonderful strands is one of my favorite things to do. In pie dough, however, too much gluten development makes tough, overworked dough. I read about a nifty little work-around from J. Kenji López-Alt to lighten up on the amount of gluten and help to make a flaky crust. The trick is in waiting to add part of the flour. I adapted his recipe a bit, and came up with my own version that I call One Cup Out Dough, because that's exactly what we'll do. We'll leave out one full cup of flour, and after we have processed the remaining flour with fat, we'll turn the dough into a mixing bowl and add that cup of flour back in, sprinkle in the water, and fold the dough over and over until it comes together. López-Alt uses a spatula, but we'll use our hands lightly. Using this handy-dandy technique, we will make dough with fewer strands of gluten.

8 tablespoons (1 stick; 112 g) butter

8 tablespoons (112 g) leaf lard

2½ cups (363 g) flour, divided

½ teaspoon salt

1 to 2 tablespoons granulated sugar (optional)

10 tablespoons (150 ml) water

1. Cut the butter and lard into tablespoon-size chunks.

2. In the bowl of a food processor, place 1½ cups (217 g) of the flour, salt, and the optional sugar, and pulse to combine.

3. Add all the fat at once and pulse until everything in the bowl turns into large smooth-ish lumps.

4. Add the remaining 1 cup (146 g) flour into the bowl of the food processor and pulse a couple of times to break up the lumps.

5. Turn the dough into a waiting bowl and sprinkle 3 tablespoons of the water over the top and 1 tablespoon or so through the middle of the dough.

6. With cool hands, continue to fold and lightly press the dough, gradually adding more water, until it can be formed into one big ball.

7. Cut the ball in half. Wrap each piece in plastic wrap, form into discs, and chill for a minimum of 2 hours.

8. When ready to roll, set the wrapped dough out on the counter and let it warm up a bit so that it is easy to roll.

VARIATION

All-Butter One Cup Out Dough
Omit the leaf lard and use ½ pound (2 sticks; 224 g) butter.

How to Get Extra Layers in Your Dough

Here are two techniques to give you some extra layers in your dough before refrigerating:

1. When the dough has nearly come together in the bowl, take the side of your hand and push halfway down in the center of the dough, sort of like a soft karate chop. Bring your hands under one edge of the dough and fold it over onto itself. Give the dough a quarter turn and repeat, five to six times in total.

2. Alternatively, you can make extra layers by rolling out a full-size dough into a 10-by-15-inch rectangle, folding the 10-inch edges to the center, folding them toward the center a second time, and finally bringing the short sides together.

How to Roll Out Dough

If dough is too cold and hard, it will not roll easily. If it feels hard, place it on the counter for 30 to 60 minutes and check on it occasionally. When it is pliable, yet still cool, it is ready to roll. If it feels too warm and greasy at any time, stop, cover your work, and place it in the fridge for the fats to chill down. I like to roll my doughs out around 54°F (12°C). When it gets to 59°F (15°C) or above, the fat will soften up too much.

1. Place a pastry cloth, silicone rolling mat, piece of plastic wrap, or parchment paper on a flat surface that is a comfortable height for you and gives you enough elbow room for rolling. Sprinkle around some flour and place a disc of dough on top of it. Sprinkle a little flour on top of the dough, too.

2. With a rolling pin, press down on the top of the dough in a few places like on the top of a peanut butter cookie. There should be some give, but not so much that your pin presses the dough right down to the rolling surface. If it does this, your dough is probably too warm, so let it chill for 10 minutes and try again.

3. Always roll out the dough from the center. Position your hands on the pin so that they are over the dough and not off to the sides. This way you can feel what is happening directly under the pin as you press down and roll.

4. Your first pass will start at the center and move out toward 12 o'clock. So that the edges of the dough don't get too thin and break, stop about 1½ inches (4 cm) from the edge. Place the pin in the center and roll back to 6 o'clock. Give the dough a quarter turn and repeat rolling from the center to 12 o'clock, picking up the pin, placing it in the center, and rolling back to 6 o'clock.

After each out-and-back roll, give the dough a quarter turn.

5. Continue to roll from the center until the dough is about 7 inches (18 cm) in diameter. Then roll all around the clock from the center until the dough is 2 inches (5 cm) larger than the diameter of the pie pan.

6. Brush off any extra flour from the top and bottom of the dough with a pastry brush.

7. Drape the dough over the rolling pin. Lightly lay the dough-covered pin on the equator of the pie pan and, with a quick and deft flick of the wrist, roll the dough toward you. Adjust the dough in the pan as needed to center it, and then let the weight of the dough settle into the corners of the pan. If you push and stretch the dough, it will shrink back during the bake.

8. Trim the edges with scissors or a knife to about a 1-inch (2.5 cm) overhang. I use culinary shears to trim excess dough from pie edges. These shears break apart in two pieces for easy cleaning. A dedicated set of craft scissors will work, too.

9. At this point, you'll either fill the pie or cover the dough with plastic wrap and place in the fridge. Then you can decide what edge you would like to make (see How to Crimp, Flute, and Edge the Crust, page 59).

FOR A SINGLE-CRUST PIE: This shell can be par-baked, blind baked, and frozen (see How to Blind Bake a Crust, page 69; and Pie Camp Tips for Blind Baking, page 70). You can also double wrap the unfilled shell and freeze for up to two months.

FOR A DOUBLE-CRUSTED PIE: If you are making a double-crusted pie, wait to trim. Finish the edges after you have added the fruit filling, rolled out the remaining dough, and carefully laid it on top of the filling.

Rolling Tips

IF THE DOUGH STICKS TO THE PIN: Wipe the dough off the pin and sprinkle a little flour over the sticky spot on the top surface of the dough. Stick happens if the fat in the dough has become too soft or if too much water was added to the dough, making it tacky.

IF THE EDGES ARE CRACKING: If the dough edges are cracking by the time it gets to be about 7 inches (18 cm) in diameter, lightly fold in the edges about 1½ inches (4 cm) (like you would do when making a crostata), flip the dough over, place your open palms on either side of the dough so that they face each other, and lightly pat the edges toward the center. Begin rolling again. This little tip has been helpful to many pie campers with cracking and breaking dough edges.

A Pictorial Guide to Rolling Out Dough

3. Roll the dough 2 inches (5 cm) larger than the diameter of the pie pan.

6. Settle the dough into the pan without stretching.

1. Place your hands on the pin and roll out to 12 o'clock.

2. Roll around the clock from the center.

4. Brush off extra flour with a pastry brush.

5. Place the dough in the pan.

7. Trim the excess dough from the edge with about a 1-inch overhang.

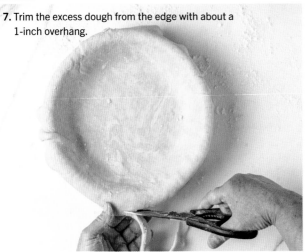

How to Make Things Go Right with Crust

Instead of looking at the side of the coin that shows how crust can go awry, these tips look at the other side of that coin and help us to make a great crust.

For a Flaky Crust

- Remember Rule #1: Keep everything chilled . . . (see page 36).

- Be sure to include some bigger pieces of fat, up to ½ inch (1.25 cm) in size. Use your knuckles and fingers to smoosh and pinch the pieces to become flat flakes. These will be the flakiest places in the crust when baked.

- When making the dough, be sure to keep some flour dry and looking white. This way the water can get to the dry flour and make enough gluten strands for our dough to hold together.

- Rule #2 in pie making: Keep your boundaries. In this case, the boundary is to stop before you think you are done. When working the dough, less is best.

- Wet dough makes tough crust. Add the minimum of water and sprinkle more, as needed, for the dough to just come together.

- Dough should feel cool like clay, and it should feel firm yet pliable as when patting a baby's bottom.

- As dough rests in the fridge, water will evenly wick through the dough, so don't worry if you have a spot that seems a little more moist or dry.

- Repeat Rules #1 and #2 often.

For a Short Tender Crust

- Rule #1 can be relaxed here and our fats can be cool or even room temperature, without melting.

- The flour and fat will be processed more than they are in flaky pastry and should look like coarse meal.

- Short and tender dough needs less gluten development. Less Water = Less Gluten. Flour, well coated with fats, will absorb less water than the dry flour we need when making flaky dough.

- Granulated sugar in dough helps to deter gluten strands.

- Adding an acid like vinegar to dough helps to deter gluten strands.

- Once the water is added, stop before you think you are done. Less Handling = Less Gluten.

For a Crisp Bottom

- Roll out the dough on finely crushed cookie crumbs.

- Use a glass pie pan so you can see if the bottom is cooked. A dark metal pan will bake a crisp crust, too.

- Always add a cold filling to your unbaked dough, because hot, or even warm, fillings will start to melt the fats in the dough before the pie has a chance to bake.

- Put a cookie sheet or pizza stone in the oven while you're preheating, then place the well-chilled pie on it to bake.

For a Crust That Holds Its Shape

- After constructing the pie, place it in the fridge for 20 to 30 minutes so it can have a little rest time after all that rolling and crimping. The fats can chill back down, too. All of this will help with pie dough shrinkage.

- Place a well-chilled pie in a hot oven 425°F (220°C) to "shock" the cold dough into holding its shape, rather than a room temperature dough that melts in an oven set at a low temperature 325°F (165°C). The hot oven will steam the layers of cold dough apart.

- Pie dough has a memory, and if it has been stretched or roughly handled, it may shrink during the bake. Handle dough with care, and let it drape and fall into a pie pan, or when covering a filling.

For a Darker Crust

- Bake in a glass, dark, or dull metal pan, as all will absorb heat more quickly than other kinds of pans.

- Sugar, egg, milk, or cream cheese in dough will add color to baked crust.

- Use a wash with egg yolk and milk.

- Bake in a high-temperature oven.

- Move the pie higher in the oven in the last part of the bake.

For a Lighter Crust

- Bake the pie in a foil "moat" that wraps around the edges of the pie dough and several inches toward the center of the pie. Toward the end of the bake, pull the foil back so the edges can get some color without burning.

- Cover the pie with a vented foil tent toward the end of the bake if needed.

- Cook at a lower temperature.

- When baked, gluten-free crusts are lighter than all-purpose flour gluten-full crusts.

For an Even Color

- Roll out dough as evenly as possible.

- Brush the wash over dough as evenly as possible.

- Sprinkle sugar lightly and evenly over dough.

- Put less sugar on the highest and thinnest parts of dough.

- If a pie is getting too dark in a bake, it may be time to pull it out of the oven or add a foil "moat" (see above).

Master Recipe: Gluten-Free Dough

Makes two dough discs; halve amounts for one dough disc

When I first started making gluten-free dough in 2006, there were few, if any, off-the-shelf gluten-free flour mixes available. So I made my own flour mix that is xanthan- and gum-free (see Gluten-Free, Gum-Free Dough in a Food Processor, page 54). Now there are some very good off-the-shelf all-purpose gluten-free mixes available, including Bob's Red Mill Gluten Free 1 to 1 Baking Flour and King Arthur Flour Gluten Free Measure for Measure. This recipe will use a total of 1 cup fat (224 g), and our choices are: all butter, a combination of half butter and half leaf lard, or vegetable shortening. It will also use either an egg or an egg replacer, and it uses some baking powder for lift. I get the most consistent results when using a food processor, but I've included by-hand instructions, too. When we use a food processor, our fats stay cooler than when we use warm hands. Gluten-free dough absorbs lots of water and becomes solid and hard the longer it sits in the fridge. So I roll these doughs out soon after they have been made and are still pliable, at about 64°F (18°C).

For even thickness, we'll roll out dough between two pieces of plastic wrap using a straight pin. The plastic wrap really helps with rolling, easing the dough into the pie pan, and finishing edges with a crimp or flute. See How to Roll Out Gluten-Free Dough on page 56 to see the steps.

3 cups (444 g) all-purpose gluten-free flour

1 cup (224 g) fat of your choice, chilled or frozen, cut into small pieces or grated

2 tablespoons granulated sugar (optional)

1 teaspoon aluminum-free baking powder

½ teaspoon salt

½ cup plus 1 tablespoon (133 ml) water

1 egg, fork beaten

1. Place all the ingredients, except the water and egg, in the work bowl of a food processor fit with a metal dough blade, or a medium bowl if making by hand.

- If using a food processor, pulse a bit to break up the butter pieces a bit more.
- If making by hand, use a mezzaluna or pastry blender to chop up the butter into small pieces, or smoosh and pinch them with your fingers. Another option is to grate frozen butter, and smoosh and pinch it into the flour.

2. Sprinkle 3 tablespoons of the water over the dough and mix and pulse by food processor, or fluff with a fork or your hands. Repeat with the remaining water in two additions.

3. Add the egg and pulse a few times if using a machine, or fluff it around with a fork, to mix into dough evenly.

4. Place the dough on a large piece of plastic wrap and tightly pull the edges up around it, pressing with the heels of your hands to mold the plastic-wrapped dough into a ball. The ball can be cut in half, and each part wrapped separately in plastic wrap. Flatten the discs to a height of about ¾ inch (2 cm) and width of 6 inches (15 cm). It is easier to form balls or discs of gluten-free dough when they are wrapped and covered, rather than placing your hands directly on the dough.

5. Chill dough for 10 to 20 minutes in the fridge or even 5 to 7 minutes in the freezer, and roll as soon as possible.

6. When rolling out any gluten-free dough, the dough should be at a pliable temperature, about 64°F (18°C), and rolled between two layers of plastic wrap. Follow the directions for How to Roll Out Gluten-Free Dough (see page 56).

VARIATION

Gluten-Free, Egg-Free Dough

1 tablespoon (10 g) Bob's Red Mill Gluten Free Egg Replacer plus 2 tablespoons water

½ cup plus 1 teaspoon (123 ml) water

After Step 1 of the recipe, add the egg replacer and the 2 tablespoons water and pulse again by machine, or mix by hand until combined. Then proceed with Step 2, using the ½ cup plus 1 teaspoon water. Omit Step 3 and go on to Step 4.

A Pictorial Guide to Making Gluten-Free Dough

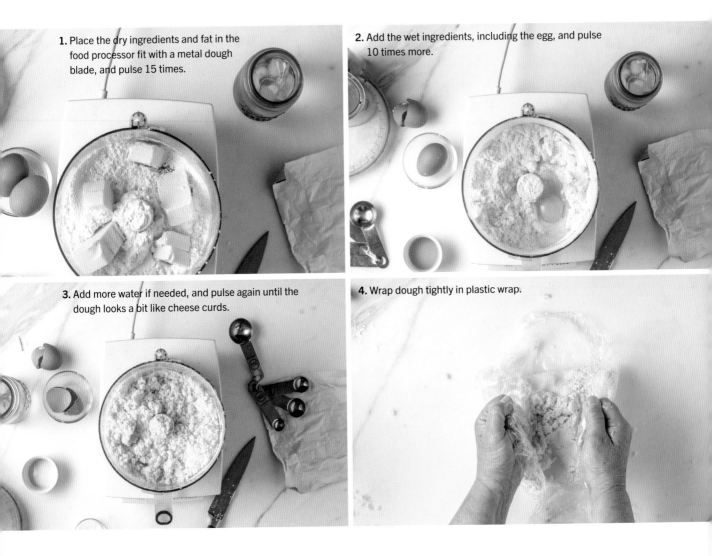

1. Place the dry ingredients and fat in the food processor fit with a metal dough blade, and pulse 15 times.

2. Add the wet ingredients, including the egg, and pulse 10 times more.

3. Add more water if needed, and pulse again until the dough looks a bit like cheese curds.

4. Wrap dough tightly in plastic wrap.

5. Form into a ball and chill.

Gluten-Free, Gum-Free Dough in a Food Processor

This recipe uses a homemade gluten-free flour mix that has no xanthan gum in it. It is the dough that I created before all-purpose gluten-free flours were available off the shelf. This recipe will use a total of 1 cup fat (224 g), and our choices are all butter, a combination of half butter and half leaf lard, or vegetable shortening. For best results, use the metal blade in your food processor.

Makes two dough discs; halve amounts for one dough disc

GLUTEN-FREE FLOUR MIX

¾ cup (95 g) tapioca starch or tapioca flour

¾ cup (98 g) cornstarch

¾ cup (116 g) sweet white rice flour

¼ cup (87 g) potato starch

DOUGH

½ teaspoon salt

1 tablespoon granulated sugar (optional)

1 cup (224 g) fat of your choice, cut into tablespoon-size pieces, chilled

2 large eggs, fork-beaten

1 tablespoon apple cider vinegar (Bragg's or another artisan apple cider vinegar)

2 to 4 tablespoons (30 to 60 ml) ice water, as needed

Additional gluten-free flour for rolling out dough

1. For the gluten-free flour mix: Mix together the tapioca starch, cornstarch, white rice flour, and potato starch.

2. Place the flour mix, salt, and optional sugar in the work bowl of a food processor.

3. Add the fat and pulse on short bursts about 15 times to break up the pieces of fat incompletely.

4. Add the eggs, vinegar, and 2 tablespoons of the ice water and pulse 5 to 10 times more until it looks like cheese curds. If it needs more water, add it now and pulse again. The dough will feel softer and moister than flaky pastry dough made with gluten-full all-purpose flour.

5. Place the dough on a large piece of plastic wrap and tightly pull the edges up around it, pressing with the heels of your hands to mold the plastic wrapped dough into a ball. The ball can be cut in half and each part wrapped separately in plastic wrap. Flatten the discs to a height of about ¾ inch (2 cm) and width of 6 inches (15 cm). It is easier to form balls or discs of gluten-free dough when they are wrapped and covered, rather than placing your hands directly on the dough.

6. Chill the dough for 10 to 20 minutes in the fridge, or even 5 to 7 minutes in the freezer, and roll.

7. When rolling out any gluten-free dough, the dough should be at a pliable temperature and rolled between two layers of plastic wrap. Follow the directions for How to Roll Out Gluten-Free Dough (see page 56).

Baking the Gluten-Free Way

After receiving the bombshell proclamation in 2006 that I was no longer able to eat gluten, I wholeheartedly turned my attention to learning the craft of baking the gluten-free way. A few years later, I was refining a new dough recipe made with different mixes of off-the-shelf gluten-free flour that hadn't been previously available to me in 2006, experimenting with different combinations of gluten-free flours, such as rice and tapioca, to see what combo tasted the best. A few different recipes were getting very good results and enthusiastic comments from tasters and testers, so when I learned of a local pie social being held to thank the volunteers of an environmental non-profit in my area, I offered to bring four pies. I thought it would be a great opportunity to get some unbiased reviews.

The last pie needed a little extra time in the oven before I saw steady bubbling coming through the vents—a sure sign that it had been baked long enough—so I arrived a little on the late side to the gathering. I turned into the parking area and saw that a special pie parking spot had been saved for me. Volunteers helped me carry the still warm pies to the picnic table, and then I stood back and took a deep breath. Folks circled over the new pies—I felt that my pie-making reputation was on the line. I saw slice after slice disappear until the pans were empty. The best compliments I received that day were from a few serious pie makers who sought me out to say how much they loved the pies and what a great crust it was. They were music to my gluten-free ears.

How to Freeze and Defrost Dough

Dough and pie can be frozen if you plan to roll out, bake, or eat it at a later time. It's quite nice to have rolled-out dough already in the freezer that is ready to go anytime the urge to make a pie strikes. I try to use filled frozen pies within one or two months. Here are some tips:

- Gluten-free dough can go straight into the freezer, but let dough made with all-purpose flour rest in the fridge for 20 to 30 minutes to allow the gluten strands to relax before freezing.

- Double wrap in plastic, date, and freeze for up to three months. I have used dough well past that time with good results, after finding them hiding in my freezer, still wrapped well and with no freezer burn.

- Defrost wrapped dough at room temperature until at a rollable temperature. I like to roll my all-purpose flour dough when it is a temperature of about 54°F (12°C), and gluten-free dough at about 64°F (18°C).

- Frozen dough can also be defrosted in the fridge overnight, and then set out on the counter to warm up before rolling.

How to Roll Out Gluten-Free Dough

1. Place the dough on lightly floured plastic wrap and sprinkle a bit more flour on top.

2. Place another layer of plastic over the top of the dough and roll dough out to desired size with a straight pin.

3. Place a dowel pin in the middle of the top layer of plastic wrap, and fold the dough across it. Carefully remove the outer plastic wrap layer using quick little tugs.

4. Center the dough over the pan but do not let the weight of the pin fall onto the edge of the pie pan as it will make an indentation in the dough. Take a hold of the edge of the uppermost part of the inner plastic layer. Lift and let it carry the dough across to the other side so that it fills the entire pan.

5. Keep the plastic layer on top of the dough, and, with your fingers, ease the dough into the pan, taking care that you fit it into the corners. Carefully remove the plastic wrap with quick little tugs.

6. Trim off extra dough. Cover a portion of the dough edge with a small piece of plastic wrap, and form fluted edges with your fingers. Move the plastic wrap as you continue to make the flutes around the entire pan.

1. Place the dough on lightly floured plastic wrap and sprinkle a bit more flour on top.

2. Lay plastic over the top of the dough and roll out with a straight pin

3. Keeping plastic wrap on, fold dough across the pin. Carefully remove outer layer of plastic wrap.

4. Lift uppermost edge of inner plastic wrap layer and carry dough across to fill the entire pan.

5. Keep the plastic layer on top of the dough and ease the dough into the pan.

6. Trim off extra dough, and use the plastic wrap to help form fluted edges. Use plastic wrap to help form fluted edges.

Cream Cheese Pie Dough

An easy-to-make dough for pies of all sizes, and especially nice for crostatas, dumplings, and hand pies. If you are using gluten-free flour, see the note below.

Makes two dough discs; halve amounts for one dough disc

2 cups (290 g) all-purpose flour or gluten-free flour mix (see Note)

2 tablespoons granulated sugar

½ teaspoon salt

½ teaspoon aluminum-free baking powder

12 tablespoons (1½ sticks; 180 g) butter, chilled and cut into ½-inch cubes

½ cup (120 g) cream cheese, chilled and cut into small pieces

1 tablespoon apple cider vinegar (Bragg's or another artisan apple cider vinegar)

3 tablespoons (45 ml) water

TO MAKE BY HAND

1. In a large bowl, place the flour, sugar, salt, and baking powder and mix together with a fork, whisk, or clean fingers.

2. Add the butter and cream cheese and, with clean hands, quickly smoosh the mixture together until it looks like coarse meal with some small peas in it. You can also use a pastry blender or a mezzaluna, chopping up and down.

3. Sprinkle the apple cider vinegar and water over the mixture and mix together with a fork or your fingers.

4. Lightly squeeze and press the dough until it all holds together. Form into a ball or rectangle.

5. Keep the dough whole or divide it in half, wrap in plastic wrap, and chill for about an hour.

TO MAKE IN A FOOD PROCESSOR

1. In the bowl of a food processor fit with the metal blade, place the flour, sugar, salt, and baking powder. Pulse two or three times to combine.

2. Add the butter and cream cheese, and pulse 10 to 15 times until it looks like a coarse meal.

3. Add the vinegar and water, and pulse five more times.

4. Turn the dough into a medium bowl and form into a disc with your hands. Wrap in plastic and place in the fridge for an hour before rolling.

NOTE: There are no gluten strands in dough made with gluten-free flour, so as soon as the fats chill back up, the dough can be rolled out. Gluten-free dough tends to get firm quickly when in the fridge overnight or even after a few hours. Set it out on the counter until it has warmed up to a pliable temperature for rolling.

A Pictorial Guide to an Easy Finish

1. Lay the upper crust on top.

2. Crimp the edge and add vents.

How to Crimp, Flute, and Edge the Crust

There are many ways to finish the edge of a pie. They include flutes, fork crimps, and braids, and shapes cut out with cookie cutters or knives. Braids and shapes are given a light brush of water on the underside before they are placed on the edge of the pie.

Any and everything is fair game for creating fancy flutes and crimps around the pie pan edge. I've used sculpting tools and wood turning and trimming tools that I've picked up at the craft store. I've used the pointy end of a bottle cap opener, vintage sterling silver cocktail and olive forks, and even the dowel handle of a wooden spoon. Look in your gadget drawer and craft box with new eyes. Maybe you'll see an item that might be repurposed to create fancy edges with very uniform shapes.

Place your pie on a rotating cake-decorating stand and spin it around as you trim, crimp, flute, and decorate. A pie camper gave me a 50-plus-year-old stand with a cast-iron base made by Ateco that will last for generations to come.

Care should be taken not to make a design either too tall or too thin, as the dough can burn. Edges can be protected with foil that is placed on at the beginning of a bake and pulled off as the bake progresses so the edges can brown. Or a piece of foil with a vent in the middle can be placed loosely over the top if the crust is browning too quickly due to temperature, oven placement, or over-sugaring (see How to Prevent a Burned Pie Top, page 95).

Cookie cutter hearts: Cut heart shapes from trimmings. Brush with water. Place the hearts on rim, slightly overlapping. Press lightly with fingertips to adhere.

Dowel handle pressed in on angle: Press the dowel into edge at an angle.

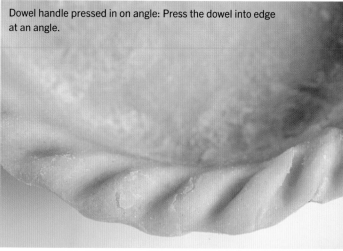

Sculpted edge: Make a stand-up rim. Press a spoon shape sculpting gauge into it.

Checkerboard: Make cuts through the dough and fold alternate sections toward the center of the shell.

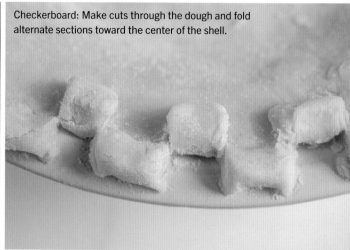

Fork crimps: Press the tines of a fork into the dough edge. If pressed too lightly, the indentation will bake out, but if pressed too deeply they will push through the dough to the pie pan. Aim for the middle ground: not too light and not too deep.

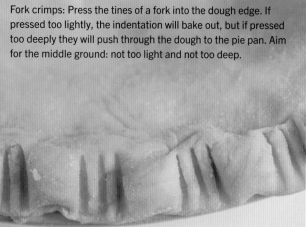

Scallops: Lightly press the tines of a fork into a fluted edge.

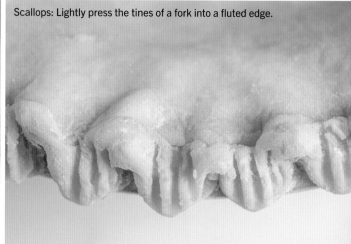

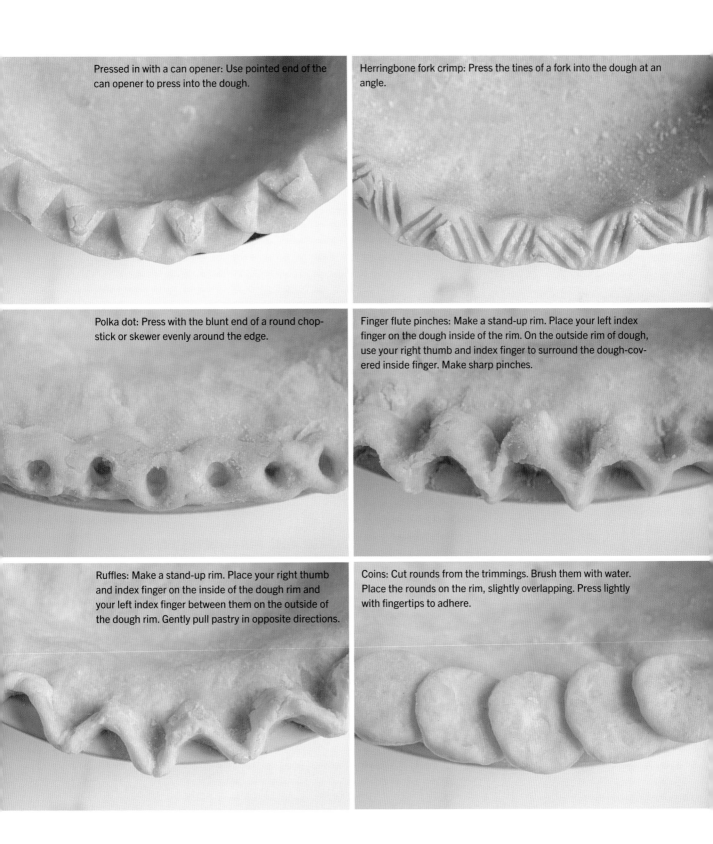

Pressed in with a can opener: Use pointed end of the can opener to press into the dough.

Herringbone fork crimp: Press the tines of a fork into the dough at an angle.

Polka dot: Press with the blunt end of a round chopstick or skewer evenly around the edge.

Finger flute pinches: Make a stand-up rim. Place your left index finger on the dough inside of the rim. On the outside rim of dough, use your right thumb and index finger to surround the dough-covered inside finger. Make sharp pinches.

Ruffles: Make a stand-up rim. Place your right thumb and index finger on the inside of the dough rim and your left index finger between them on the outside of the dough rim. Gently pull pastry in opposite directions.

Coins: Cut rounds from the trimmings. Brush them with water. Place the rounds on the rim, slightly overlapping. Press lightly with fingertips to adhere.

How to Make a Braided Edge

I love the look of a three-strand braid around the edge of a pie. The length of the braid needed will differ as the circumference of pie pans are different. Pie top artist Jessica Leigh Clark-Bojin shared with me the math for how to do this. Now, I am by no wild stretch of the imagination a math wiz. In fact, when I was at college, my math requirements were satisfied by keeping a journal of my thoughts in a class called Math for Liberal Arts Majors. But this calculation harkens back to the days of high school geometry taught by Sister deSales, who I'm sure would be thrilled to know that I am actually using something she taught me way back then.

To find the circumference of your specific pie pan, we'll first need to know its diameter. Take a ruler or a tape measure, and measure how far it is across from outside rim to outside rim, as if it were the equator. Assuming your pie pan is round, this is the diameter of the circle. Now, multiply the diameter by 3.14, which just happens to be pi, the symbol of which is π.

I'll walk you through a sample using an Emile Henry 9-inch (23 cm) deep-dish pie pan. The diameter across the equator of the pie pan is 11⅜ inches. I'm going to round it up to 11½ (29 cm) so our calculation will be 11½ by 3.14 inches = 36 inches (29 cm by 8 cm). This is now the length we will need for one strand of braid. There are three strands in a braid, so we will need 108 inches (2.7 m) . . . or so.

Rolling out a piece of dough into the shape of a skinny, yard-long rectangle is a bit much. So let's splice the ends of shorter lengths together so we can braid in a saner manner like this:

1. Roll out the dough and cut it into equal length strands that are manageable for you.

2. Place a tiny dab of water on the top of one end.

3. Place a bit of the end of a second strand over the damp end of the first strand.

4. Use a gentle but firm touch to press the splice together, taking care that the strip keeps its shape. You can trim it up with a knife or pizza wheel cutter if it gets messy. The main thing is to try and keep the thickness of the dough the same and the strip tidy.

5. Take three spliced strands and braid them into one long length, or braid them into two or three lengths and neatly splice as you go.

6. Brush a little water all the way around the edge of the dough that the braid will sit on.

7. Place the braid on top of the damp edge, and neatly splice the ends as in Steps 3 and 4 so it makes an unbroken circle on top of the dough. With your fingers, lightly press down to secure the braid in place.

NOTES:

- Place the strips on a sheet pan or cookie tin so if the dough begins to warm up, we can cover the pan with plastic wrap, place it in the fridge to chill up a bit, and then continue when it is easier to work.

- Braids add a thicker crust along the edge so unless you, or the folks who will be eating your creation, really love a thick crust edge, I suggest that the width of the strips be no more than ½ inch (1.25 cm), and preferably a little less.

A Pictorial Guide to Making a Lattice Top

Lattice strips can be cut from wide to thin, have wavy or straight edges, and can be made with braided or twisted strips. For thin strips, cut as many ¼ to ½ inch (6 mm to 1.25 cm) wide strips as possible. For medium strips, cut 12 to 14 strips that are ¾ to 1 inch (2 to 2.5 cm) wide. For wide strips on a 9-inch (23 cm) pie pan, I suggest you cut six strips that are about 2 inches (5 cm) wide. Whatever width, edge, or braid you choose, the steps will be the same. We will place our strips on a diagonal to give a little diamond shape when they are woven. We will also turn the pie around 180 degrees in Step 7.

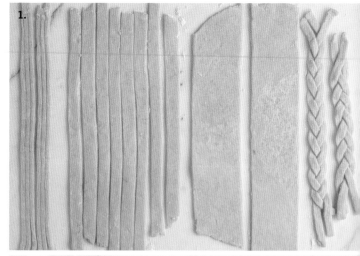

1.

4.

1. Cut strips.

2. Lay half the strips across the pie top with a little space in between.

3. To create the diamond pattern, strip 1 (wide) is folded nearly all the across the pie, strip 3 (triple) a bit more than half way across, and strip 5 (braid) a bit less than half way across. Lay a new strip (plain) on the diagonal crossing strips, 2, 4, and 6 (plain). These are the strips that we did not fold yet.

4. Unfold strip 1 (wide), 3 (triple), and 5 (braid) over the new strip (plain) we placed on the diagonal in step 3, and then fold up strips 2, 4, 6 (all plain) across it as well. Place a new strip (triple) on the diagonal so that it crosses strips 1, 3, and 5.

5. Unfold strips 2, 4, and 6 (plain) over the strip (triple) we placed on the diagonal at the end of step 4. Lay a new strip (plain) on the diagonal so that it crosses strips 2, 4 and 6 (plain).

6. Unfold strip 1 (wide), 3 (triple), and 5 (braid) over the new strip (plain) that we placed on the diagonal at the end of step 5. Place another new strip (plain) on the diagonal so that it crosses strips 1 (wide), 3 (triple), and 5 (braid). Fold strips 2, 4, and 6 down over this new strip (plain).

CONTINUED

7. Turn the pie around 180 degrees; fold back strips 2 (braid), 4 (triple), and 6 (wide), and make sure that strips 1, 3, and 5 (plain) are down.

8. Place a new strip (braid) across strips 1, 3, and 5 (plain).

9. Fold strips 1, 3, and 5 (plain) up across the new strip (braid) we placed on the diagonal at the end of step 8; and unfold strips 2 (braid), 4 (triple), and 6 (wide) down across it. Place a new strip (plain) on the diagonal so that it crosses strips 2 (braid), 4 (triple), and 6 (wide).

10. Unfold strips 1 (plain), 3 (plain), 5 (plain). Trim the extra dough and finish with whatever edge you like.

11. Ta-da! You've made a lattice pie!

7.

8.

9.

10.

11.

No-Weave Lattice

1. Place half the strips going north–south evenly spaced.

2. Top with the remaining strips laid east–west and evenly spaced.

Single Trellis Top

Twist the strips as you lay them across the pie top about 1¼ inches (3.2 cm) apart, going one way only.

No-Weave Trellis Top Lattice

1. Twist the strips as you lay them across the pie top about 1¼ inches (3.2 cm) apart.

2. Twist and lay the remaining strips so that they cross the first strips at 90 degrees.

3. Trim the extra dough and finish with whatever edge you like.

Full Top Triple Lattice

You will need to make 1½ times the roll-out dough recipe for this one.

1. Cut 30 to 36 strips that are ½ to ¾ inch (1.25 to 2 cm) wide.

2. Place 18 strips on top of the pie so that the top is completely covered.

3. Weave the lattice top with the remaining 18 strips, using three strips together as if they were one strip.

Easy Art Tops

Here are a few ideas for easy pie tops that can look quite spectacular.

- Use cookie cutters that are all one geometric shape and place the shapes in patterns.
- Cut out strips that are all big, all little, or some of each, and lay them haphazardly wherever you want, à la Jackson Pollock.
- Instead of a full top crust with vents, cut out a larger circle in the center of your dough to make one big vent, while leaving a 2- to 3-inch (5 to 7.5 cm) border.
- Cut out the dough with heart-shaped cookie cutters and place on top of the filling, in either a symmetrical mandala pattern or randomly. Use the same size or different size heart cutters.
- Before laying the dough on top of the filling, cut out heart shapes, and let them be vents.
- Cut out circles with a biscuit cutter, and use a smaller circle to cut out the middle so that you have a round border, and smaller circles. Make a slice through each of the border pieces and fit them together like a chain. Gently splice each open edge back together with your finger. Place the chain in a circle pattern on top, with the smaller circle pieces around the edge. Be sure to brush the back of each circle with a little water to "glue" it in place.
- Before laying the dough on top of the filling, use a small to medium cookie cutter shape to cut out shapes on half of the dough, and save the shapes. Place the dough on top of the filling so that the open cut outs cover half the pie. Place the saved dough cutouts on top of the plain half of the dough. Be sure to brush the back of each shape with a little water to "glue" in place.
- Make a lattice top alternating thick and thin strips.
- Make a lattice with braided strips going one direction, and plain unbraided strips going the other.
- Make a lattice top with thin strips placed right next to each other. Hold two or more strips together as if they were one, and weave them up and down.
- Make one dough braid long enough to coil around a pie top. Splice edges as needed.
- Cut out the dough with leaf-shaped cookie cutters and place the leaves all over the top of the pie. If you want, cut out a trunk and some branches. Brush the back of each leaf with a little water and "glue" them on the branches.
- Cut out the dough with flower-shaped cookie cutters and place the flowers all over the top of the pie.

How to Blind Bake a Crust

A pre-baked and cooled crust is used for pies with fillings that require no baking at all. Fully baking a crust with no filling is called blind baking. When an unfilled piecrust is partially baked, it is called par-baking. The process for both is simple, but there are a few things to know.

WE WILL NEED

1 pie pan

½ recipe Roll-Out Dough (1 disc of dough; see Roll-Out Dough recipes, pages 38–58)

A fork or dough docker

Plastic wrap

Sheet pan

Parchment paper, sheet pan liner, aluminum foil, or a commercial paper coffee filter with a flat bottom

Pie weights (rice, beans, lentils, or a combination of them, granulated sugar, or ceramic or metal pie weights)

1. Place a pie pan in the fridge or freezer to chill.

2. Roll out the dough to about 2 inches (5 cm) larger than the size of your pie pan. If using a rolling dough docker, dock it now.

3. Gently place the dough in a chilled pie pan. Flute or crimp the edges (see How to Crimp, Flute, and Edge the Crust, page 59). The dough may shrink some in the bake so be sure it extends all the way to the edge of the pie pan.

4. If you are docking by a fork, lightly pierce the bottom and sides of the dough all over.

5. Cover with plastic wrap and place in the freezer for 30 minutes.

6. Place a sheet pan on the lowest rack in the oven and preheat to 375°F (190°C).

7. Remove the plastic wrap and cover the dough with a sheet of parchment paper, sheet pan liner, commercial paper coffee filter with a flat bottom, or lightly buttered piece of foil. Whatever you choose, cut it about 2 inches (5 cm) larger than the pie pan so you can lift the hot pie weights out without spilling them after the first bake.

8. Fill the pie pan with pie weights of choice, which can be rice, beans, lentils, or a combination of them, granulated sugar, or commercially purchased ceramic or metal pie weights.

9. Place the pie pan in the preheated oven and bake for 20 to 25 minutes.

10. Remove from the oven and set on a rack.

11. Carefully remove the liner with the pie weights and place in a large bowl.

12. If a par-baked crust is needed, let cool completely before filling.

13. If fully baking the crust, lower the temperature to 350°F (175°C), return the partially baked pie to the oven, and bake for another 7 to 10 minutes until the crust is a light golden brown. If the crust needs more color, blind bake it longer.

14. Remove from the oven, set on a rack, and let cool before filling.

NOTE: An old-fashioned dough docker looks like a big wooden-handled comb, with tines for pressing into the dough. There are also rolling dockers made out of plastic.

Pie Camp Tips for Blind Baking

Here are a few handy hints for ensuring a successful blind-baked crust.

- Air bubbles, also called blisters, can form while unfilled dough bakes. To avoid these, once the dough is placed in the pan, prick it all over with a fork. This is called docking the dough.

- To decrease shrinkage during a bake, after docking the dough, place the pie pan with dough in the freezer for 30 minutes while you preheat the oven. I have never had a pie pan shatter on me during a blind bake, but I don't suggest blind baking or par-baking in a pan that has great sentimental value or is irreplaceable.

- To avoid a meltdown or slump during a blind bake, remove the pan from the freezer, cover the dough with parchment, a sheet pan liner, a flat bottom coffee filter, or a lightly buttered piece of foil, and fill with pie weights. Be sure the liner is big enough so that after it is filled with weights, everything can be lifted away from the baked crust without anything spilling into it, or onto the counter or floor.

- You can purchase ceramic or metal pie weights, or use dry beans, lentils, or rice from your pantry, which can be reused. So as not to use them in soups and stews, I place the beans, lentils, or rice in a special storage container marked "Pie Weights." It takes about 1¼ to 1½ pounds of weights for a 9-inch (23 cm) shallow pan, and 2 pounds for a 9-inch (23 cm) deep-dish pan. Adjust as needed for smaller or larger pans.

- Try using granulated sugar as a pie weight. It will toast as it bakes, and after can be cooled, stored, and used as an ingredient in any recipe that might benefit from sugar with a slightly toasted flavor.

- Place the weights on top of the liner that covers the rolled-out dough in the pan. Liners can be parchment paper, sheet pan liner, aluminum foil, or a commercial paper coffee filter with a flat bottom. A coffee filter has the added benefit of soaking up extra butter and fat. With your hands, smooth the weights up along the sides so that they come almost to the top and are placed evenly on the bottom.

- Another option that some do, although I have not, is to place unbaked dough in a pie pan, fit a sheet of foil on top of the dough, set an empty pie pan on top of it, and blind bake. The extra pie pan placed on top will hold the shape of the dough.

- To give the bottom of the pie dough a good bake, preheat a sheet pan and bake the filled pie pan on it.

- So as to avoid the baked crust getting soft, set the par-baked or blind baked crust on a rack and let cool before filling.

- If a bit of the dough has stuck onto the backside of the parchment, sheet pan liner, foil, or coffee filter because of the pie weights, gently scrape it off while it is still warm and pliable. Then pat it onto the spot in the crust where it came from. As it will be under the filling, no one will be the wiser.

- For extra crispness and flavor, roll out the dough on finely crushed cookie crumbs. Optionally, spread a light coating of egg wash on the inside of the blind-baked crust, and then place it back in the oven for an additional 3 to 5 minutes. This will provide a barrier between the crust and the filling to keep the crust crisp.

- To freeze a blind-baked pie shell, let the baked shell cool completely. Double wrap in plastic wrap, mark with the date of baking, and freeze for up to three months. To defrost when ready to use, remove the shell from the freezer and unwrap. Place in a preheated 450°F (230°C) oven for 8 to 10 minutes. The shell is now ready to be filled according to whatever recipe you are using.

1. A docked dough with fluted edges.

2. Dough lined with parchment, filled with beans for pie weights, and ready to be baked.

Master Recipe: Press-In Crumb Crust

Makes one 9-inch (23 cm)
deep-dish pie (amounts for other size
pies to follow)

I still remember the sound the wax paper made when a new pack of honey grahams was opened. Even though the wrapping has changed and it makes a different sound now, when I'm making crumb crusts with graham crackers I steal away at least one section of a cracker to dunk in milk, just like I did when I was a little girl. Use gluten-free cookies for a gluten-free version. Your own recipes for crisp homemade cookies will be just fine, too. The weight of cookie varieties will be different, so in this instance, using a measuring cup may be the way to go. This is a quick and easy crust to make. Just whirl up some cookies in a food processor until they are fine crumbs, mix in a bit of sugar and melted butter, press into a pie pan, and pop into the oven for a short bake.

2½ cups (300 g) cookie crumbs (graham
cracker, peanut butter, chocolate, or vanilla
wafers)

3 tablespoons (37 g) granulated sugar

6 tablespoons (84 g) butter, melted

A FEW OPTIONAL EXTRAS

1 teaspoon cinnamon, ginger, or cardamom

½ teaspoon vanilla or other extract of your
choice

½ teaspoon orange zest

½ cup chopped nuts

½ cup shredded sweetened coconut

1. Preheat the oven to 350°F (175°C).

2. Make the cookie crumbs by processing them in a food processor or placing them in a large resealable bag and rolling with your pin until finely crushed.

3. Place the cookie crumbs, sugar, and optional extras into a bowl. Add the melted butter and distribute it well with clean hands or a fork.

4. Turn the mixture into the pie pan and evenly spread it out over the bottom and up the sides, but do not spread on top of the rim. You can use your fingers, the back of a spoon, or even the rounded side of a coffee cup or a small bowl. Try to make the depth of the crust even on the sides and the bottom.

5. Bake for 6 to 8 minutes until the edges have gained a little color. Remove from the oven and set aside to cool.

VARIATIONS

For a 9-Inch (23 cm) Shallow Pie or 8-Inch (20 cm) Deep-Dish Pie

1¾ cups (213 g) cookie crumbs

2 tablespoons granulated sugar

4 tablespoons (56 g) butter, melted

For a 10-Inch (25 cm) Pie

3 cups (360 g) cookie crumbs

¼ cup (50 g) granulated sugar

8 tablespoons (1 stick; 112 g) butter, melted

PRESS-IN CRUMB CRUST VARIATIONS

Vanilla Macadamia Nut Crust
Makes one 9-inch (23 cm) shallow pie or one 8-inch (20 cm) deep-dish pie

Use this variation for the Coconut Mascarpone Cream Pie (page 262) and Red Goose Pie (page 195).

1¾ cups (180 g) vanilla wafer crumbs (for gluten-free, use Kinnikinnick Gluten Free Vanilla Wafers)

½ cup (75 g) finely chopped macadamia nuts

2 tablespoons granulated sugar

5 tablespoons (70 g) butter, melted

½ teaspoon orange zest (optional)

Chocolate Sandwich Cookie Crumb Crust
Makes one 9-inch (23 cm) shallow pie or one 8-inch (20 cm) deep-dish pie

This press-in crust uses the entire sandwich cookie including the filling. Use this variation for an Ice Cream Pie (page 302).

1¾ cups (227 g) chocolate sandwich cookie crumbs (for gluten-free use Mi-Del Chocolate Sandwich Cookies)

2 tablespoons granulated sugar

4 tablespoons (56 g) butter, melted

Gingersnap Crumb Crust
Makes one 9-inch (23 cm) shallow pie or one 8-inch (20 cm) deep-dish pie

Use this variation for the Triple Ginger Cream Pie (page 185) or an Ice Cream Pie (page 302).

1¾ cups (213 g) gingersnap cookie crumbs

2 tablespoons granulated sugar

5 tablespoons (70 g) butter, melted

½ teaspoon orange zest (optional)

Oatmeal Crumb Crust

Makes one 9-inch (23 cm) deep-dish pie

Another easy-to-make press-in crust is made with old-fashioned rolled oats and brown sugar. In this recipe, I process the oats to make them smaller. If you are gluten-free, be sure to use gluten-free oats. Add a teaspoon of cinnamon, or ½ teaspoon of vanilla or orange zest, for some extra flavor.

2½ cups (270 g) old-fashioned rolled oats

½ cup all-purpose (70 g) or gluten-free flour (55 g; weight may vary by brand)

½ cup (100 g) brown sugar, packed

½ teaspoon salt

6 tablespoons (84 g) butter, melted

1. Preheat the oven to 350°F (175°C).

2. Place the rolled oats in the bowl of a food processor and process until they are the size of crumbs. It's okay to have some smaller pieces of oat flakes remaining.

3. Add the flour, brown sugar, and salt and process again to mix thoroughly.

4. Add the melted butter and process again to mix thoroughly.

5. Turn the mixture into the pie pan and evenly spread it out over the bottom and up the sides, but do not spread on top of the rim. You can use your fingers, the back of a spoon, or even the rounded side of a coffee cup or small bowl. Try to make the depth of the crust even on the sides and the bottom.

6. Bake for 12 minutes. Remove from the oven, let cool, and fill.

NOTE: This baked and cooled crust can be made ahead and frozen. Place plastic wrap around the filled pie pan and place in the freezer for up to one month.

Coconut Almond Oat Crust

Makes one 9-inch (23 cm) deep-dish pie or one 10-inch (25 cm) tart

I once needed to make an entire pie, from crust to filling, in just one hour to take to a potluck supper. I looked in my cupboard to see what I had on hand. Partial bags of shredded coconut, almond flour, and old-fashioned rolled oats. I used the oats whole since I didn't have time to use the food processor to make a little smaller. I combined everything with some sugar and melted butter, pressed the mixture into a 10-inch (25 cm) tart pan, and gave it a quick bake in the oven. The result was amazing. This crust has since become one of my all-time favorites. You can size down the ingredients for a smaller pan, or use it all in the smaller pan and make the crust a bit thicker. Be creative and add extra flavor with a teaspoon of cinnamon, ginger, or cardamom.

1 cup (110 g) shredded sweetened coconut

1 cup (100 g) almond flour

1 cup (100 g) old-fashioned rolled oats

2 to 4 tablespoons granulated sugar (depending on how sweet you would like it)

5 tablespoons (70 g) butter, melted

1. Preheat the oven to 350°F (175°C).

2. Pour the coconut, almond flour, oats, and sugar into a bowl. Add the melted butter and distribute well with clean hands or a fork.

3. Turn the mixture into the pie pan and evenly spread it out over the bottom and up the sides, but do not spread on top of the rim. You can use your fingers, the back of a spoon, or even the rounded side of a coffee cup or small bowl. Try to make the depth of the crust even on the sides and the bottom.

4. Bake for 15 to 18 minutes, until the crust looks golden brown and the tips of the coconut are beginning to darken.

5. Remove from the oven and set aside.

VARIATIONS

Coconut Almond Oat Ginger Crust

Add 1 teaspoon ground ginger.

Coconut Almond Oat Cinnamon Crust

Add 1 teaspoon cinnamon.

Coconut Almond Oat Cardamom Crust

Add 1 teaspoon cardamom.

Hazelnut Meal or Almond Flour Crust

Nut crusts are made in the same way as cookie crumb crusts. You'll find hazelnut meal and almond flour (almond meal) online or at some grocery stores. Store any extra nut flours in tightly sealed containers in the fridge.

Makes one 9-inch (23 cm) shallow pie, but you might be able to stretch it to fit a 9-inch (23 cm) deep-dish pie

2 cups (224 g) hazelnut meal or almond flour

3 to 4 tablespoons granulated sugar (depending on how sweet you would like it)

½ teaspoon salt

½ teaspoon cinnamon (optional)

5 tablespoons (70 g) butter, melted

1. Preheat the oven to 350°F (175°C).

2. Place the hazelnut meal, sugar, salt, and optional cinnamon into a medium bowl. Add the melted butter and distribute well with clean hands or a fork.

3. Turn the mixture into the pie pan and evenly spread it out over the bottom and up the sides, but do not spread on top of the rim. You can use your fingers, the back of a spoon, or even the rounded side of a coffee cup or small bowl. Try to make the depth of the crust even on the sides and the bottom.

4. Bake for 6 minutes for the hazelnut meal crust or 10 minutes for the almond flour crust, until the edges get a bit of color. Remove from the oven and set aside to cool.

Classic Fruit Pies

Fruity

Pies

Classic Fruit Pies

How to Make a Fruit Pie Filling in Five Easy Steps

1.
Measure.

2.
Sweeten.

3.
Season.

4.
Thicken.

5.
Taste.

Classic Fruit Pies

Now that we have learned to make dough, let's move on to making fruit pie filling. We will learn to make a fruit pie filling in Five Easy Steps. Our goal is to become adept and confident in the making of fruit pies no matter what season or variety of fruit. Years after attending Pie Camp, pie campers send me photos of beautiful pies they have made with just-picked fruit, telling me how they enjoy sharing them with friends and family. You can do this, too. Pie does not need be complicated to be delicious.

I'll walk you through each of these steps. But first, an important public service announcement about flavor.

Flavorful Fruit = Flavorful Pie

Use the best tasting fruit you can find and use no fruit before its time. Taste before buying, harvesting, and adding to your filling. Yes, you can add sugar and spice, but neither will do much of anything if your fruit is lacking in flavor. Tasteless Fruit = Tasteless Pie, and tasteless fruit is best repurposed to the compost bin. Let these words be your mantra: Flavorful Fruit = Flavorful Pie.

Step One: Measure: How Much Fruit To Use

I use either a 9-inch (23 cm) shallow pie pan or a 9-inch (23 cm) deep-dish pie pan. In the recipes I will tell you which pan I specifically use and the exact amounts of ingredients. I've also made a chart for you that you might want to bookmark (see Ingredients and Amounts for Fruit Pie Fillings, page 85), so that once you've learned the Five Easy Steps of fruit pie filling, you can turn to it and be on your way to making any fruit pie.

Fruits like cherries, berries, peaches, and other stone fruits are super juicy, and if we mound them up in the pie pan like a mountain, chances are they will overflow during the bake and give us a smoking oven that will need to be cleaned. Not my favorite chore and likely not yours, either. So let's remember Rule #2: Keep Your Boundaries. This rule tells you the amount of fruit needed for just about any fruit pie.

- For a 9-inch (23 cm) shallow pan, the total fruit needed will be 4 cups.
- For a 9-inch (23 cm) deep-dish pan, the total fruit needed will be 6 cups.

Our practice pie will use any single fruit or a mix, and can be either fresh or frozen. If using frozen fruit, we won't thaw it because thawed fruit lets loose its juice before it is baked.

My rule of thumb method for measuring fruit for all fruit pies is to place the fruit in the pie pan and then take a look at how high it is filled. For juicy fruit like berry, cherry, rhubarb, peach, plum, and such, the height should average out to slightly below the rim of the pan, with some pieces a little higher, and some a little lower. Apple and pear fillings can be mounded higher above the rim. I do like to include a little extra for tasting purposes. Now, turn the fruit into your bowl, wipe out the pie pan, and set it aside or underneath your bowl if you are short on counter space. Let's go on to Step Two.

Step Two: Sweeten

The purpose of sweetener is to exalt the flavor of the fruit, but never to mask it so much that the result is cloying. The best words of advice I can share with you are this: you can always add, but it is difficult, if not impossible, to remove. On occasion, a fruit is perfect just as it is and may not need any sweetener at all, but most fruits will require some sweetener. There are many options for sweeteners. They include brown, granulated, turbinado, maple, and date sugars, and liquid sweeteners like maple syrup and honey (see section on Sweetener, page 26). Today, we'll use granulated sugar like my grandmother did.

- For our fruit pie made in the 9-inch (23 cm) shallow pan, add ⅜ to 1¼ cups (75 to 250 g) granulated sugar.
- For our fruit pie made in the 9-inch (23 cm) deep-dish pan, add ½ to 1½ cups (100 to 300 g) granulated sugar.

Reserve some of the sugar before adding it to the fruit in the mixing bowl. After we have taste tested in Step Five, we can add it in. This is what is called adjusting for taste.

Step Three: Season

Like sugar, seasoning should exalt a filling, and not mask or overpower it. Whether cinnamon, allspice, nutmeg, ginger, cardamom, salt, lemon or vinegar, or liqueurs, to name a few, seasonings used are your own choice. You'll find suggestions for seasoning specific fruits in the chart on page 85. Use a light hand when adding seasoning, and after taste testing in Step Five, you can add more to your own taste.

It's just fine to experiment with spices or liqueurs. Nothing ventured, nothing gained, right? You might create something that I never would have thought of, get rave reviews at your own dining table, or win first place in a pie contest. Just go slow and remember that you can always add more, but that it's hard to take it out. It's a Rule #2 thing.

Step Four: Thicken

To thicken, we have three different options: all-purpose or gluten-free flour, cornstarch, or tapioca (either flour or quick-cooking). Each one will thicken our filling when it is baked and cooled.

- For our fruit pie filling in a shallow pan, use 3 tablespoons to ½ cup (25 to 70 g) all-purpose flour or gluten-free flour, or 1½ to 2½ tablespoons tapioca (either flour or quick-cooking), or 2½ teaspoons to 2½ tablespoons cornstarch, or a mixture of thickeners as suggested in the chart on page 85.
- For our fruit pie filling in a deep-dish pie pan, use ¼ to ½ cup (35 to 70 g) all-purpose flour or gluten-free flour, or 2½ to 3 table-spoons tapioca (either flour or quick-cooking), or 1 to 3 tablespoons cornstarch, or a mixture of thickeners as suggested in the chart on page 85.

Notes on Thickeners

- When using quick-cooking tapioca, let the mixed filling sit for 10 to 15 minutes. The little pieces of tapioca will soften up some during that time, although some may still be visible when baked.
- Gluten-free flour tends to soak up more liquid, so use up to a tablespoon less flour in either size pan.

- If the fruit is exceptionally juicy, I suggest using two different thickeners (see the chart on page 85).

Step Five: Taste

Remember that taste is totally subjective.

- With fingers, a spoon, or a fork, lightly mix everything together in the bowl.
- Now taste.
- If that first taste makes you want to have another one, your filling is good to go.
- If you want more sweetener or seasoning, add what you reserved in Steps Two and Three, or even more. When you arrive at the moment where you want to keep taking more bites because you love it, your filling is ready to go into a chilled pie shell, topped with a lattice or full top crust, and placed in a preheated oven.

What about Dotting with Butter?

This is usually done after the filling goes into the pie pan, but I mention it here because 95 percent of the time I forget to do it! So that you won't forget, take a knob of butter (the size of a small walnut), break or cut it up into a few tiny pieces, and mix it right into the filling before turning it into the chilled pie shell.

How to Choose Thickener for Fruit Pie Filling

I stick with three main thickeners: flour, cornstarch, and quick-cooking tapioca.

FLOUR: I use flour in many fruit pie fillings, and I find it does especially well for apple and pear. Mix it well into the filling. Look for some slight bubbling to come out of the vents or lattice when the filling is done.

CORNSTARCH: When making a stove-top fruit filling, I use cornstarch. Cook the filling until it is opaque and shiny, and make sure the filling is bubbling before removing it from the oven. Cornstarch can also be used for an oven-baked fruit filling. Using too much cornstarch or under-baking can make for a gloppy filling. Cornstarch is ideal for a creating shiny filling in a cherry pie, and great for a cranberry pie, too.

TAPIOCA (QUICK-COOKING AND FLOUR): This is especially great for juicy fruit fillings like berries and stone fruits. When using quick-cooking tapioca, I place all the ingredients in the bowl, mix, and then let sit for 10 to 15 minutes. The little pieces of tapioca will soften up some during that time. You may still see some pieces floating around in your pie, but they will be soft. Tapioca must reach a temperature that is high enough for it to thicken a filling properly. Look for steady bubbling coming through the vents or lattice.

COMBINING THICKENERS: It is fine to use more than one thickener with fruit that is especially juicy, like rhubarb. Some quick-cooking tapioca or cornstarch, in addition to flour, will help that filling thicken up. Always look for bubbling coming through the vents or lattice.

How Much Does That Pie Pan Hold?

I bake in pans that are round, oval, square, rectangular, and hexagonal. I even have one that is in the shape of the pi symbol for use on March 14. Roughly, my collection is a bit over 100 pie pans, but the number fluctuates—sometimes a pie pan doesn't make it back home after it leaves my kitchen. I don't worry too much about it, as usually another shows up to takes its place. What I have noticed in having a collection of this size is that there is some variation in how much a pie pan holds. So keep that in mind and make a note for yourself for the next time you use that pan.

Ingredients and Amounts for Fruit Pie Fillings

- A 9-inch deep-dish pie pan will hold about 6 cups, about 1½ to 2 pounds of fruit.
- A 9-inch shallow pie pan will hold about 4 cups of fruit, about 1 to 1½ pounds fruit.
- Use the smaller amounts of sugar, seasoning, and thickener for a shallow pie pan.
- Apples and pears can be mounded up in the pie pan, but don't mound juicy fruits.
- Sugar amounts are suggestions and should be based on the sweetness of the fruit.
- Seasonings are also suggestions. Feel free to add other spices you like.
- Always take a taste of the filling to adjust amounts to your own taste before baking.

FRUIT	SUGAR	SEASONING	THICKENER	OPTIONAL
Apple/Pear 6–10 cups (5–10 apples or pears depending on size of fruit)	⅜–½ cup (75–100 g)	1 teaspoon cinnamon, ½ teaspoon allspice, a pinch nutmeg, ½ teaspoon salt, 1 tablespoon lemon juice or apple cider vinegar	⅓–½ cup (50–70 g) all-purpose flour	Apple or pear liqueur, walnuts or pecans, cranberries, quince
Berry (can be mixed) 4–6 cups blackberry, raspberry, loganberry, strawberry, blueberry, mulberry	⅔–¾ cup (130–150 g)	A pinch nutmeg, a squeeze of ½ lemon, or 1½ teaspoons to 1 tablespoon fruit-flavored vinegar, ¼–⅓ teaspoon salt	¼–⅓ cup (35–50 g) all-purpose flour or 2–2½ tablespoons tapioca (flour or quick-cooking)	Orange liqueur
Cherry 4–6 cups sour or sweet cherries	Sour: ⅞–1 cup (175–200 g), Sweet: ⅝–⅔ cup (120–135 g)	A pinch nutmeg, a squeeze of ½ lemon, ¼–⅓ teaspoon salt	2½–3 tablespoons tapioca (flour or quick-cooking) or cornstarch	Almond or orange liqueur
Stone fruit 4–6 cups peach, nectarine, apricot, plum	½–¾ cup (100–150 g)	A pinch nutmeg, a squeeze of ½ lemon, ¼–⅓ teaspoon salt	3 tablespoons–¼ cup (25–35 g) all-purpose flour plus 1½–2 tablespoons tapioca (flour or quick-cooking) if fruit is especially juicy	Orange liqueur
Rhubarb 4–6 cups	1–1¼ cups (200–225 g)	A pinch nutmeg, a squeeze of ½ lemon, ¼–⅓ teaspoon salt	⅓–½ cup (50–70 g) all-purpose flour plus 1½–2 teaspoons tapioca (flour or quick-cooking)	Orange liqueur
Mixed fruit juicy 4–6 cups strawberry-rhubarb, apricot-raspberry, peach-blackberry, blueberry-peach	⅔–¾ cup (130–150 g)	A pinch nutmeg, a squeeze of ½ lemon or 1½ teaspoons–1 tablespoon fruit-flavored vinegar, ¼–⅓ teaspoon salt	2½ tablespoons tapioca (flour or quick-cooking) or ¼ cup (35 g) all-purpose flour	Fruit liqueur
Cranberry 4–6 cups	1¼–1½ cups (250–300 g)	A pinch nutmeg, a squeeze of ½ lemon, ¼–⅓ teaspoon salt	2½ teaspoons–1 tablespoon plus ½ teaspoon cornstarch	Orange liqueur, walnuts
Fejoia (Pineapple Guava) 4–6 cups	⅔–¾ cup (130–150 g)	A squeeze of ½ lemon or lime, or 1–2 teaspoon splash of citrus vinegar, ¼–⅓ teaspoon salt	¼–⅓ cup plus 1 tablespoon (45–55 g) all-purpose flour, plus ½ teaspoon tapioca (flour or quick-cooking)	Fruit liqueur
Currant 4–6 cups red, black, or white currants	1–1¼ cups sugar (200–225 g)	A pinch nutmeg, a squeeze of ½ lemon, ¼–⅓ teaspoon salt	¼–⅓ cup (35–50 g) flour or 2½ tablespoons tapioca (flour or quick-cooking)	Cream de cassis
Gooseberry 4–6 cups	¾–1 cup (150–200 g)	A pinch nutmeg, a squeeze of ½ lemon, ¼–⅓ teaspoon salt	2–2½ tablespoons tapioca (flour or quick-cooking) plus 1½–2 tablespoons all-purpose flour	Orange liqueur
Loquat 4–6 cups	⅔–¾ cup (130–150 g)	A squeeze of ½ lemon	1–1½ tablespoons tapioca (flour or quick-cooking)	Orange liqueur

What Is Pectin?

Pectin is a plant-based gelling substance that naturally occurs in some fruits. We usually think of pectin when making jams and jellies, which require an addition of sugar to set.

A list of fruits with high levels of pectin include:

- Apple
- Blackberry, unripe
- Cranberry
- Currant
- Gooseberry
- Quince
- Citrus peel, from which commercially available pectin is made.

J. Kenji López-Alt writes in *The Food Lab* that tart apples have a lower pH and contain more pectin. Because of this, the tart apple bakes more firmly than its sweet sister. The pectin acts as "molecular glue that holds together an apple's cells." I would add that sometimes in a bake, firm apples never seem to soften up at all. So using a mix of apples, some for tart (that hold their shape) and some for sweet (that soften up to become a little smooshy and juicy), makes for a nicely textured filling with exciting flavor.

You'll see that some recipes in these pages call for optional peeling of apples. Pectin is contained in apple peels as well, along with some flavor. Though fruits with naturally occurring pectin like those listed in the preceding list can help with thickening, let us not completely forgo the use of flour, tapioca, or cornstarch in our fillings, as their addition will benefit greatly the end result.

Master Recipe: Fruit Pie

Makes one 9-inch (23 cm) deep-dish or shallow pie

Fruit, sweetener, seasoning, thickener, and taste are the key elements to making fruit pie. With the simple steps in this master recipe, we can use any fruit—either fresh or frozen—and choose and adjust sweeteners and seasonings to our own taste, for limitless variations of easy-to-make delicious pie. If using frozen fruit, don't defrost beforehand, as doing so let loose its juice before the pie is ready to be baked. Use frozen fruit exactly as if it were fresh. Okay, now let's get creative with fruit pie.

1 recipe Roll-Out Dough (see Roll-Out Dough recipes, pages 38–58)

4 to 6 cups fruit (see chart on page 85)

⅜ to 1¼ cups granulated sugar (75 to 225 g) (see chart)

¼ to ½ teaspoon salt

¾ teaspoon spices of choice (see chart)

1 to 2 gratings or pinch of nutmeg (if using, see chart)

Thickener (see chart)

Lemon, apple cider, or other fruit-flavored vinegar (see chart)

Liqueur (optional; see chart)

2 teaspoons (9 g) butter, chopped into little pieces

1 to 2 teaspoons granulated or demerara sugar, for sprinkling on top of the pie

EGG WASH

1 egg white plus 2 teaspoons water, fork beaten (or other wash of your choice; see Washes for the Top, page 90)

1. Make the pie dough and chill in the fridge while you make the filling. Also place the pie pan in the fridge or freezer to chill.

2. Prepare the fruit:

- Apples: should be peeled if the skin seems thick, as on Granny Smiths or Cosmic Crisps, then slice or chunk them up into pieces you can comfortably get into your mouth, but not so big that they may still be crunchy at the end of the bake time.

- Stone fruits, such as peaches, nectarines, plums, and cherries, will need to be pitted and, if needed, chopped or sliced into a smaller size.

- Berries, unless exceptionally large like some strawberries, can be kept whole.

- Rhubarb should be cut into pieces about ¾ inch (2 cm).

3. In a large mixing bowl, place the fruit, sugar, salt, spices, optional liqueur, and thickener and mix lightly until most of the surfaces are covered. Taste the filling and adjust the sweetener and seasoning to your own taste.

4. Roll out one disc of the dough and place in the chilled pie pan.

5. Pour the filling into the unbaked pie shell and dot with the butter.

6. Roll out the remaining dough, lay it over the fruit, and cut five or six vents on top, or make a lattice top (see A Pictorial Guide to Making a Lattice Top, pages 64–67.) Trim the excess dough from the edges and crimp (see How to Crimp, Flute, and Edge the Crust, page 59).

7. Cover the pie and chill in the fridge while you preheat the oven to 425°F (220°C).

8. Bake for 20 minutes.

9. Turn the oven down to 375°F (190°C) and bake for another 20 minutes.

10. Open the oven, carefully remove the pie, set it on a heat-safe surface, and close the oven to keep the heat inside. Quickly and carefully brush the top of the pie with the egg wash and then sprinkle lightly with sugar. Return the pie to the oven and continue baking at 375°F (190°C) for an additional 20 minutes.

11. Look for steam and a slight bit of juice coming out of the vents before removing it from the oven. Get your ear right down almost to the top of the pie and listen for the sizzle-whump (see below), which some call the pie's heartbeat.

12. Cool for at least 1 hour before slicing.

The Sound of Sizzle-Whump

sizzle-whump | si-zəl (h)wəmp | noun

The sound a double-crusted pie makes when it is ready to come out of the oven. The crust makes a sizzling sound and the bubbling filling hits the inside of the upper crust, making a whumping noise. Some people refer to the sizzle-whump as the pie's heartbeat.

Tips for the Tops

Vents

Rule #3 of pie making: Vent. A fruit pie needs vents to allow the heat and steam to come out so a boiling filling won't burst through unexpectedly in a weak spot. It's important to let the heat out in ourselves, too, and creating vents on top of a pie is a way to vent in a positive manner. Vents are a pie maker's signature. They can be simple slashes in various shapes: arrows, herringbone, star, A for apple, or X, Y, or Z. Intricate designs, using cookie cutters or a sharp knife, can also be achieved by cutting through the top of a rolled-out dough when it is still on the rolling mat. The top is then carefully transferred and centered to cover a filling. Of course, a few slashes with a knife, or pokes with the tines of a fork, on a pie top just before it goes into the oven are fine, too.

Here are some other ideas for creative venting:

- A sunburst with ½-inch (1.25 cm) strips that meet in the middle and are topped with a circle.
- Pinwheel shapes that meet in the middle.
- A long 1-inch- (2.5 cm) wide strip that starts in the center and spirals out to the edge. Splice together strips with a little water as needed.

Washes for the Top

To apply a wash, use a brush that is made of either natural bristle or easy-to-clean silicone. A crushed-up piece of parchment paper or sheet pan liner works, as will your fingers. Each wash or glaze will give a slightly different look to the top of a pie. Here are a few to choose from and how to make them.

WHOLE EGG WITH WATER: In a small bowl, place a whole egg (both yolk and white) and fork beat with 1 tablespoon water until mixed and spreadable.

EGG YOLK WITH WATER: In a small bowl, place an egg yolk and fork beat with 1 tablespoon water until mixed and spreadable.

EGG WHITE ONLY: In a small bowl, place an egg white and fork beat until spreadable.

EGG YOLK WITH MILK: In a small bowl, place an egg yolk and fork beat with 1 tablespoon milk until mixed and spreadable.

EGG WHITE WITH WATER: In a small bowl, place an egg white and fork beat with 1 tablespoon water until mixed and spreadable.

NOTE: Gluten-free dough does not brown as well as dough that is made with all-purpose flour, so I suggest using a wash with an egg yolk to get more color.

No wash on dough

Whole egg with water

Egg white with water

Egg yolk with milk

Egg yolk with water

Egg white only

How to Prevent a Soggy Bottom

We all would like to avoid the dreaded soggy bottom. Here are a few tips that will help us to bake up crisp crust:

- When the oven is preheating, place on the bottom rack an uncovered sheet pan or cookie sheet, which all the generations of bakers in my family call cookie tins. When ready to bake the pie, remove the pan and cover it with parchment paper or a sheet pan liner. Set the pie on top, and bake on the lowest rack for 20–30 minutes. Move to the middle rack and bake until done.

- Bake on a preheated pizza stone.

- Roll out the dough on a layer of finely crushed cookie crumbs.

- If you are using extremely juicy fruit, bake your pie as soon as possible so the juices won't soak into the bottom crust.

- Never put a hot filling into an unbaked pie shell as the fats will melt.

- Blind bake the crust (see How to Blind Bake a Crust, page 69) and fill with a cooled stove top filling (see Stove-Top Fruit Filling, page 306).

- Sprinkle some dried breadcrumbs or cookie crumbs inside the unbaked pie shell before adding the filling. They will soak up some of the liquid.

- Before filling the bottom crust, brush it with a fork-beaten egg white and let the crust chill back up in the fridge.

- Avoid shiny pie pans. Shiny deflects heat. Opt for the pie pan that is darker or has a matte finish.

- Glass pans transfer heat slowly and evenly, and as they are see through it is easy to gauge if the bottom has the right color and is sufficiently baked. When removing a hot pie from the oven, be sure to place the pan on a towel or pot holder to avoid the pan possibly shattering.

- Ceramic pans take longer to heat up, but they give even heat distribution and hold heat longer so that the bottom crust will keep baking a bit longer after the pie is removed from the oven.

- Cool your just-baked pie on an elevated wire rack. This gives some airspace underneath the hot pie plate.

During the Bake

How to Catch Filling Drip

One of our pie-making goals is that the pie filling does not bubble out or spill onto the oven floor. If a pie pan is overfilled, there are a few things to do to help prevent a smoking mess in the oven.

A sheet pan placed underneath a pie can catch extra drips that might bubble over the rim of the pie pan during a bake. I have eighth-, quarter-, and half-size sheet pans. Rack holders inside your oven may cut down the actual space on your rack, so be sure to get a size that will actually fit into your oven. For easy cleanup, line the sheet pan with a Silpat (a silicone mat that is safe for baking), aluminum foil, a piece of parchment, or a sheet pan liner. Place a filled pie pan on a preheated sheet pan for an immediate blast of heat to the bottom crust. A hot sheet pan right out of the oven can warp if placed directly under cold water, so cool before washing.

A drip catcher, also called splatter guard, is a 12-inch- (30 cm) round metal pan with a slightly raised lip around its edge. In the middle there is an opening, also with a raised lip. The pie is set on top of the middle opening, which allows heat to reach the bottom of the pie. The raised outside edge catches any potential splatters and drips.

Bake the 20-20-20 Way

The full bake will take about one hour, during which time you'll set your timer for three 20-minute intervals. This is known as the 20-20-20 Method, or the Pie Camp Shuffle. Why do we do it this way? Over years of baking, I've found that if sugar goes on toward the later part of the bake instead of at the beginning, then there is less chance for a burned top. Trust me on this. Here's how it works:

FIRST 20: Bake in an oven preheated to 425°F (220°C) for 20 minutes.

SECOND 20: Turn the oven down to 375°F (190°C) and bake for a second 20 minutes.

THIRD 20: This one has four easy steps for you to do:

1. Open the oven, carefully remove the pie, set it on a heat-safe surface, and close the oven to keep the heat inside (see Why Opening the Oven Door Is Venting to Avoid, page 96).

2. Quickly and carefully brush the top of the pie with an egg white wash made of 1 egg white and 1 tablespoon water, fork beaten. There are some other washes you can check out at Washes for the Top (page 90).

3. Sprinkle lightly with 1 to 2 teaspoons of granulated, sparkling, or demerara sugar.

4. Place the pie back in the oven, close the oven door, and continue baking for the final 20 minutes.

How to Make a Foil Pie Shield

Aluminum foil was called tin foil by both my mom and grandmom. Whatever the name, with it we can make a foil pie shield to cover the crust of any size pie that may be browning too quickly.

WE WILL NEED

1 square piece of foil large enough to cover the entire pie top, including the edges (most aluminum foil is 12 inches (30.5 cm) wide, so it's fine to use a 12-inch square and crimp extra foil over the edge of the pie)

1. Tear off a square piece of foil large enough to cover the entire pie top, including the edges.

2. Fold the foil in half. In the middle of the fold, make a 3-inch- (7.5 cm) long tear.

3. Open up the foil. Fold the foil the opposite way, and in the middle of the fold, make another 3-inch (7.5 cm) long tear.

4. Unfold the foil and you should have a square opening in the center.

5. Place the foil over the pie top, making sure to cover the edges of the dough.

6. Fold back the edges of the center so that some of the dough is exposed.

7. Fold down the outer edge over the rim of the pie a bit so it doesn't fall off.

8. Put this shield on to protect the top of a pie anytime you feel it is getting too brown, or during the last 20 minutes of the bake. It's also fine to put this on at the beginning of the bake, and then pull it off for the last 20 minutes of the bake (see Bake the 20-20-20 Way, page 93).

9. Carefully remove the foil, cool, refold in quarters, and save to use again.

NOTE: Never place aluminum foil directly on the oven floor, because in some ovens it may start a fire and void the warranty.

How to Prevent a Burned Pie Top

Pie tops that are overly browned and blistered can be a disappointment. Here are a few ways to help avoid a crust that is too dark:

- Use a pie shield or make your own (see How to Make a Foil Pie Shield, opposite).

- A pie shield can be placed on the rim of a pie at the beginning of a bake, and it can be removed during the last 20 minutes so that the pie top and edges will get some color. Or the pie can bake uncovered, and then the pie shield can be added during the last 20 minutes of the bake, or sooner if the pie top has attained the desired color.

- If baking in a pie pan that is exceptionally large, by the time the center is done the edges may be too brown. Loosely cover the edges with a foil pie shield and continue to bake until the pie is done.

- Don't make edges, flutes, and crimps too thin. All the fat may bake out, resulting in a very dry and overly brown crust.

- Wait until the last 20 minutes of the bake to brush on a wash and sprinkle with sugar.

- As an alternative to using a foil pie shield, place a sheet pan or cookie tin on the rack above the baking pie.

- Check the oven temperature. I once accidentally set the oven at 525°F (about 275°C) instead of 425°F (220°C) and very quickly had burned crust.

- When sprinkling with sugar, use a lesser amount on the edges and the center, if mounded. These are the highest places on a pie top and they will brown first.

Why Opening the Oven Door Is Venting to Avoid

My pie-making Rule #3 is Vent. Venting is important in pie making, as we need to let the steam escape from a bubbling fruit filling or it will find the weak spots in the dough and burst through, or out the sides if not sealed well. A very important exception to the venting rule is the oven door during the bake. It's very tempting for pie campers to open the oven door to check on their pies, but opening and closing the oven door lets heat out, and oven temperatures can drop rapidly. I have found that an oven door that is open for 30 seconds can drop a bake temperature by 100°F (37°C), and more if open longer. This can really affect the timing on a bake.

Oven temperatures fluctuate when baking. The oven is set to rapidly rise in temperature during the preheat. Once the preheat is complete, the heating element will go on and off. When the oven cools down below the set point the heating element will turn on, and once the temperature is brought back up a bit above the set point the heating element will go off again.

An oven with a window and light inside is a thing of wonder and has become my favorite TV show. You can oftentimes find me gazing adoringly at a pie baking inside of my two ovens, named Thing One and Thing Two, as I chant, *They bake pies, they bake pies fast. Thing One and Thing Two will last and last.* You can chant these words, too. Just keep that heat inside and only open the oven door when needed.

Is It Ready?

How to Tell When a Fruit Pie Is Ready

There are a few ways to tell when your pie is ready to come out of the oven, and our senses are important in all of them.

SCENT: You are getting close when your house smells like a bakery.

SIGHT: The look of both the crust and filling will tell you a lot.

- For the crust: I like my pies to have a golden brown color. Check it during the bake to see if it is browning too quickly (see How to Prevent a Burned Pie Top, page 95).
- For the fruit filling: Look for steady bubbling coming through the vents. If there is none, place it back in the oven and check it every 3 to 5 minutes.

SOUND: For a double-crusted pie, get your ear close to the top of the upper crust and listen for the sounds of bubbling underneath. I call this the sizzle-whump (see page 89).

TOUCH: The crust should feel baked. If it is still dough-like, bake it longer.

Let It Cool, Let It Cool, Let It Cool

Take the pie out of the oven, set it on a cooling rack, and let it cool so the filling can set up. A just-baked fruit pie needs to cool so the filling can set well. If you cut a pie too soon, the filling may still be runny, in which case serve the pie in a bowl and eat with a spoon. It will still taste delicious. When the pie is cool, make three cuts, forming two adjacent pieces of pie. This will make it easier for you to lift that first piece out. A thin offset elbow spatula is great for lifting the first slice of pie out of the pan, and you can use it to spread and smooth whipped cream or meringue on a pie top, too.

Boiled Cider Apple Pie

Makes one 9-inch (23 cm)
deep-dish pie

The essence of apple is intensified in boiled cider, giving a delicious depth of flavor to an apple pie like no other. It's also good spooned over vanilla ice cream. For this pie I don't mound the apple filling up high in the pan, but instead lay sliced apples in flat layers up to the rim of the pie pan so that there is less chance of getting a gaping space between the filling and crust when baked.

1 recipe Roll-Out Dough (see Roll-Out Dough recipes, pages 38–58)

6 large apples (about 6 cups), peeled or unpeeled, quartered, and cored

½ cup (50 g) granulated sugar, plus more for sprinkling on top of the pie

2 to 4 tablespoons boiled cider (see How to Make Boiled Cider, opposite)

1 teaspoon cinnamon

½ teaspoon allspice

½ teaspoon salt

⅓ cup (50 g) flour

1 tablespoon butter, chopped into little pieces

EGG WASH

1 egg white plus 2 teaspoons water, fork beaten (or other wash of your choice; see Washes for the Top, page 90)

1. Make the pie dough and chill in fridge while you make the filling.

2. Slice the apples into ½-inch- (1.25 cm) thick slices.

3. In a large mixing bowl, put the apples, sugar, boiled cider, cinnamon, allspice, salt, and flour, and mix lightly until most of the apple surfaces are covered with what looks like wet sand.

4. Roll out half the pie dough and place in the pie pan.

5. Lay the apple slices flat in the unbaked piecrust and dot with butter.

6. Roll out the remaining dough, lay over the fruit, and cut 5 to 6 vents on top. Trim excess dough from the edges and crimp (see How to Crimp, Flute, and Edge the Crust, page 59).

7. Cover and chill in the fridge while you preheat the oven to 425°F (220°C).

8. Bake on the middle rack of oven for 20 minutes.

9. Reduce heat to 375°F (190°C) and bake for 20 more minutes.

10. Open the oven, carefully remove the pie, set it on a heat-safe surface, and close the oven to keep the heat inside. Quickly brush the top of the pie with the egg wash and sprinkle lightly with sugar. Return the pie to the oven and continue baking at 375°F (190°C) for an additional 20 minutes, or until the pie is done.

11. Look for steam and a slight bit of juice coming out of the vents before removing it from the oven. Get your ear right down almost to the top of the pie and listen for the sizzle-whump (see page 89).

12. Cool for at least 1 hour before slicing.

How to Make Boiled Cider

Boiled cider is one of the best things ever to boost the flavor of an apple pie. It gives a filling what food professionals call "depth of flavor." The best part of boiled cider is how very easy it is to make. We'll need a stainless steel or enameled stockpot, spoon, stove, and some sterilized jars to transfer the cider to after it has reduced slowly for hours. I buy a gallon of apple cider, pour the entire thing into the pot, and cook over medium heat, stirring occasionally, until that gallon has reduced to just about a pint. One caution—if the cider cooks down too long and gets too thick, you'll end up with sort of an apple caramel that is too solid to drizzle over a filling and is very hard to get out of the pan.

WHAT YOU'LL NEED

1 gallon (3.78 L) organic apple cider

A large noncorrosive pot (stainless steel or enameled cast iron)

Spoon

Stove

Clean and sterilized jars with lids

1. Pour the cider into the pot.
2. Turn the heat to medium-high and bring to a boil.
3. Turn the heat down to medium-low and let the cider cook until reduced to about 2 to 3 cups. This will take 4 to 5 hours. Stir every once in a while. I set a timer for every 60 minutes and stir. Skim off the foam and sediments that may rise to the top with a sieve or cone strainer.
4. Watch and stir more during the last half hour so that it doesn't scorch or get too thick. The boiled cider is done when it is reduced down to approximately 2 cups.
5. Pour into sterilized jars. It will thicken as it cools. That's it.

Apple Blackberry Pie

Makes one 9-inch (23 cm)
deep-dish pie

During late summer Pie Camps, I have many times led groups of campers to one of my secret blackberry spots so we can "pick a pie." We make quite the parade carrying loppers for thinning, and baskets and buckets for harvesting. When we return to Pie Cottage, our hands are stained from juicy sweet berries, and sometimes our faces, too. Blackberries ripen sooner than apples, so after they are picked, freeze them on flat trays covered with a sheet pan liner or parchment paper, and then transfer the frozen fruit into freezer bags that are marked and dated. When using frozen berries, do not defrost; use them just as if they were fresh. Oh, one other thing. Be sure to wear long sleeves when picking in the blackberry brambles.

---

1 recipe Roll-Out Dough (see Roll-Out Dough recipes, pages 38–58)

5 large apples (about 5 cups), peeled or unpeeled, quartered, and cored

¾ cup (150 g) granulated sugar, plus 1 to 2 teaspoons for sprinkling on top of the pie

¼ teaspoon salt

¾ teaspoon cinnamon

2 gratings or a pinch of nutmeg

⅓ cup (45 g) flour

A small squeeze of half a lemon

1 cup (145 g) blackberries, fresh or unthawed frozen

1 to 2 tablespoons black currant wine, crème de cassis, or blackberry liqueur (optional)

2 teaspoons (9 g) butter, chopped into little pieces

EGG WASH

1 egg white plus 2 teaspoons water, fork beaten (or other wash of your choice; see Washes for the Top, page 90)

1. Make the pie dough and chill in the fridge while you make the filling.

2. Slice the apples into ½-inch- (1.25 cm) thick slices, or chunk them up into pieces you can comfortably get into your mouth, but not so big that they may still be crunchy at the end of the bake time.

3. In a large mixing bowl, place the apples, sugar, salt, cinnamon, nutmeg, flour, and squeeze of lemon, and mix lightly until most of the surfaces are covered.

4. Add the blackberries and optional wine, and mix lightly to combine.

5. Roll out half the dough and place in the pie pan.

6. Pour the filling into the unbaked pie shell and dot with the butter.

7. Roll out the remaining dough, lay it over the fruit, and cut five or six vents on top, or make a lattice top (see A Pictorial Guide to Making a Lattice Top, pages 64–67.) Trim the excess dough from the edges and crimp (see How to Crimp, Flute, and Edge the Crust, page 59).

CONTINUED

8. Cover the pie and chill in the fridge while you preheat the oven to 425°F (220°C).

9. Bake for 20 minutes.

10. Turn down the oven to 375°F (190°C) and bake for 20 more minutes.

11. Open the oven, carefully remove the pie, set it on a heat-safe surface, and close the oven to keep the heat inside. Quickly brush the top of the pie with egg wash and then sprinkle lightly with sugar. Return the pie to the oven and continue baking at 375°F (190°C) for an additional 20 minutes.

12. Look for steam and a slight bit of juice coming out of the vents before removing it from the oven. Get your ear right down almost to the top of the pie and listen for the sizzle-whump (see page 89).

13. Cool for at least 1 hour before slicing.

NOTE: If the top of the pie looks like it is browning too quickly, cover with a piece of vented foil placed shiny side down, or place a sheet pan or cookie tin on the rack above the pie to shield it. Think of it as a sunscreen or an umbrella.

VARIATIONS

Apple Blackberry Pie with an Orange Twist

1. Substitute 1 tablespoon Cointreau, or other orange-flavored liqueur, for the black currant wine, crème de cassis, or blackberry liqueur.

Apple Elderberry Pie

1. Substitute 2 cups elderberries for the blackberries.

2. Use ½ cup (100 g) brown sugar and ¼ cup (50 g) granulated sugar

3. Substitute 2½ tablespoons cornstarch for the flour.

Classic Apple Pie

1. Leave out the blackberries and add 1 to 2 more apples.

2. Use only ½ cup (100 g) granulated sugar.

3. Season with 1 teaspoon cinnamon, ½ teaspoon allspice, a grating of nutmeg, and ½ teaspoon salt.

4. Increase the flour to ½ cup (70 g).

5. Add 1 to 2 tablespoons Calvados instead of black currant wine, or crème de cassis.

Apple Ginger Maple Bourbon Pie

At Pie Camp, we adjust sugar and spice in our filling by tasting it before it goes into the pie pan. Start with the smaller amounts listed for ginger and bourbon, and add more if you like. You'll know it is just right when you want to take another bite.

Makes one 9-inch (23 cm) deep-dish pie

½ recipe Roll-Out Dough, adding ½ teaspoon ground ginger to the dry ingredients (see Roll-Out Dough recipes, pages 38–58)

1 recipe Crumble Topping, adding 1 teaspoon ground ginger (see Master Recipe: Crisp or Crumble Topping, page 160)

6 large apples (about 6 cups), peeled or unpeeled, quartered, and cored

⅓ cup (80 ml) maple syrup

¼ teaspoon salt

2 to 3 tablespoons finely chopped candied ginger

1 cup (120 g) chopped pecans (optional)

1 to 2 tablespoons bourbon

A small squeeze of lemon, about ½ teaspoon

⅓ cup (50 g) flour

1 tablespoon butter, chopped into little pieces

1. Make the pie dough and chill in the fridge.

2. Make the Crumble Topping and place in the freezer.

3. Slice the apples into ½-inch- (1.25 cm) thick slices, or chunk them up into pieces you can comfortably get into your mouth, but not so big that they may still be crunchy at the end of the bake time.

4. In a large mixing bowl, place the apples, maple syrup, salt, candied ginger, optional pecans, bourbon, lemon, and flour, and mix lightly until most of the surfaces are covered.

5. Roll out the pie dough and place in the pie pan. Trim the excess dough from the edges and crimp (see How to Crimp, Flute, and Edge the Crust, page 59).

6. Pour filling into the unbaked pie shell and dot with butter.

7. Chill in the fridge while you preheat the oven to 425°F (220°C).

8. Bake the pie for 20 minutes.

9. Turn down the oven to 375°F (190°C) and bake for 20 more minutes.

10. Open the oven, carefully remove the pie, set it on a heat-safe surface, and close the oven to keep the heat inside. Evenly sprinkle the frozen Crumble Topping over the filling. Return to the oven and bake for an additional 20 minutes.

11. Remove from the oven and let the pie cool for at least an hour so it can set up before eating.

Classic Blackberry Pie

Makes one 9-inch (23 cm) shallow pie

One of my favorite pies to make, bake, and share is blackberry. Use the sweetest berries and then season them with a little nutmeg, a squeeze of lemon, and a little orange liqueur or some orange zest. A mix of berries, totaling 4 cups, can be used, too. No blackberries? Feel free to substitute marionberries, raspberries, blueberries, and even elderberries.

1 recipe Roll-Out Dough (see Roll-Out Dough recipes, pages 38–58)

4 cups (about 1¼ lbs, 480 g) blackberries

⅔ cup (130 g) granulated sugar

A small grating of nutmeg

¼ teaspoon salt

1 teaspoon fresh-squeezed lemon juice

3 tablespoons flour or 2 tablespoons tapioca (quick-cooking or tapioca flour)

1 tablespoon orange liqueur or zest of ½ orange

2 teaspoons (9 g) butter, chopped into little pieces

1 to 2 teaspoons granulated or demerara sugar, for sprinkling on top of the pie

EGG WASH

1 egg white plus 2 teaspoons water, fork beaten (or other wash of your choice; see Washes for the Top, page 90)

1. Make the pie dough and chill in the fridge while you make the filling.

2. Put the blackberries, sugar, nutmeg, salt, lemon, flour, and liqueur in a big bowl and mix lightly until the fruit is well coated.

3. Roll out half the dough and place in the pie pan.

4. Pour the filling into the pan and dot with butter.

5. Roll out the remaining dough, lay it over the fruit, and cut five or six vents on top, or make a lattice top (see A Pictorial Guide to Making a Lattice Top, pages 64–67). Trim the excess dough from the edges and crimp (see How to Crimp, Flute, and Edge the Crust, page 59).

6. Cover the pie and chill in the fridge while you preheat the oven to 425°F (220°C).

7. Bake for 20 minutes.

8. Turn down the oven to 375°F (190°C) and bake for 20 more minutes.

9. Open the oven, carefully remove the pie, set it on a heat-safe surface, and close the oven to keep the heat inside. Quickly brush the top of the pie with egg wash and sprinkle lightly with sugar. Return the pie to the oven and continue baking at 375°F (190°C) for an additional 20 minutes, or until the pie is done.

10. Remove the pie from the oven and cool for at least an hour so it can set up before eating.

Peaches and Cream Pie

Makes one 9-inch (23 cm)
deep-dish pie

I wait for sweet juicy peaches all year long. During the summer everything pretty much stops for me when they are ripe and I find as many ways as possible to use and share what I create. After an August Pie Camp concluded, I had just enough Summer Lady peaches from Frog Hollow Farm on hand to create this sweet and juicy pie. The sour cream, flavored with a bit of lime and cardamom, blended with the peach juice and gave the pie a creamy tanginess. Don't be shy about adding a little sour cream to other fruit pie fillings. Serve slightly warm, with a cold glass of prosecco, while sitting on the deck looking at sparkling stars.

1 recipe Roll-Out Dough (see Roll-Out Dough recipes, pages 38–58)

½ cup (56 g) almond meal

1 cup (200 g) granulated sugar, divided

6 large peaches (about 6 cups), sliced

½ cup (4 ounces, 120 ml) sour cream

1 teaspoon fresh-squeezed lime juice

⅛ teaspoon salt

3 tablespoons tapioca starch or ¼ cup (35 g) flour

½ teaspoon cardamom

Sparkling sugar

EGG WASH

1 egg white plus 2 teaspoons water, fork beaten (or other wash of your choice; see Washes for the Top, page 90)

1. Make the pie dough and chill in the fridge.

2. Preheat the oven to 400°F (205°C).

3. Roll out the dough and place in the pie pan.

4. Put the almond meal and ¼ cup (50 g) of the sugar on top of the dough. Mix around with your fingers a bit to combine and spread out evenly.

5. Place the peach slices on top of the almond meal–sugar mixture.

6. In a small bowl, place the remaining ¾ cup (150 g) sugar, sour cream, lime juice, salt, tapioca starch, and cardamom, and mix well to combine. Pour evenly over the peaches.

7. Roll out the remaining disc of dough and place it on top. Trim the excess dough from the edges and crimp (see How to Crimp, Flute, and Edge the Crust, page 59). Cut some steam vents on top.

8. Lightly brush the egg wash on top of the pie. Sprinkle with the sparkling sugar.

9. Bake for 60 minutes, or until you see some steaming and bubbling coming through the vents.

VARIATION

Substitute lemon juice for the lime juice, and cinnamon for the cardamom.

Ginger Cardamom Peach Pie

Makes one 9-inch (23 cm) deep-dish pie

Many pie campers are surprised that I don't peel peaches. I find the entire process of giving a peach a short bath in boiling water, slipping the skin off when it comes out, and finally trying to get the peach pit out adroitly while the juice is dripping all over the place, just plain messy. So, unless it really will make a difference in a pie, I leave the skin on. You'll be happy to know that you won't have to peel the peaches in this pie, or do too much in the way of chopping, either.

½ recipe Roll-Out Dough (see Roll-Out Dough recipes, pages 38–58)

1 recipe Crumble Topping (see Master Recipe: Crisp or Crumble Topping, page 160)

¼ cup finely chopped candied ginger

½ cup (60 g) chopped pecans

¼ cup (35 g) flour

⅔ cup (130 g) granulated sugar

2 teaspoons cardamom

2 teaspoons ground ginger

4 large freestone peaches (about 2 lbs, 1 kg), cut in half with pit removed (see Note)

1 recipe Ginger Whipped Cream (see Master Recipe: Whipped Cream chart, page 183) or Ice Cream (see Master Recipe: Ice Cream, page 300) for serving

NOTE: The pit of a freestone peach will come out easily with fingers. The pit of a cling peach "clings" to the flesh and must be cut or pried out, which can damage the flesh.

1. Make the pie dough and chill in the fridge.

2. Preheat the oven to 425°F (220°C).

3. Make the Crumble Topping, adding the candied ginger and pecans. Place in the freezer.

4. Roll out the dough and place in the pie pan.

5. In a small bowl, mix together the flour, sugar, cardamom, and ground ginger.

6. Evenly sprinkle half the flour-sugar mixture over the dough.

7. Fit the peach halves into the pie dough, cut side down. If they are large, you may have to cut them in quarters.

8. Evenly sprinkle the remaining flour-and-sugar mixture over and around the peaches.

9. Bake in the oven for 20 minutes.

10. Open the oven, carefully remove the pie, set it on a heat-safe surface, and close the oven to keep the heat inside. Sprinkle the Crumble Topping over the peaches. Turn down the oven to 350°F (175°C), and return the pie to bake for another 30 to 35 minutes. You should see some of the filling bubbling up through the topping.

11. Remove the pie from oven and let cool.

12. Serve warm or at room temperature with the Ginger Whipped Cream or Ice Cream.

Blueberry Plum Crumb Pie

Makes one 9-inch (23 cm) shallow pie

When I have a bounty of blueberries and a plethora of plums, I look for ways to use them. Both fruits hold up well in the fridge, but when fresh is not available, then frozen unthawed blueberries work just fine. The addition of both orange zest and orange juice brightens up the fruit, and the gingersnap cookie crumbs on the bottom of the baked crust are a nice surprise. Be sure to let the pie cool completely to let the filling set up.

½ recipe Roll-Out Dough (see Roll-Out Dough recipes, pages 38–58)

½ cup finely crushed gingersnap cookie crumbs

1 recipe Crumble Topping (see Master Recipe: Crisp or Crumble Topping, page 160)

FILLING

2 cups (about 10 oz, 250 g) blueberries, fresh or unthawed frozen

2 cups (about 10 oz, 250 g) halved and pitted Italian plums

¾ cup (165 g) brown sugar, packed

3 tablespoons quick-cooking tapioca or cornstarch

1 teaspoon orange zest

1 teaspoon cardamom

1 teaspoon ginger

¼ teaspoon salt

2 tablespoons fresh-squeezed orange juice

1 to 2 teaspoons (5 to 9 g) butter, chopped into little pieces

1. Make the pie dough and chill in the fridge.

2. Roll out the pie dough. On the last roll, sprinkle the gingersnap crumbs over the pie dough and firmly roll them into the dough. Flip the dough over and lay the dough into the pie pan so that the cookie crumb side is on the bottom and touching the pie pan.

3. Trim the excess dough from the edges and crimp (see How to Crimp, Flute, and Edge the Crust, page 59). Place in the fridge to chill for 30 minutes.

4. Pour the Crumble Topping mixture into a bowl or plastic bag and chill in the freezer for at least 15 minutes while you make the filling.

6. Preheat the oven to 425°F (220°C).

7. In a large bowl, place the blueberries and cut plums. Set aside.

8. In a medium bowl, mix together the brown sugar, tapioca, orange zest, cardamom, ginger, and salt with a fork. Sprinkle the mixture over the blueberries and plums, and mix lightly until well coated.

9. Add the orange juice and mix again.

10. Place the filling in the rolled out piecrust and dot with 1 to 2 teaspoons butter.

11. Bake for 20 minutes. Turn down the oven to 375°F (190°C) and bake for 20 more minutes.

12. Open the oven, carefully remove the pie, set it on a heat-safe surface, and close the oven to keep the heat inside. Evenly sprinkle the Crumble Topping over the hot filling. Return the pie to the oven and bake for 20 minutes more.

13. Remove the pie from the oven and let cool.

Green Tomato Pie

Makes one 9-inch (23 cm) shallow pie

This old-fashioned pie from the 1800s is one that deserves to be brought back to the table. Made from unripe green tomatoes, it is seasoned much like an apple pie. This basic version uses cinnamon, allspice, a bit of nutmeg, and apple cider vinegar. I think that you could probably substitute green tomatoes for apples in any basic apple pie recipe and it would come out a winner. A pie camper, who has become a very good friend and pie-making buddy, said it smelled and tasted just like the one her grandmother made. If you like, you can make variations with up to 2 cups of sliced apples, a half cup of raisins, or a tablespoon or two of diced up candied ginger. As the *Washington Post* wrote in 1901, green tomato pie "bids fair to be in for a new lease of popularity." It's up to you if you prefer to skin the tomatoes or leave their jackets on (see How to Peel Green Tomatoes, opposite).

1 recipe Roll-Out Dough (see Roll-Out Dough recipes, pages 38–58)

4 cups (about 1 lb; 460 to 500 g) green tomatoes, skinned (optional)

¾ cup (150 g) granulated sugar, plus a few teaspoons for sprinkling on top

¼ cup (50 g) brown sugar

1 rounded teaspoon cinnamon or more to taste

½ teaspoon allspice

A pinch of freshly grated nutmeg

¼ teaspoon salt

1 tablespoon good-quality apple cider vinegar (Bragg's or another artisan apple cider vinegar)

¼ cup (25 g) tapioca starch

Half-and-half for brushing on top

1. Make the pie dough and chill in fridge.

2. Preheat the oven to 400°F (205°C).

3. Roll out half the dough, place in the pie pan and place in the fridge to chill while you make the filling.

4. Quarter the tomatoes, cut out and discard most of the firm center core. Slice the tomatoes to a thickness of about ¼ inch (6 mm) and place in a medium bowl.

5. Add the white and brown sugars, cinnamon, allspice, nutmeg, salt, apple cider vinegar, and tapioca starch. With a spoon, mix to coat well.

6. Turn the tomato filling into the chilled pie pan and return it to the fridge while you roll out the top dough.

7. Lay the rolled out dough on top of the filling, and trim and crimp or flute the edges (see How to Crimp, Flute, and Edge the Crust, page 59). Cut some steam vents on top. You can also make a lattice top (see A Pictorial Guide to Making a Lattice Top, pages 64–67).

8. Sprinkle the top of the pie with a few teaspoons of sugar and brush with half-and-half.

9. Place in the oven and bake for about 55 minutes. About halfway through the bake, check to make sure the top is not overbrowning. If it is, use one of the techniques in How to Prevent a Burned Pie Top (see page 95).

10. Remove from the oven when you see the filling peeking through the edges and vents with some bubbling.

11. Let cool for about an hour. This pie is very good eaten while it is still slightly warm.

VARIATIONS

Ginger Green Tomato Pie

1. Add 2 tablespoons diced candied ginger to filling.

2. Add ½ teaspoon powdered ginger to filling.

Green Tomato and Apple Pie

Add 2 cups sliced apples.

How to Peel Green Tomatoes

EQUIPMENT NEEDED

Saucepan

Slotted spoon

Large bowl filled with ice water, a.k.a. an ice water bath

Knife

1. Fill a medium or large saucepan with water and bring to a rolling boil.

2. With a knife, score the smooth end, opposite the stem end, of each green tomato with an X just so it breaks the skin.

3. With a slotted spoon, lower the scored tomatoes into the boiling water. Let boil for 2 minutes. Lift the tomatoes out with the spoon and place into the ice water bath.

4. Remove the green tomatoes from the ice water. Starting at the corners of the X, pull the skin off the tomato. Discard the skin.

Apple Rum Raisin Custard Pie

Makes one 9-inch (23 cm)
deep-dish pie

What better way to celebrate apple season than with this special apple pie? It uses just three apples, sliced crosswise to a width of about ¼ inch (0.6 cm) and a basic custard, plus some rum for extra flavor. During the spring of 2020, when we were sheltering in place and eating down our pantries, I found this pie to be exceptionally adaptable: I chopped up some dried plums to replace the raisins, apple pie liqueur for the rum, and 2-percent milk for the half-and-half. However you make it, I think you will find that this pie will quickly became a very enjoyable keeper.

½ recipe **Roll-Out Dough** (see **Roll-Out Dough** recipes, pages 38–58)

3 apples, peeled, cored and halved

1 teaspoon fresh-squeezed lemon juice

½ cup (100 g) granulated sugar, divided

3 tablespoons flour

¾ teaspoon cinnamon

½ teaspoon allspice

A pinch of freshly grated nutmeg

A pinch of salt

¾ cup (120 g) raisins

CUSTARD

2 eggs

⅔ cup (160 ml) half-and-half

3 tablespoons granulated sugar

2 tablespoons (30 ml) dark rum

3 tablespoons (42 g) butter, melted

1. Preheat the oven to 400°F (205°C).

2. Roll out the pie dough and place it in a pie pan or 9-inch square or rectangular baking dish. Crimp or flute the edges (see How to Crimp, Flute, and Edge the Crust, page 59). Cover and set in the fridge to chill.

3. Place the apple halves flat side down onto a cutting board and slice crosswise to about ¼-inch (6 mm) width, holding the apple with your fingers as best you can so that it still looks like half an apple when the slices are cut and gathered together. Cut in half again across the waistline of the apple. Squeeze a teaspoon of lemon juice on top of the apples.

4. In a small bowl, mix together the sugar, flour, cinnamon, allspice, nutmeg, and salt.

5. Evenly sprinkle half of the sugar-flour mixture and half of the raisins in the bottom of the dough-filled pie pan.

6. Tuck groups of sliced apples snuggly into the pie pan, with their curved backs on top in a pleasing pattern.

7. Evenly top the apples with the remaining raisins and sugar-flour mixture.

8.   Place in the preheated oven and bake for 20 minutes while you make the custard.

9.   To make the custard, whisk the eggs in a medium bowl. Add the half-and-half, 2 tablespoons of the sugar, dark rum, and melted butter and whisk again to blend.

10.   After the pie has baked for 20 minutes, open the oven, carefully remove the pie, set it on a heat-safe surface, and close the oven to keep the heat inside. Pour the custard mixture over the apples, and carefully return to the oven, trying not to spill as you do so.

11.   Bake for 20 to 25 minutes more until the top is a golden color and has puffed up around the edges. There will be a slight jiggle in the middle.

12.   Remove from the oven and immediately sprinkle with the remaining 1 tablespoon sugar evenly over the top.

13.   Let cool. Serve warm, room temperature, or chilled.

VARIATIONS

Apple Jack Raisin Custard Pie

Substitute 2 tablespoons Calvados or Laird's Applejack for the rum.

Apple Rum Raisin Walnut Pie

1.   Add ½ cup (60 g) chopped walnuts in Step 5.

2.   Add another ½ cup (60 g) chopped walnuts in Step 7.

"The Bramley Apple Tree was grown from a pip by a young lady, Mary Anne Brailsford between 1809 & 1815. It was thought it came from an apple grown on a tree at the bottom of her garden. . . . One seedling produced very fine apples in 1837 when the new occupier was Mr. Matthew Bramley. A local gardener, Henry Merryweather, later obtained permission to take cuttings from the tree and it was duly registered as the Bramley Seedling."

—INFORMATION FROM THE HERITAGE LOTTERY FUND

Irish Apple Tart with Custard Sauce

Makes one 10-inch (25 cm) tart

In Ireland, sweet pies are usually called tarts, seasoned simply, and served with lightly sweetened whipped cream or a delicious custard sauce. On each of the days during a three-week journey on the Emerald Isle, my dear friend Cindy and I stopped into the bake or teashop of whatever village we happened to be passing through. "Tea" became our code word for pulling off the road to enjoy numerous apple tarts, all in the name of research, of course. If the baker was on site, it was an opportunity to chat about recipes, techniques, and differences in US, EU, and UK ingredients. Now home, a slice of this tart with a cuppa tea brings fond memories of rural landscapes, winding lanes, and the gracious hospitality of the Irish people. The baking apple of choice in the British Isles is the tangy Bramley, which on occasion I find at farmers' markets in America.

1 recipe Irish Tart Dough (recipe follows)

4 tangy tart apples (about 1 lb, 500 g), peeled, cored, and sliced (Bramleys, if you can get them)

¼ cup plus 2 tablespoons (75 g) granulated sugar, plus more for the top of the pie

A small pinch salt

A small pinch of cloves, ground (optional)

¾ teaspoon cinnamon (optional)

1 tablespoon boiled cider (optional; see **How to Make Boiled Cider**, page 99)

Custard Sauce (recipe follows) for serving

EGG WASH

1 egg white plus 2 teaspoons water, fork beaten (or other wash of your choice; see **Washes for the Top**, page 90)

1. Preheat the oven to 350°F (175°C).

2. Roll out half of the tart dough and place it in the tart pan.

3. Spread the apples evenly in the tart pan.

4. Mix together the sugar, salt, and the optional cloves, cinnamon, and boiled cider, and evenly sprinkle over the apples.

5. Roll out the top dough and lay it over the apples. Trim and crimp the edges (see How to Crimp, Flute, and Edge the Crust, page 59). Cut out optional dough trimmings in shapes of apples or leaves.

6. Brush the top of the pie with the egg wash. Place the optional dough cutouts on top and brush with the egg wash.

7. Bake for 50 to 60 minutes. If you like a richer color, you can brush the top of the pie a second time about 25 minutes into the bake.

8. Remove the pie from the oven and sprinkle lightly with sugar.

9. Let cool. Serve with Custard Sauce (recipe follows).

Irish Tart Dough

Makes one double-crust 10-inch (25 cm) tart

A little confectioners' sugar to sweeten and a bit of vanilla highlight this dough, which holds the filling for an Irish Apple Tart. I've sized this dough to make a double-crusted tart, made in a 10-inch (25 cm) tart pan.

8 tablespoons (1 stick; 112 g) butter, cut into 1-inch (2.5 cm) pieces

1¾ cups (225 g) flour

2 tablespoons confectioners' sugar

A small pinch of salt

2 extra large egg yolks (you can reserve the egg whites to be used in the egg wash)

½ teaspoon vanilla (optional)

2½ tablespoons milk

1. Place the butter in the freezer to chill for about 10 minutes while you get everything else ready.

2. Place the flour, confectioners' sugar, and salt in a medium bowl and mix with a fork until well blended.

3. Add the cold butter pieces to the bowl and with your fingertips and knuckles, smoosh and pinch them into the flour until it is crumbly and looks like coarse meal.

4. In a small bowl, whisk the egg yolks and optional vanilla with a fork. Make a well in the center of the dry ingredients and pour the yolks into it. Lightly mix with a fork to combine.

5. Add the milk and lightly mix with a fork to combine.

6. Using your hands, bring the dough together and form into a rectangle about 1 inch thick. Wrap tightly with plastic and chill for 30 minutes.

Apple Mulberry Tart

Substitute 1 cup (about 145 g) mulberries, fresh or frozen (unthawed), for 1 cup apples.

Custard Sauce

Makes about 2 cups

This sauce is also known as crème anglaise, but every place I traveled to in Ireland called it custard sauce. When we make the custard for Duncan's recipe of vanilla Ice Cream (see Master Recipe: Ice Cream, page 300), we will learn that a custard must be watched carefully, and stirred constantly and gently, so as to make sure the yolks do not curdle into tiny pieces of cooked egg and the sauce doesn't break. Making the sauce in a double boiler does take a bit longer, but it lessens the possibility of the eggs curdling. A sauce that has broken can usually be saved and no one will be the wiser as described in the directions of this recipe. For a variation, instead of vanilla add a tablespoon of Grand Marnier, brandy, rum, cognac, or Irish whiskey before cooling.

2 cups (about 480 ml) whole milk

1 teaspoon vanilla extract

4 egg yolks

¼ cup (50 g) granulated sugar

1 tablespoon heavy cream

1. In a medium saucepan, place the milk and vanilla extract and heat over medium-low until the liquid begins to tremble. Stop before it comes to a boil. Remove from the heat and let cool while you beat the eggs.

2. Place the egg yolks and sugar in a medium bowl. Beat with an electric mixer on high until the mixture has increased about threefold in volume and becomes thick and pale. When you lift the beaters you should be able to see a "ribbon" of the mixture on top for a second or so before it settles back down and disappears into itself.

3. A bit at a time, gently whisk in the slightly cooled milk into the bowl of yolks and sugar.

4. Pour the mixture back into the saucepan. Heat over very low heat, while stirring gently and constantly in the shape of a figure eight with a wooden spoon for 8 to 9 minutes. The sauce will thicken a bit to coat the back of the spoon. When you feel a slight drag on the spoon, remove from the heat immediately. As mentioned above, you may want to do this step in a double boiler so as to lessen the possibility of the eggs curdling, which can happen very quickly.

5. If the eggs do curdle at this step, or after you are gently heating in Step 6, turn the mixture into a mixing bowl, and with an electric beater on medium, mix until everything is smooth again. This won't take too long. Turn it back into the saucepan or double boiler.

6. Add the heavy cream and heat for 1 minute more over very low heat, while stirring very gently.

7. Set a large fine sieve strainer on a bowl and pour the heated custard through it. You can use a spatula or wooden spoon to help it through. Discard any solids in the strainer.

8. Let the sauce cool. It can be served warm or chilled.

NOTE: During the writing of this book in 2019 and 2020, the price of vanilla, both extract and beans, skyrocketed due to the weather in Madagascar, which destroyed much of this highly prized and most labor-intensive crop. That being said, without breaking the bank, for the best flavor, buy the best vanilla you can.

Summer Solstice Strawberry Pie

Makes one 9-inch (23 cm) shallow pie

June 21 is the summer solstice in the northern hemisphere, and on that day I can count on having enough ripe homegrown strawberries to make at least one pie if not more. Each area of the country will have regional favorites. In the Pacific Northwest where I live, my favorite is the Shuksan. Its large and luscious red fruits hide under vibrant green leaves. Although they don't hold up as well as commercially grown berries—really only one day after they are plucked from the plant—the three-week harvest window lets me share a sweet bounty with family, neighbors, and friends. This shiny red pie sure tastes like summer to me.

1 recipe Hazelnut Meal or Almond Flour Crust (page 76)

1 cup (8 oz, 227 g) mascarpone cheese

2 to 3 tablespoons granulated sugar, depending on how sweet you like it

One 8-ounce (227 g) jar good-quality strawberry jam

3 cups (about 20 oz, 566 g) ripe, unblemished strawberries, cleaned and hulled

2 to 3 tablespoons orange liqueur or 1 teaspoon orange extract

1. Make, pre-bake, and set aside the crust to cool.

2. Place the mascarpone, sugar, and orange liqueur in a medium bowl and whip on high with a handheld mixer until well combined and spreadable.

3. Turn the whipped mascarpone onto the top of the cooled crust and spread lightly and evenly with a spatula.

4. Turn the strawberry jam into a small saucepan and heat slowly over low heat, while stirring. When the jam loosens and becomes more liquid, pour it through a sieve strainer to remove the solids. Let the liquid cool to room temperature and spoon on top of the whipped mascarpone.

5. Arrange the strawberries on top of the jam in a pleasing pattern with the pointy side up.

6. Place in the fridge and chill for 2 or more hours.

Pie-Lets & Crostatas

Pie-Lets & Crostatas

I have been asked many times what I do with all the pies I make and bake, and why don't I weigh more than I do with all those pies around? Now I do love a slice of a freshly baked pie still warm from the oven, and, as you are reading this book, I would imagine that you do, too. But when an entire home-baked pie on the counter is just begging to be eaten, we can easily move out of that "healthy" zone. So what to do when a full-size recipe is just too darn big?

There are so many different options: crostatas, smaller pies that I call "pie-lets," and tiny pies made in muffin tins and canning lids. All are just the right size dessert for one or two. You can get your pie on without feeling like you will need to diet for the next two weeks. Small pies are a wonderful way to experiment with different filling combinations, to try out new ideas for pie-top decorating, and they are easy to share with pie-loving friends, neighbors, and countrymen as we practice our pie-making craft. Let's begin by making a pie-let . . .

A Few Fancy and Fun Pie-Let Edges

Here are a few other dough ideas to make your pie-lets pretty special.

- Circles: Cut out 3- to 4- inch (7.5 to 10 cm) dough circles. Six circles should do it. Lay one in the bottom of the pie pan, and lay the others around the sides so that they overlap out to the edge. Press lightly to adhere.

- Squares: Cut four 5-inch (12.5 cm) dough squares. Lay them in the bottom of the pie pan so that the corners meet in the center, and the corner opposite covers and stands up along the edge.

- Hole in the middle: Cut a circle the size that will cover the top of the pie-let, and then cut out the center with a biscuit cutter.

How to Make a Pie-Let

We'll make dough, sized to make one pie-let. It's also easy enough to make a full-size pie dough recipe and divide it into quarters for multiple pie-lets. That way, we can make one or two now, double wrap the remaining quarters in plastic wrap, and tuck them into the freezer for up to three months. The smaller quartered pieces will defrost and be ready to roll in less time than full-size discs of dough, too.

Here's the basic game plan:

1. Make a pastry dough recipe for a single pie-let (see Pie-Let Dough, page 125).

2. Cut in two equal pieces. Roll out one piece and place in a mini pie pan. I use a brightly colored 5½-inch (14 cm) ceramic pan.

3. Place in the fridge while you make a small filling. Is there just one peach left on your counter, and a handful of blueberries? That should be enough (see Basic Pie-Let Fruit Fillings, page 126). I've included specifics for cherry-peach, apple, and ginger-pear fillings to get you started.

4. Roll out the remaining piece of dough and place it on top. Cut a few vents and, if you like, decorate with dough shapes cut from cookie cutters or make a mini lattice crust on top.

5. When ready to bake, preheat the oven to 400°F (205°C) and place the pie-let on a pre-heated sheet pan or cookie tin. Instead of the hour-long bake time that most fruit pies take, a pie-let will take about 35 minutes. It takes less time to cool, too, so you can enjoy your sweet treat more quickly.

Fillings for Pie-Lets

A pie-let will take less filling than that which goes into a full size pie. It will take about 1 cup (240 ml) of filling to fill one 4-inch (10 cm) tart pan, and 1½ cups (360 ml) of filling to fill one 5½-inch (14 cm) pie pan. The fruit fillings in the recipes that follow can also be used to make Muffin Tin Pies (page 128).

Other Ways to Make Pie-Lets

MUFFIN TINS: A mini-size muffin tin makes bite-size treats. A standard-size muffin tin is great for creating individual serving pies and also butter tarts. A jumbo muffin tin will serve one very generously, or two rather modestly (see Muffin Tin Pies, page 128).

CANNING LID RING: Wide mouth canning rings take on a new life when they are filled with dough and filling for tiny pies (see Canning Lid Pies, page 131).

DOUGH PRESS: I have multiple sizes of dough presses from 3 inches (7.62 cm) to 6 inches (15.24 cm), but most often I use the smaller ones for hand pies. The backside of the press has a circle edge to cut out the round shape from rolled-out dough. Fill with one of the fruit fillings, seal the edges, and bake on a parchment-covered sheet pan like you do for Fruitful Crostatas (page 134).

Now let's learn how to make the dough and some basic fruit filling for pie-lets.

Pie-Let Dough

Makes one 5½-inch (14 cm) double-crusted pie

Making a small amount of dough like this is a great way to experiment using other fats such as goose, duck, bacon, or, if you know someone who hunts, even bear (see Note).

½ cup plus 2 tablespoons (90 g) flour

A pinch of salt

2 tablespoons (28 g) butter or 4 tablespoons (56 g) if making an all-butter dough, chopped small and chilled

2 tablespoons (28 g) leaf lard (omit if making an all-butter dough), chopped small and chilled

2 tablespoons plus 1 teaspoon ice water (more or less)

1. Place the flour, salt, cold butter, and lard (or all butter if making an all-butter dough) in a small to medium bowl.

2. With clean hands, quickly smoosh the mixture together, or use a pastry blender with an up and down motion, until the ingredients look like cracker crumbs with lumps the size of peas and almonds. These lumps will make your crust flaky.

3. Sprinkle the ice water over the mixture, fluffing and tossing lightly with a fork as you do.

4. Squeeze a handful of dough to see if it holds together. Sprinkle over more water and fluff with a fork as needed until it holds together.

5. Form into one disc, wrap in plastic wrap, and chill for about an hour before using.

NOTE: From personal experience, I can attest that bear fat does make a very flaky piecrust; in fact it makes one of the best I've had. Bear fat is not commercially available. If you know someone who hunts bear, ask that the fat be saved and rendered for you. You will want fat from an end-of-summer bear that has been feasting on roots and berries, and not fish.

Basic Pie-Let Fruit Filling

Makes 1½ cups (360 ml) filling

Pie-let fillings are a great way to use up small amounts of fruit. This basic filling is a version of our master recipe for fruit pie, but scaled down to fill one 5½-inch (14 cm) pie pan. Always use the most flavorful fruit available.

1½ cups fruit

2 to 3 tablespoons granulated sugar, depending on sweetness of fruit

A tiny pinch of salt

Seasoning of choice (for example, a pinch of nutmeg, ¼ teaspoon cinnamon, or ¼ teaspoon cardamom, or a combination)

A tiny squeeze of fresh lemon juice

1 teaspoon fruit liqueur of choice (optional)

1 teaspoon quick-cooking tapioca

1. Place the fruit, sugar, salt, seasoning, lemon juice, optional liqueur, and tapioca in a small to medium bowl and mix lightly until the fruit is well coated.

2. Adjust the sweetener and seasoning to your taste. When it makes you want to have a second taste, it is ready to fill the pie-let.

Now let's get on to some specific fillings for pie-lets.

Cherry Peach Filling

Makes about 1 cup (240 ml) filling

The season for both cherries and peaches is fleeting, so pit and freeze the cherries, and then add them to one perfectly sweet peach when it ripens in the summer. You can use a paperclip, chopstick, or eraser on the end of a pencil to pit cherries for one or two pies. But if you have an abundant harvest of cherries, a cherry pitter will be an indispensable tool. One of the best is the Leifheit 37200.

1 ripe peach, cut into bite-size pieces

½ cup sour or sweet cherries, pitted, frozen, or fresh

3 tablespoons granulated sugar (for sweet cherries, reduce to 1½ tablespoons)

A tiny pinch of salt

A tiny grating of nutmeg

¼ teaspoon cinnamon

A tiny squeeze of fresh lemon juice

½ teaspoon quick-cooking tapioca.

1. Place the peach, cherries, sugar, salt, nutmeg, cinnamon, lemon juice, and tapioca in a small to medium bowl and mix lightly until the fruit is well coated.

2. Adjust the sweetener and seasonings to your taste.

Apple Filling

Makes 1 to 1½ cups (240 to 360 ml) filling

Peeled or unpeeled? That is the question. I don't peel mine unless it has a thick skin, like that of a Granny Smith or Cosmic Crisp.

1 or 2 apples, cored and chopped to total 1 to 1½ cups

1 tablespoon granulated sugar

1 tablespoon brown sugar

¼ teaspoon cinnamon

⅛ teaspoon allspice

A very tiny grating of nutmeg

A tiny pinch of salt

½ teaspoon apple liqueur, such as Calvados (optional)

2 tablespoons flour

1. In a small bowl, place the chopped apples, sugars, cinnamon, allspice, nutmeg, salt, optional liqueur, and flour. Mix with a spoon or clean hands to combine.

2. Adjust the sweetener and seasonings to your taste.

Ginger Pear Filling

Makes 1 to 1½ cups (240 to 360 ml) filling

A lovely pairing of ginger and pear fills this little pie-let. Pears are another fruit that I don't peel.

1 or 2 pears, cored and chopped to total 1 to 1½ cups

1 teaspoon finely diced candied ginger

2 tablespoons granulated sugar

¼ teaspoon cinnamon

⅛ teaspoon ground ginger

A very tiny grating of nutmeg

A tiny pinch of salt

½ teaspoon ginger liqueur or rum (optional)

1 tablespoon tapioca starch or cornstarch

1. In a small bowl, place the chopped pears, candied ginger, sugar, cinnamon, ground ginger, nutmeg, salt, optional ginger liqueur, and tapioca starch. Mix with a spoon or clean hands to combine.

2. Adjust the sweetener and seasonings to your taste.

Muffin Tin Pies

Makes 6 muffin tin pies

These little pies can be baked open faced, have a lattice with strips cut from leftover dough, have dough shapes cut out using a cookie cutter, or have a crumble topping. One little pie makes a serving for two . . . or one. An ice cream trigger scoop can be used to add just the right amount of filling into each of our dough-filled muffin tins.

½ recipe Roll-Out Dough (see Roll-Out Dough recipes, pages 38–58)

1 recipe Basic Pie-Let Fruit Filling (page 126) or other filling of choice

Sugar for sprinkling the top of the crust

EGG WASH

1 egg white plus 2 teaspoons water, fork beaten (or other wash of your choice; see Washes for the Top, page 90)

1. Butter six cups and the top of a regular-size muffin tin.

2. Roll out the dough to about 12 inches (30 cm) in diameter.

3. Cut into 4-inch (10 cm) rounds and save the trimmings for the tops.

4. Fill the cup of each buttered muffin tin with one 4-inch (10 cm) round. Overlap the dough as needed. It's okay if they don't look perfect.

5. Fill with ⅓ cup (80 ml) filling.

6. Roll out the the scraps of dough. Cut in ¼-inch (6 cm) wide strips and weave a mini lattice top (see A Pictorial Guide to Making a Lattice Top, pages 64–67), or cut shapes with a cookie cutter and place on top of the filling.

7. Place the muffin tin in the fridge to chill while you preheat the oven to 400°F (205°C).

8. Before baking, brush the tops with an egg wash, and lightly sprinkle with sugar.

9. Bake for about 30 minutes, or until you see bubbling and the tops are a golden brown.

10. Remove the muffin tin from the oven and place on a rack to cool.

11. When cool enough to touch, loosen the edges of each mini pie with a knife and gently lift out from the muffin tin. Serve warm or at room temperature.

VARIATION

Crumble Tin Pies

1. Make one-quarter of the recipe for Crumble Topping (see Master Recipe: Crisp or Crumble Topping, page 160).

2. Evenly sprinkle Crumble Topping, instead of crust, over the filling.

3. Bake as above.

Canning Lid Pies

Yield varies

Another variation on the pie-let theme, and a fun way to use up dough scraps and extra filling, too, are these little pies that use a canning jar ring for a mold. Dough is fitted inside the ring, blind baked, cooled, and filled with an already-cooked stove top filling, or with ice cream and various toppings to create tiny ice cream pies.

EQUIPMENT NEEDED

Multiple 3½-inch (9 cm) wide-mouth canning jar rings (you won't need the flat lid that fits inside of it)

A sheet pan or cookie tin covered with parchment or a sheet pan liner

INGREDIENTS

Pie dough scraps

Leftover fruit filling (optional; see Basic Pie-Let Fruit Filling, page 126) or cream filling (optional; see Master Recipe: Pastry Cream, page 178)

Chantilly Cream (optional; see Master Recipe: Whipped Cream chart, page 183) for serving

Ice Cream flavor of choice (optional; see Master Recipe: Ice Cream, page 300) with a variety of toppings (optional) for serving

1. Place the canning jar rings on the sheet pan or cookie tin covered with parchment paper or a sheet pan liner.

2. Roll out the dough scraps and cut into 5½-inch (14 cm) circles.

3. Lay one circle of dough inside each canning jar lid.

4. Fold the extra dough over into the inside of the pie dough.

5. Press gently around the rim and raise the dough so it is a bit higher than the rim of the ring.

6. Place in the fridge for about 10 to 15 minutes so the dough can chill back down.

IF BLIND BAKING

1. Preheat the oven to 400°F (205°C).

2. Dock the bottom of the dough with a fork.

3. Bake for 10 to 12 minutes. As all ovens are not the same, so take a look at 10 minutes and remove if the dough is getting too dark.

4. Remove from the oven and let cool.

5. Fill with leftover fruit or cream filling and top with Chantilly Cream. They can be also be filled with a few tablespoons of softened Ice Cream and your choice of toppings, then pop them back into the freezer until ready to serve.

IF BAKING WITH FILLING

1. Preheat the oven to 375°F (190°C).

2. Fill with a few tablespoons of fruit filling, taking care not to mound it up too high or it will spill all over the baking pan as it bakes.

3. Bake open faced for about 40 minutes, or until you see some bubbling.

4. Let cool and serve with a small scoop of Ice Cream or Chantilly Cream.

Pie Camp Questions

There is something very special about pie. Here are a few questions to ponder both at and away from the baking counter.

- Is pie one of my family traditions?
- What are my pie memories?
- What excites me about pie making?
- What scares me about pie making?
- What is my favorite pie to make?
- Do I feel at ease making pie?
- Do I find pie making fulfilling?
- If I could gift someone a homemade pie, who would it be?
- Is there a time that I have received a pie?
- Who are my pie teachers?
- What lessons have I learned from pie?
- How much time do I take for making pie and doing other things I love?
- Does pie making bond me to my family or community? How?
- What opportunities do I have in my family or community to share pie making?
- Can something as simple as pie make a difference in the world? How?

Creamy Little Berry Bites

These bites are lovely for a light dessert during berry season. They can hold up in the fridge for a few hours until you are ready to serve.

Makes 6 berry bites

½ recipe Cream Cheese Pie Dough (page 58)

2 to 3 tablespoons (28 to 42 g) butter, melted

4 ounces (110 g) mascarpone cheese

⅓ cup (80 ml) heavy whipping cream

¼ teaspoon vanilla extract or other extract of your choice, such as orange, lemon, or coconut

2 tablespoons confectioners' sugar

¼ cup lemon curd

1 cup (150 g) strawberries, raspberries, blueberries, blackberries, other seasonal berries, or a mix

1. Make the Cream Cheese Pie Dough.

2. Brush the melted butter in 6 cups of a regular-size muffin tin and set in the fridge while you roll out the dough.

3. On a flat surface, sprinkle some flour, roll out the dough, and cut out 4-inch (10 cm) circles with the back of a dough press (see Dough Press, page 124). If you don't have a dough press, invert a 4-inch bowl over the top of the dough, and cut around it with a knife or pizza cutter.

4. Tuck the dough circles into the muffin tin cups. Place in the fridge for about 30 minutes until well chilled.

5. In a medium bowl, place the mascarpone cheese. Using an electric hand mixer, whip for about 1 minute to add some air and loft.

6. Add the heavy whipping cream, vanilla extract, and confectioners' sugar and whip again until combined. Set in the fridge to chill.

7. Preheat the oven to 325°F (165°C). Place a paper cupcake liner in each of the dough-filled muffin tins, and fill with pie weights.

8. Place in the oven and bake for 20 minutes. Remove from the oven and carefully take out the filled cupcake liners.

9. Place the muffin tin back in the oven for another 3 to 5 minutes to dry out the dough and give it a bit more color if needed. Remove from the oven and let cool. It is easiest to get the baked shells out of the muffin tins when they are still warm.

10. When the baked shells are completely cool, place 2 teaspoons of the lemon curd in the bottom of each shell.

11. Divide the mascarpone filling equally and place on top of the lemon curd.

12. Place the sliced strawberries or berries on top of the mascarpone filling.

Fruitful Crostatas

Makes 6 to 7 crostatas

One of my favorite combinations of fruit for this open-faced hand pie is rhubarb and berry. I use 3 cups rhubarb cut in ½-inch (1.25 cm) pieces, plus 1 cup berries, but you can use whatever sweet and ripe fruits are available. The filling will hold up in the fridge for up to three days. It can also be used for Pie Deconstructed (page 304) or as a fruit topping on ice cream.

1 recipe Cream Cheese Pie Dough (page 58) or other Roll-Out Dough (see Roll-Out Dough recipes, pages 38–58)

3 tablespoons water

¼ cup (32 g) cornstarch

4 cups fruit (about 1 lb; 500 g), such as rhubarb, strawberries, blueberries, raspberries, blackberries, peaches, plums, nectarines, cherries, or a combination

¾ cup (150 g) granulated sugar, plus more for sprinkling on top of the crostatas

A small pinch of salt

A small squeeze of lemon

A small grating of nutmeg

A few teaspoons of orange or other liqueur (optional)

EGG WASH

1 egg white plus 2 teaspoons water, fork beaten (or other wash of your choice; see Washes for the Top, page 90)

1. Make the dough and place in the fridge to chill while you make the fruit filling.

2. Place the water in a small bowl and, with a whisk or fork, briskly whisk in the cornstarch. Set aside.

3. In a medium heavy saucepan, place the fruit, sugar, salt, lemon, nutmeg, and optional orange liqueur. Be creative here and use other seasonings that you like. Place on medium heat and cook for about 6 minutes, stirring occasionally.

4. Add the cornstarch mixture, bring to a boil, and cook for 2 minutes more, while stirring.

5. Remove from the heat. Turn the filling into a bowl and let cool completely. It takes at least 40 minutes to chill in my fridge. Meanwhile, you can begin making the crostata crust.

6. Remove the dough from the fridge and divide into four equal pieces. Roll out each piece of dough to roughly a 7-inch (18 cm) circle.

7. Place one dough circle on a parchment-covered baking sheet. Fill with ⅓ to ½ cup of the filling in the center, leaving a 1- to 2-inch (2.5 to 5 cm) border.

8. Fold in and pleat the edges of dough over the filling, leaving an opening in the center.

9. Lightly brush some of the egg wash over the edges and sprinkle with some extra sugar.

10. Repeat with the remaining dough circles and filling.

11. Place in the fridge while you preheat the oven to 425°F (220°C). Bake for 15 minutes, then turn down the oven to 375°F (190°C) and bake for an additional 15 minutes until golden brown.

Peach Crostatas

Makes 4 crostatas

If you are looking for a special dessert to share with friends, you've found it. Peach crostatas are high up on my list of delicious. I've sized this recipe for four, but it can easily be doubled. You can put any extras in the freezer for another day, or whenever you are craving a little baked treat for yourself.

½ recipe Cream Cheese Pie Dough (page 58) or other Roll-Out Dough (see Roll-Out Dough recipes, pages 38–58)

¼ cup plus 1 tablespoon cornstarch

5 tablespoons (75 g) granulated sugar, plus 1 tablespoon for sprinkling on top

1 teaspoon cinnamon

A tiny pinch of salt

2 sweet ripe peaches, halved, pitted, and sliced

1 teaspoon (5 g) butter

4 teaspoons lemon curd

EGG WASH

1 egg white plus 2 teaspoons water, fork beaten (or other wash of your choice; see Washes for the Top, page 90)

1. Make the dough and place in the fridge to chill.

2. In a small bowl, mix the cornstarch, sugar, cinnamon, and salt together with a fork or whisk. Set aside.

3. Remove the dough from the fridge and divide into four equal pieces. Roll out each piece of dough to roughly a 7-inch (18 cm) circle.

4. Place one dough circle on a parchment-covered baking sheet. Evenly sprinkle 1 tablespoon of the dry mixture on top of the dough, leaving a 1- to 2-inch (2.5 to 5 cm) border. Arrange the slices of one peach half on top.

5. Sprinkle 1 teaspoon of the dry mixture over the fruit.

6. Dot with ¼ teaspoon butter and 1 teaspoon lemon curd.

7. Fold in and pleat the edges of dough over the filling, leaving an opening in the center.

8. Repeat with the remaining dough circles and filling.

9. Lightly brush some of the egg wash over the edges and sprinkle with some extra sugar.

10. Place in the fridge while you preheat the oven to 425°F (220°C). Bake for 15 minutes, then turn the oven down to 375°F (190°C) and bake for an additional 15 minutes until golden brown.

NOTE: You can substitute 2 nectarines or 4 to 6 apricots for the peaches.

Honey Hazelnut Fig Crostatas

Makes 4 crostatas

Figs drizzled with honey have been enjoyed for centuries. Here, we'll enjoy them baked in a crostata over a bed of hazelnut frangipane. No hazelnuts or Frangelico on hand? Just substitute ground almonds or almond meal and 1 tablespoon brandy and ¼ teaspoon almond extract.

½ recipe Cream Cheese Pie Dough (page 58) or other Roll-Out Dough (see Roll-Out Dough recipes, pages 38–58)

1 recipe Hazelnut Frangipane (recipe follows)

8 to 12 ripe figs (2 to 3 for each crostata)

¼ cup hazelnuts, roasted and roughly chopped (see How to Roast Hazelnuts, Pecans, or Walnuts, page 314)

4 to 8 teaspoons honey for drizzling on top of the crostatas

Sugar for sprinkling on top of the crostatas

EGG WASH

1 egg white plus 2 teaspoons water, fork beaten (or other wash of your choice; see Washes for the Top, page 90)

1. Make the dough and place in the fridge to chill.

2. Remove the dough from the fridge and divide into four equal pieces. Roll out each piece of dough to roughly a 7-inch (18 cm) circle.

3. Place one circle on a parchment-covered baking sheet. Evenly spread 2 tablespoons of Hazelnut Frangipane, leaving a 1-inch (2.5 cm) border.

4. Cut the figs in quarters and arrange on top.

5. Sprinkle a tablespoon of hazelnuts and drizzle 1 to 2 teaspoons of honey over the figs.

6. Fold in and pleat the edges of dough over the filling, leaving an opening in the center.

7. Repeat with the remaining dough circles and filling.

8. Lightly brush some of the egg wash over the edges and sprinkle with some extra sugar.

9. Place in the fridge while you preheat the oven to 425°F (220°C). Bake for 15 minutes, then turn down the oven to 375°F (190°C) and bake for an additional 15 minutes until golden brown.

Hazelnut Frangipane

4 tablespoons (½ stick; 60 g) butter

½ cup (100 g) granulated sugar

¾ cup (80 g) finely ground hazelnuts or hazelnut meal

1 egg

A pinch of salt

1 tablespoon flour

1 tablespoon Frangelico

¼ teaspoon vanilla extract

1. In a medium bowl, place the butter and sugar. With a hand or stand mixer, beat until pale and fluffy.

2. Add the hazelnuts, egg, salt, flour, Frangelico, and vanilla extract and mix well until completely combined.

Peach Packets

Makes 4 packets

This is actually a dumpling, but when I sliced the peaches in half and wrapped them in dough, they looked little gift packages, so I renamed them Peach Packets. With some dough trimmings cut extra thin, you can even fashion a bow to place on top where all the points come together. If your peaches are exceptionally large, make a full dough recipe, since the squares will need to be cut larger to make the packet for the peach. Save the extra for another project.

¼ recipe Orange Crisp Topping (see Master Recipe: Crisp or Crumble Topping variation, page 161)

½ recipe Roll-Out Dough (see Roll-Out Dough recipes, pages 38–58)

2 peaches

Sugar for sprinkling: granulated, sparkling, or demerara

Raspberry fruit powder (optional; see How to Make Fruit Powder, page 309)

EGG WASH

1 egg white plus 2 teaspoons water, fork beaten (or other wash of your choice; see Washes for the Top, page. 90)

1. Make the Orange Crisp Topping and place in the freezer to chill.

2. Make the dough and place in the fridge to chill.

3. Cut the peaches in half, remove and discard the pits.

4. Cut the dough in four equal pieces. Roll each piece into a square that is 7½ inches (17 cm) per side.

5. In a small bowl, mix the egg white and water together with a fork.

6. With a silicone brush, or one you don't mind getting wet, brush one rolled-out square with the egg wash, and then sprinkle with some Orange Crisp Topping, making a little mound in the middle that the peach will be placed over.

7. Place the cut side of half a peach on top of the topping.

8. Brush the edges of the dough with a little water. Bring two opposite corners together at the top of the peach, and then pinch lightly to hold together. Repeat with the remaining corners.

9. With your fingers, pinch the four dough seams, from the top of the peach to the bottom, to seal the peach inside.

10. Make an optional bow, leaf, or other decoration, and place near the top of the packet where the corners meet. This can be "glued" on with a little water or egg wash.

11. Repeat Steps 6 through 9 with the remaining three peach halves.

12. Place the packets on a sheet pan or cookie tin covered with a sheet pan liner or parchment paper, and place in the fridge to chill while you preheat the oven to 400°F (205°C).

13. Just before baking, brush the dough all over with egg wash, and sprinkle with sugar and a light coating of optional raspberry fruit powder.

14. Bake for 25 to 30 minutes. Test to see if the peach is done by sliding a thin skewer at an angle at the top of the packet so it goes into the baked peach easily. Let cool and serve on individual plates.

VARIATION

Whole Peach Dumpling

1. Remove the pit by gently sliding an apple corer halfway through the peach at the top. Remove the apple corer, turn the peach over, and slide the apple corer halfway through the peach at the bottom. When you pull out the corer, the peach pit should come out. Be sure to use ripe peaches.

2. Roll out the dough into a square that is 8½ to 9 inches (21 to 23 cm) per side.

3. Brush the dough with the egg wash. Place a gingersnap, or a lemon or vanilla wafer, in the middle of the dough square as a platform for the cored peach to sit on.

4. Fill the hollowed-out cavity of the peach with Crisp Topping.

5. Brush the edges of the dough with a bit of water. Bring opposite corners to meet at the top of the peach and press firmly but gently to seal. Repeat with the remaining corners.

6. Smooth the dough around the peach, taking care to make sure the seams are firmly but gently pressed together. Trim extra dough and firmly but gently press together again.

7. Top with two leaves cut out from the remaining dough and "glue" on with water or egg wash.

8. Place the peaches on a sheet pan or cookie tin covered with a sheet pan liner or parchment paper, and place in the fridge to chill while you preheat the oven to 400°F (205°C).

9. Just before baking, brush the dough all over with egg wash and sprinkle with sugar. A light coating of optional raspberry fruit powder mixed with sugar is lovely on top.

10. Bake for 25 to 30 minutes. Test to see if the peach is done by sliding a thin skewer at an angle at the top of the dumpling so it goes into the baked peach easily. Let cool and serve on a pretty plate.

Baked Apple Granola Dumplings

Here's another way to enjoy the "old faithful" apple pie flavors of autumn. Wrap dough strips around cored and peeled apples, fill with a crumble-style topping made with granola, and bake. For fun, if you like, you can paint the apples and leaves with colored edible food gels. These dumplings are delicious to eat whether hot, warm, or cool.

Makes 4 dumplings

½ recipe Roll-Out Dough (see Roll-Out Dough recipes, pages 38–58)

½ cup granola

¼ cup plus 2 tablespoons (75 g) granulated sugar

½ teaspoon cinnamon

A very small pinch of salt

⅛ teaspoon apple cider vinegar (Bragg's or another artisan apple cider vinegar) or fresh-squeezed lemon juice

1 teaspoon Calvados or apple jack (optional)

4 apples, cored and peeled

1 teaspoon (5 g) butter

Sugar for sprinkling: granulated, sparkling, or demerara

1 or 2 cinnamon sticks or 4 straight pretzels

EGG WASH

1 egg yolk plus 2 teaspoons water, fork beaten (or other wash of your choice; see Washes for the Top, page 90)

1. Make the dough and place in the fridge to chill.

2. Preheat the oven to 400°F (205°C).

3. In a medium-small bowl, mix together the granola, ¼ cup (50 g) of the sugar, cinnamon, salt, apple cider vinegar, and optional Calvados and set aside.

4. Divide the dough into four equal pieces. Roll out each piece and cut into long ¾- to 1-inch (2 to 2.5 cm) strips. Cut four 1½-inch (4 cm) circles and eight leaves out of scraps.

5. Place each cored and peeled apple on top of a dough circle.

6. Starting at the bottom of the apple, wrap strips of dough around the apples, splicing ends and overlapping edges of strips as needed. Cup your hands around the apple and lightly, but firmly, press into the strips to help secure them in place. Turn the apple over and make sure that the edges of the bottom dough circle are underneath the dough strips; press to secure.

7. Place the apples on a sheet pan, cookie tin, ovenproof baking dish, or pie pan lined with parchment paper or a sheet pan liner.

8. Fill the cored cavities of the apples with the granola filling and dot with ¼ teaspoon butter each.

CONTINUED

9. Put a dab of water on each leaf and place over the top of the filling, pressing lightly but firmly so that it stays in place. If the leaves aren't glued on well, they may melt down the side of the apple.

10. Lightly brush the egg wash over the wrapped apple and leaves.

11. Bake for 20 minutes. After 20 minutes, remove the tray from the oven, brush the apples again with the egg wash, and sprinkle with sugar. Return to the oven and continue baking for 20 to 25 minutes. If the dough is browning too quickly, cover with a vented tent made with a piece of foil (see How to Make a Foil Pie Shield, page 94). Use a toothpick or skewer to make sure the apples are cooked and soft.

12. For the stem, place a piece of cinnamon stick into the filling.

NOTE: If you have Custard Sauce on hand, put a pitcher of it on the table to pour over the apple dumplings (see Custard Sauce, page 118).

Easy Tart Shells

Makes twelve 2½-inch (6.35 cm) tart shells

Many of us make pastry dough by hand or with a food processor, but I wanted to see if it would be possible to make dough using a handheld electric beater. After some trial and error, here's what I came up with. Quick and easy to make, these little tart shells are perfect for Lemony Quick Tartlets (page 147). You can omit the leaf lard and use all butter if you like.

3 tablespoons (42 g) butter

2 tablespoons (30 g) leaf lard

1 tablespoons granulated sugar

1 egg, fork beaten

1 cup (150 g) flour

2 tablespoons milk or half-and-half

1. Preheat the oven to 375°F (190°C).

2. In a medium bowl, place 2 tablespoons of the butter, lard, sugar, and fork-beaten egg.

3. Mix with a handheld electric beater on a low-ish setting until, more or less, it is combined.

4. Add the flour alternately with the milk, mixing lightly after each addition.

5. Gather into a ball and flatten out a bit. Cover with plastic and chill for about 30 minutes.

6. Melt the remaining 1 tablespoon butter. Brush the melted butter in each well of a regular-size muffin tin.

7. Roll out the dough and cut into 4-inch (10 cm) circles. Gather the scrap dough together lightly and roll out again and cut until you have 12 circles.

8. Place a circle of dough in each of the buttered cups. Use your fingers to gently smooth it along the sides. It is okay if there are a few folds in the dough.

9. Fill each of the paper baking cups with about 2 tablespoons of pie weights and carefully place inside the dough-filled cups.

10. Bake on the bottom rack of the preheated oven for 15 minutes.

11. Remove the tin from the oven and remove the paper baking cups, taking care not to spill the weights. Save the baking cups as they can be used again.

12. Remove the tart shells from the muffin tin and set on a cooling rack.

Plum Raisin Tartlets

Makes about 6 tartlets

One rainy Sunday afternoon, when the season was hovering between summer and fall, I looked in my larder in hopes of spying something that I could use to cap off a family supper. I didn't want to go out to the store in the downpour, and when I found a bag of dried plums on my baking shelves, I set it on the counter, along with raisins, an orange, and the last of a bottle of brandy. With these ingredients I made a quick filling to fill some easy-to-make tart shells.

6 Easy Tart Shells (page 144; and see How to Blind Bake a Crust, page 69)

1 cup (200 g) roughly chopped dried pitted plums (prunes)

½ cup (80 g) seedless raisins

¼ cup (60 ml) brandy or rum

⅓ cup (80 g) water

½ cup (50 g) granulated sugar

1 tablespoon (14 g) butter

Zest of one orange

A little cinnamon

¼ recipe Whipped Cream (see Master Recipe: Whipped Cream, page 182)

1. Make, pre-bake, and set aside the crust to cool.

2. In a medium bowl, place the dried plums and raisins, and pour the brandy over them. Let them soak for an hour or more, stirring occasionally.

3. In a medium saucepan, pour the plums, raisins, and brandy, and then add the water and sugar. Turn the heat to medium and cook about 5 minutes until thick, stirring occasionally.

4. Remove from the heat and stir in the butter and orange zest. Set aside to cool.

5. Sprinkle each cooled tart shell with a little cinnamon and then fill with about 2 tablespoons of filling.

6. Make the Whipped Cream and pipe or spoon a dollop on top.

Lemony Quick Tartlets

Making this recipe is an easy way to fill little Easy Tart Shells. If you have only lemons on hand, use one for zest and two for juice.

Makes 8 to 9 tartlets

8 to 9 Easy Tart Shells (page 144; and see How to Blind Bake a Crust, page 69)

A pinch of cinnamon

One 14-ounce (396 g) can sweetened condensed milk

2 eggs, whisked

Zest of 1 lemon, finely chopped

Zest of ½ orange, finely chopped

Zest of ½ lime, finely chopped

Juice of 1 lemon, freshly squeezed

Juice of ½ orange, freshly squeezed

Juice of ½ lime, freshly squeezed

1 recipe Whipped Cream (see Master Recipe: Whipped Cream, page 182)

Candied lemon peel (optional; see Candied Citrus Peels, page 313) for garnish

1. Make, pre-bake, and set aside the crust to cool.

2. Preheat the oven to 350°F (175°C).

3. Place the pre-baked tart shells on a parchment-lined baking sheet, or slip them into paper baking cups and place them back inside a cupcake or muffin tin. Sprinkle each tart shell with a little cinnamon.

4. In a small saucepan, place the milk, eggs, zests, and juices. Turn the heat to medium and cook for 5 minutes, stirring constantly.

5. Pour the filling into the tart shells and bake for 10 minutes. Remove from the oven and let cool completely.

6. Make the Whipped Cream and pipe or spoon a dollop on top. Garnish with optional candied lemon peel.

VARIATION

Lemon Curd Tartlets

No time to make a filling? Here's an idea for an instant dessert.

Open a jar of store-bought lemon curd, fill the baked tartlet shell, place a sliced strawberry on top, and sprinkle with confectioners' sugar.

Butter Tarts

These classic Canadian treats are tiny, delicious, and perfect with a cup of tea. I've included a pair of variations, too.

Makes 10 to 12 tarts

BUTTER TART DOUGH

1½ cups (190 g) flour, plus a little more for rolling

A pinch of salt

8 tablespoons (1 stick; 112 g) cold butter, cubed

¼ cup (60 ml) ice water

1 egg yolk

1 teaspoons white vinegar or fresh-squeezed lemon juice

BUTTER TART FILLING

1 cup (200 g) brown sugar

A pinch of salt

4 tablespoons (½ stick; 56 g) butter, softened

1 egg, fork beaten

1 teaspoon vanilla extract

½ cup (100 g) raisins or currants

TO MAKE THE DOUGH

1. In a large bowl that you can comfortably get your hands in, place the flour and salt. Fluff with a fork or your clean hands to mix.

2. Add the cold butter, and smoosh and pinch it into the flour with your fingertips, or cut it in with a pastry cutter. The pieces of fat should be no larger than pea size with flakes the size of oats.

3. In a small bowl, mix together the water, egg yolk, and white vinegar with a fork. Pour over the flour and fat mixture, and fluff with a fork or fingers to mix in.

4. Bring the dough together and knead it three or four times with the heel of your hand. Pat it out into a flat rectangle, wrap in plastic, and refrigerate for 20 to 30 minutes.

5. On a well-floured surface, roll out the dough to a rectangle about 12 by 18 inches (30 by 46 cm) and ¼ inch (6 mm) thick. As you roll out the dough, be sure that it isn't sticking and you can move it on the surface. Add a bit more flour if needed.

6. Cut the dough into 4-inch (10 cm) circles. Gather the scrap dough together lightly and roll out again and cut until you have 12 circles.

7. Place a circle of dough in each of the buttered cups. Use your fingers to gently smooth it along the sides. It is okay if there are a few folds in the dough.

CONTINUED

8. Place the dough-filled muffin tin in the fridge while you go on to make the filling.

TO MAKE THE FILLING

1. Preheat the oven to 450°F (230°C).

2. In a medium bowl, add the brown sugar, salt, and softened butter. With an electric hand mixer, mix on low until the butter and sugar are well combined.

3. In a small bowl, mix the egg and vanilla together with a fork. Add to the butter and sugar mixture and, using a big spoon, mix until combined.

4. Stir in the raisins.

5. Fill each tart shell with 1 scant tablespoon filling.

6. Bake for about 15 minutes.

7. When the tin comes out of the oven, run the blade of a knife around the edge of the tarts so they won't stick. Let cool and then remove from the muffin tin.

VARIATIONS

Plain Jane Butter Tarts

Omit the currants or raisins.

Wise Pies

In Ireland, it is believed that if one eats a hazelnut, wisdom and inspiration will be received. In case you would like to see if it is so, make these little tarts.

Omit the currants or raisins, and place one or two roasted and chopped hazelnuts in the tart shell before filling and baking (see How to Roast Hazelnuts, Pecans, or Walnuts, page 314).

Pies by Any Other Name

Pies by Any Other Name

I am always on the lookout for high-quality fruit. I search for flavor in the produce aisles of grocery stores, big and small, and at farmers' markets where I have been known to engage in discussions that start out with the question, "What's sweet today?" Sometimes I use a refractometer, the little tool that looks like a 6-inch spy glass that winemakers and fruit growers use to measure sweetness. But there are other ways to gauge a fruit's pie-worthiness, as most of us do not carry this tool around with us. I always try to find the heaviest fruit, as it will have more sugar. The aroma of the fruit is another great indicator of flavor. And, of course, tasting samples that are offered is a good example of what you will be bringing home. I love watching the faces of youngsters as they taste fruit: if it's sweet, they may ask for another sample. Finding the sweetest fruit is an endless quest, and a worthy one at that. Tasting your filling is an important step in pie making.

The part of the country where I live allows me to grow my own cherries, berries, plums, apples, and pears. At times, I find myself overwhelmed with fruit reaching its peak and needing to be used immediately. Fortunately, the high summer—when so much of this abundant harvest ripens—is also peak pie season, when picnics, backyard barbecues, and potlucks take place and I liberally utilize the recipes that follow. I think of the pandowdy, sonker, crisp, crumble, cobbler, and slump as pies by another name. They are first cousins of fruit pies as they share the same basic ingredients—fruit, flour, butter, and sugar. The pandowdy will use any roll-out dough placed on top of the filling (see Roll-Out Dough recipes, pages 38–58). For a sonker, we'll cut wide strips from a blended biscuit and pie–style dough and place them on top in a rustic lattice. Crisps and crumbles use the crisp toppings that we've enjoyed on our fruit pies. Finally, we'll make some cobblers and slumps with a batter that turns golden brown in the oven. All of these pie cousins are quick to make and bake, and, like any good pie, are very easy to share and enjoy any time of the year.

Apple Pandowdy

Makes one 9- to 10-inch (23 to 25 cm) deep-dish pie

A pandowdy is a very humble looking pie baked with only a top crust in a deep-dish baking dish or even a cast-iron skillet. I did read once that after a pandowdy is baked, it should be deftly inverted onto a platter, much like a Tarte Tatin. If your flipping nerve is a bit on the wane, simply remove the pandowdy from the oven and let it cool. You can then make it look a little dowdy by breaking up the top of the crust a bit with a spoon. Serve with scoops of vanilla ice cream. This is delicious made with pears, too.

½ recipe Roll-Out Dough (see Roll-Out Dough recipes, pages 38–58)

Butter for greasing baking dish or cast-iron skillet

6 to 8 apples, peeled or unpeeled, quartered, cored, sliced or chopped

½ cup (100 g) granulated sugar, plus 2 teaspoons or more for sprinkling on top

½ teaspoon salt

1 teaspoon cinnamon

2 gratings of nutmeg

½ teaspoon allspice

1 tablespoon apple cider vinegar (Bragg's or another artisan apple cider vinegar) or 1 to 2 teaspoons fresh-squeezed lemon juice

1 to 2 tablespoons Calvados or boiled cider (optional; see How to Make Boiled Cider, page 99)

¼ cup (35 g) flour

1 tablespoon (14 g) butter, melted

Ice Cream (see Master Recipe: Ice Cream, page 300) for serving

1. Make the dough and place in the fridge to chill.

2. Place a sheet pan or cookie sheet on the lowest rack in the oven and preheat to 425°F (220°C).

3. Butter well a 9- to 10-inch (23 to 25 cm) deep-dish baking dish or cast-iron skillet.

4. In a large mixing bowl, put the apples, sugar, salt, cinnamon, nutmeg, allspice, vinegar, Calvados, and flour, and mix lightly until most of the surfaces are covered with what looks like wet sand.

5. Pour the mixture into the buttered baking dish or skillet.

6. Roll out the dough 1 inch (2.5 cm) larger than the pie pan and lay it over the apple filling. Tuck the edge of the dough down and inside the baking dish or skillet. Cut a few rustic vents on top of the crust.

7. Brush the top with some melted butter and sprinkle with sugar.

8. Place the pandowdy on the heated sheet pan and bake for 20 minutes.

9. Turn down the oven to 375°F (190°C), then open the oven and move the pan onto the middle rack and bake for an additional 25 to 30 minutes more until you see some steady bubbling around the sides and coming through the vents.

10. Remove from the oven and let cool for a bit.

11. Before serving, break up the top crust a bit with a spoon, spoon into bowls, and serve with scoops of Ice Cream.

Kate's Peach Berry Sonker

Makes one 9-by-13-inch (23-by-33 cm) sonker

From the western counties of Surry and Wilkes in North Carolina, a sonker uses dough that is more like a biscuit, then rolled out, cut in strips, and placed along the sides of the baking pan. A fruit filling is added and some dough strips are laid over the fruit in a quasi-lattice. The filling is very juicy, and it is served with a sweet sauce called a dip. One July weekend, pastry chef and good friend Jenni Field followed the North Carolina Surry County Sonker Trail with her husband. I eagerly followed the updates and pictures she posted on social media. The day after she returned, and while her sonker experience was still fresh in her senses, we chatted about the finer points of sweetness, texture, and temperature. Each of us then set out to create our own versions of this regional dessert. The filling is very adaptable, and you can use whatever is available. Try peaches, berries, or cherries mixed together, or a single fruit filling. One filling I made used a combination of green gooseberries, white currants, red currants, peaches, and a few tart cherries. It was spectacular.

DOUGH

½ pound (2 sticks; 224 g) butter, cold and cut into tablespoon-size pieces, plus more to butter the baking dish

2½ cups (363 g) flour

1 tablespoon aluminum-free baking powder

½ teaspoon salt

1 cup (240 ml) milk

FILLING

2½ tablespoons flour

1¼ cups plus 2 tablespoons (275 g) granulated sugar, divided

4 to 5 cups (1 very generous qt, 1 L) peaches

3 cups (about 300 g) blackberries

1 tablespoon vanilla extract

5 tablespoons (70 g) butter

2 tablespoons sparkling sugar or demerara sugar

½ cup (118 g) Milk Dip (recipe follows)

EGG WASH

1 egg white plus 2 teaspoons water, fork beaten (or other wash of your choice; see Washes for the Top, page 90)

TO MAKE THE DOUGH

1. Preheat the oven to 375°F (190°C).

2. Grease the sides of a 9-by-13-inch (23 by 33 cm) baking dish with butter.

3. In a medium bowl, place the flour, baking powder, salt, and pieces of cold butter. With a pastry cutter, knives, mezzaluna, or your fingers, cut and smoosh the butter into the dry ingredients until it is roughly mixed.

4. Add the milk and mix until the dough is tacky.

5. Place half the dough on a floured board. Pat the dough out a bit, roll it out to about ⅜ inch (1 cm) thick, and cut into long 2½-inch (6 cm) wide strips.

6. Lift a strip and tuck it around the sides of the pan. Repeat with the other strips until the pan is encircled with the wide strips. It's okay if you have to piece them together. The bottom of the pan will be doughless.

TO MAKE THE FILLING

1. Place the flour and 1¼ cups (250 g) sugar in the baking dish and mix around a bit with your fingers or a fork to combine.

2. In a medium bowl, place the peaches, black-berries, and vanilla, and gently mix together. Turn the filling onto the top of the flour and sugar in the baking dish.

3. Sprinkle the remaining 2 tablespoons sugar over the top of the fruit.

4. Break up the butter into small pieces and place over the top of the fruit evenly.

TO MAKE THE TOP

1. Roll out the remaining dough to ⅜ inch (1 cm) thick and cut into long 2½-inch- (6 cm) wide strips. Lay the strips over the top of the filling to form a rough lattice. An offset spatula is a great help in getting the rolled out strips onto the top of the filling.

2. In a small bowl, mix the egg and water together with a fork and brush some on top of the lattice strips. Sprinkle with 2 tablespoons of sparkling sugar.

3. Place the sonker in the oven and bake for the first 30 minutes of the bake. The total time will be 60 minutes. While the sonker is baking, make the Milk Dip (recipe follows).

4. After the sonker has baked for 30 minutes, carefully remove it from the oven, set on a flat surface, and close the oven door. Pour ½ cup (118 g) of the hot Milk Dip over the top.

5. Return the sonker to the oven and bake for an additional 30 minutes, or until the filling is bubbling around the edges and up through the crust. The crust should be a beautiful golden brown when finished. If it is browning too quickly, place a piece of foil loosely over the top and continue to cook.

6. Let cool for 20 to 30 minutes and serve warm or at room temperature. Pass a pitcher of addi-tional warm Milk Dip to pour over the servings.

CONTINUED

Peach Currant Gooseberry Sonker

Use a combination of sliced peaches, white and red currants, and green gooseberries to total 7 to 8 cups (about 2 qts, 1.8 L) fruit.

Milk Dip

Makes about 1½ cups (360 ml)

Some of this will be poured into the sonker halfway through the bake. Pour the rest in a pretty pitcher and pass at the table. Milk dip should be served warm or at room temperature.

2½ teaspoons cornstarch

¼ cup (50 g) plus 2 tablespoons granulated sugar

A pinch of salt

1½ cups (360 ml) milk

1 teaspoon vanilla extract

1. In a medium saucepan, mix together the cornstarch, sugar, and salt with a whisk.

2. Whisk in the milk.

3. Turn the heat to medium-high and bring to a boil while whisking constantly. Cook for 2 minutes more while whisking. Remove from the heat.

4. Stir in the vanilla and set aside to cool. Extra milk dip can be refrigerated.

Master Recipe: Crisp or Crumble Topping

Makes about 3 cups of crisp topping

Makes a generous 2 cups crumble topping

Fruit filling, with a crumbly topping that is baked in the oven to a lovely golden brown color, is either a crisp or a crumble. The difference is that a crisp topping includes oats and optional nuts, and a crumble topping is made without oats. Make your topping first and then give it a chill for 15 minutes in the freezer so the butter won't be soft when it goes into the oven.

CRISP TOPPING

½ cup (100 g) packed brown sugar

¼ teaspoon salt

½ cup (70 g) flour

1 teaspoon ground ginger or cinnamon (optional)

1½ cups (160 g) old-fashioned rolled oats

8 tablespoons (1 stick; 112 g) butter, chilled

½ cup (60 g) chopped pecans or walnuts (optional)

CRUMBLE TOPPING

½ cup (100 g) packed brown sugar

¼ teaspoon salt

1½ cups (160 g) flour

1 teaspoon ground ginger or cinnamon (optional)

8 tablespoons (1 stick; 112 g) butter, chilled

1. In the bowl of a food processor, combine the sugar, salt, flour, and cinnamon or ginger, if using. If you are making the Crisp Topping, add the oats.

2. Divide the chilled butter into eight large pieces and add to the food processor bowl.

3. Pulse the food processor about 20 times to cut the butter into the dry ingredients. It should look crumbly. Pulse more if needed.

4. If you are making the Crisp Topping, add the chopped nuts, if using, and pulse a few more times.

5. Turn the mixture into a bowl or freezer bag and let chill for at least 15 minutes.

NOTE: The desired depth of a crisp or crumble topping is a personal preference. I like my toppings to be thick, but if you like yours to be thinner, save the extra topping in the freezer and use for another time or to make additional smaller pies.

VARIATION

Orange Crisp Topping
Use this topping for Peach Packets (page 138).

1. Roast the nuts, cool, and add (see How to Roast Hazelnuts, Pecans, or Walnuts, page 314).

2. Add 1 tablespoon Cointreau or other orange liqueur.

Old-Fashioned Apple Crisp

Makes one 9-inch (23 cm) crisp

For an exceptionally delicious crisp, use a variety of apples, some for sweet and some for tart. I think crisps are best eaten the day they are made, while still warm. You can either put the entire Crisp Topping on at the beginning of the bake, or you can add it halfway through so that the topping holds more clumpy shapes.

1 recipe Crisp Topping (see Master Recipe: Crisp or Crumble Topping, page 160)

Butter for greasing the baking dish

6 to 8 apples, peeled, quartered, cored, and sliced

⅓ to ½ cup (66 to 100 g) granulated sugar, depending on how sweet or tart the apples

1 teaspoon cinnamon (optional, as there will also be cinnamon in the topping)

A squeeze of half a lemon (about 1 teaspoon), more if you like a really bright taste

1 to 2 tablespoons apple liqueur such as Calvados or Clear Creek Distillery Eau de Vie (optional)

2 tablespoons flour

Half-and-half, Whipped Cream (see Master Recipe: Whipped Cream, page 182), or vanilla Ice Cream (see Master Recipe: Ice Cream, page 300) for serving

1. Make the Crisp Topping and place in the freezer.

2. Preheat the oven to 375°F (190°C). Butter a 9-inch (23 cm) square baking dish and set aside.

3. In a medium bowl, place the apples, sugar, optional cinnamon, lemon juice, optional apple liqueur, and flour. Mix with a spatula, spoon, or your clean hands until everything is well combined. Let sit for 10 to 15 minutes, mixing occasionally with a spoon.

4. Turn the apple filling into the buttered baking dish.

5. Now you have a choice:

   • Add the Crisp Topping now and bake for 50 to 55 minutes, until the filling is bubbling around the edges and the top of the crisp is golden.

   OR

   • Bake without the Crisp Topping for 25 minutes. Open the oven, carefully remove the pie, set it on a heat-safe surface, and close the oven to keep the heat inside. Sprinkle the frozen Crisp Topping over the top of the apples. Return the baking pan to the oven and continue to bake for an additional 25 to 30 minutes, until the filling is bubbling around the edges and the top of the crisp is golden.

6. Remove from the oven and let cool for a bit.

7. Serve with half-and-half poured over the top, Whipped Cream, or a scoop of vanilla Ice Cream.

Buttery Blackberry Crisp

Makes one 8-inch (20 cm) square crisp

What you'll need first are some freshly picked blackberries. On the Olympic Peninsula in Washington State where I live, just about every alley and roadside has brambles in the late summer and early fall with beautiful berries begging to be picked. When picking berries, wear an old long sleeve shirt so as not to get your arms too scratched up, and look for the blackberries that are big, plump, and come off of the vine easily. You won't have to pick too many, either. A quart of berries will do just fine . . . plus a few more for sampling. If blackberries don't grow near you, you can find them in season in your grocery produce section, and frozen blackberries will do just fine any time of the year.

---

1 recipe Crisp Topping (see Master Recipe: Crisp or Crumble Topping, page 160)

4 cups (about 400 g) fresh or frozen blackberries

¾ cup (150 g) granulated sugar

⅛ teaspoon salt

A small grating of nutmeg

¼ teaspoon cinnamon

Juice of ½ small lemon or lime

1 tablespoon orange liqueur or 1 teaspoon grated orange zest (optional)

Ice Cream (optional; see Master Recipe: Ice Cream) for serving

1. Preheat the oven to 400°F (200°C).

2. Make the Crisp Topping and set in the freezer while you make the filling.

3. Put berries, sugar, salt, nutmeg, cinnamon, lemon juice, and optional orange liqueur into a bowl and gently mix with a spoon until the berries are well coated. Set aside.

4. Place the filling into an 8-inch (20 cm) square baking dish or a tart or pie pan of similar size.

5. Spread the Crisp Topping over the blackberry filling evenly. Save any extra in the freezer for another bake.

6. Pop the pan into the center of the preheated oven and bake for 30 to 35 minutes.

7. You'll want to let the crumble sit a bit before serving, but if you just can't wait, place a scoop of Ice Cream on top to help it cool down.

VARIATION

Individual Servings
Divide the filling into ramekins, top with the Crisp Topping, place on a baking sheet, and bake as above.

Banana Rhubarb Crisp

Makes one 8-inch (20 cm) square crisp

Before flying to New York City for the first week-long photo shoot with Andrew Scrivani for *Art of the Pie*, our first book together, I paid a visit to my friend Melissa's farm to harvest some of her rhubarb. She had no idea what variety it was, just that it was big—sometimes up to one pound per stalk. I carefully trimmed and wrapped it, and the following day, carried it right on the plane. By the time the book was released, Melissa had had a stroke and was no longer able to live on her beautiful farm. Her daughter and son-in-law, both avid gardeners, took it over, and they were kind enough to give me a root division from the plant from which I loved to pick. It's thriving in my Pie Cottage garden, and I've taken to calling it Melissa. This crisp uses bananas and lightly stewed rhubarb, and it is excellent with either custard sauce or a scoop of ice cream.

---

1 recipe Crisp Topping (see Master Recipe: Crisp or Crumble Topping, page 160)

About 2 pounds (1 kg) rhubarb, sliced to approximately 1-inch (2.5 cm) size

1 cup (200 g) granulated sugar

½ cup (120 ml) water

2 large ripe bananas

¾ teaspoon ground ginger

1 tablespoon orange liqueur (optional)

Custard Sauce (see Custard Sauce, page 118) or Ice Cream (see Master Recipe: Ice Cream, page 300) for serving

1. Preheat the oven to 350°F (175°C).

2. Make the Crisp Topping and place in the freezer.

3. In a medium saucepan, place the rhubarb, ½ cup (100 g) of the sugar, and the water.

4. Turn the heat to low, cook for 6 to 10 minutes, until the rhubarb gets soft. Remove from the heat.

5. Slice the bananas into ½-inch (1.25 cm) moons.

6. Place the stewed rhubarb, banana slices, remaining ½ cup (100 g) sugar, ginger, and optional orange liqueur into an 8-inch (20 cm) square baking dish. Mix gently to combine.

7. Evenly spread the Crisp Topping over the filling. Save any extra in the freezer for another bake.

8. Bake for 30 to 35 minutes, until the top is lightly browned and you see some of the juicy filling bubbling up around the edges of the crisp.

9. Serve hot, warm, or cool with Custard Sauce or Ice Cream.

Stoned Fruit Crisp

Makes one 8-inch (20 cm) square crisp

With tongue in cheek, I give you a crisp that might be the perfect edible to quell the munchies. Using whatever stone fruits are ripe and available, make this with apricots, peaches, nectarines, plums, pluots, cherries, or a colorful combination of some or all of them. It's up to you if you add some cannabis into the mix.

1 recipe Crisp Topping (see Master Recipe: Crisp or Crumble Topping, page 160)

4 cups (1 qt, 1 L) stone fruit of any variety or combination, sliced

¾ cup (150 g) granulated sugar

⅛ teaspoon salt

¼ teaspoon cinnamon

Juice of ½ small lemon

1 tablespoon orange liqueur

Ice Cream (optional; see Master Recipe: Ice Cream, page 300) for serving

VARIATION

Individual Servings

Divide the filling into ramekins, top with Crisp Topping, place on a baking sheet, and bake as above.

1. Preheat the oven to 400°F (200°C).

2. Make the Crisp Topping and set in the freezer while you make the filling.

3. In a medium bowl, place the fruit, sugar, salt, cinnamon, lemon juice, and orange liqueur. Mix gently with a spoon until the slices of fruit are well coated.

4. Turn the filling into an 8-inch (20 cm) square baking dish.

5. Spread the Crisp Topping over the fruit filling evenly. Save any extra in the freezer for another bake, or munch on it while the crisp bakes.

6. Pop the pan into the center of the oven and bake for 30 to 35 minutes.

7. You'll want to let the crisp sit a bit before serving, but if the munchies have gotten the better of you and you just can't wait, add a scoop of Ice Cream on top of the crumble, and dig into the baking dish with a spoon.

Apple Pear Triple Ginger Crumble

Makes one 9-inch (23 cm) square deep-dish crumble

The scent of apples and pears baking with ginger is such a warming and seasonal fragrance. If you are a ginger fan, you'll love that this crumble uses ginger in three ways—ground, candied, and in a liqueur. For an all-pear version, make the Crumble Topping with cinnamon and optional nuts, omit all the ginger, and instead add 2 teaspoons of fresh-squeezed lemon juice and 2 teaspoons of vanilla extract.

1 recipe Crumble Topping (see Master Recipe: Crisp or Crumble Topping, page 160)

Butter for greasing the baking dish

3 apples, peeled, quartered, cored, and sliced

3 pears, peeled quartered, cored, and sliced

½ cup (100 g) granulated sugar

1 teaspoon cinnamon, ground

1 teaspoon ginger, ground

¼ teaspoon salt

2 tablespoons diced candied ginger

1 to 2 tablespoons ginger liqueur (optional)

2 tablespoons all-purpose or gluten-free flour

Half-and-half, Whipped Cream (see Master Recipe: Whipped Cream, page 182), or Ice Cream (see Master Recipe: Ice Cream, page 300) for serving

1. Make the Crumble Topping and place in the freezer.

2. Preheat the oven to 375°F (190°C). Butter a 9-inch square deep-dish baking dish and set aside.

3. In a medium bowl, place the apples, pears, sugar, cinnamon, ground ginger, salt, candied ginger, optional ginger liqueur, and flour. Mix with a spatula, spoon, or your clean hands until everything is well combined. Let sit for 10 to 15 minutes, mixing occasionally.

4. Turn the filling into the buttered baking dish.

5. Evenly spread the topping over the filling and bake for 50 to 55 minutes, until you see some bubbling around the edges.

6. Remove from the oven and let cool for a bit.

7. Serve with half-and-half poured over the top, Whipped Cream, or a scoop of Ice Cream.

Mixed Berry Slump

Makes one 1½-quart (2.3 L) slump

A slump uses sweetened and seasoned fruit that's placed in a skillet and topped with plops of biscuit dough. It then goes into the oven to bake uncovered. You'll need a baking dish that can go from the stovetop to the oven. A cast-iron skillet works great for this. If you want to make a bigger slump, double the amounts.

FILLING

½ cup (100 g) granulated sugar

½ cup (120 ml) water

A squeeze of ½ small lemon (about 1 teaspoon juice)

1 tablespoon orange liqueur (optional, but really nice)

4 cups (1 qt, 1 L) mixed berries (strawberry, blackberry, blueberry, raspberry, or huckleberry)

DOUGH

1 cup (145 g) flour

1½ teaspoons aluminum-free baking powder

1½ teaspoons granulated sugar, plus 1 tablespoon (demerara is preferred) for sprinkling

¼ teaspoon salt

2 tablespoons (28 g) butter, cold

½ cup (120 ml) milk or half-and-half

1 tablespoon (14 g) butter, melted

TO MAKE THE FILLING

1. Preheat the oven to 400°F (205°C).

2. In a 1½-quart (2.3 L) baking dish that can go from the stovetop to the oven, add the sugar, water, lemon, and optional orange liqueur, and place on the stovetop. Turn the heat to medium and mix until the sugar dissolves.

3. Add the berries to the dish, and let cook on medium to medium-low while you make the dough.

TO MAKE THE DOUGH

1. In a medium bowl, place the flour, baking powder, sugar, and salt, and mix with a fork to combine.

2. Cut the cold butter into small pieces and, with clean fingertips, pinch and rub them into the flour mix until it looks like coarse meal.

3. Add the milk or half-and-half, and combine with a fork until it just comes together.

4. Form the dough into about eight pieces that are the size of small eggs. Place the dough pieces evenly over the top of cooking berries.

5. Brush the melted butter over the top of the dumplings and sprinkle with the remaining sugar. Bake for 25 minutes.

6. To serve, spoon the fruit and a dumpling or two into a bowl, and top with more of the cooked fruit.

Hestia and Angel: Pie Camp Angels

By the time 2010 rolled around, I was teaching three Art of the Pie day camps each weekend in Seattle, and the more sessions I offered, the faster they seemed to fill. Including the ferry ride, it was more than a three-hour journey for me. I would load my pie-making gear and ingredients into the back of my pie-mobile, and then teach at Seattle's iconic Pike Place Market. At the end of the day, after cleaning up, I would head home, only to turn around the next day and do it all again. The couches and guest rooms of friends were greatly appreciated, as staying in town was so much easier. Something had to give, and I hoped that it would not be me.

I lit candles one evening and petitioned Hestia, the goddess of the hearth, to please help me find a place in the city that would be as welcoming and homey as my sweet cottage at the foot of the Olympic Mountains. The next morning at 6:00 am, I received an email from Mari, a pie camp graduate who has become a friend, telling me how she had this odd feeling and didn't know why, but she felt she had to tell me about a place that was coming up for rent in Seattle. I replied to her immediately and contacted the owner posthaste.

Before the sun came up the next morning, I was on my way to Seattle to meet the owner and see the house. When I pulled up, I saw a vintage cottage, surrounded by tidy gardens that looked sweet, warm, and very inviting. There were lovely old wood floors, lots of light, and, just off the living room, a kitchen with enough counter space for teaching. It was perfect. We set the date that I would move in with my dog, cat, and grand piano. I couldn't help but think that Hestia had heard my petition. Later that day when I returned to Pie Cottage, I lit another candle to thank her. During that year, I rented out my own home in Port Angeles. Pie Camps continued to fill, including ones that I was now traveling to teach up and down the West Coast, and across the country. I even traveled to Gascony in southwest France to teach.

When my renter shared the news that she would be moving on from my home, I immediately wondered if I moved back, would campers make the three-hour trek for Pie Camp? Always being one who jumps in with both feet, even when I don't know quite how I'll be landing, I decided to give it a try and moved home. I was amazed and overjoyed when the first Pie Camp, filled with pie makers who had found me on the internet,

traveled from as far away as Ohio, Massachusetts, Texas, and Dubai to learn to make pie. If this wasn't an affirmation of doing what you love, I don't know what is. Then came the news that *USA Today* was sending a reporter to attend a 4-Day Pie Camp.

I wanted my gardens to be at their best, but after my time away, they needed lots of attention. When I lit a candle this time, I also put a plea out on social media that I was in immediate need of a garden angel. Within minutes, a longtime friend put me in touch with someone who could help. The pairing couldn't have been more perfect, and her name was Angel. In just two weeks, she rescued my gardens and had them in tip-top shape by the time the reporter arrived at my door. Over the years, Angel and I have become very good friends, sharing stories of our lives, along with laughter, a few tears, hugs, and this recipe for her Creeping Crust Peach Cobbler.

Angel's Creeping Crust Cobbler

Makes one 8-inch (20 cm) square cobbler

Cobblers usually use biscuit-type batter that is dropped on top of fruit, but Angel's cobbler tops the batter with the fruit. During the bake, the batter rises and creeps up around the fruit. Angel sifts the dry ingredients for the batter, because that's how she's always done it, but she said it's okay not to sift, too. This filling calls for peaches, but I once cobbled together a double-sized recipe using rhubarb and mixed berries, took it to a wedding potluck, and came home with a baking dish that was scraped clean down to the bottom.

BATTER

8 tablespoons (1 stick; 112 g) butter, unsalted

1 cup (145 g) flour

1 teaspoon aluminum-free baking powder

¾ cup (150 g) granulated sugar or less, depending on the sweetness of the fruit

½ cup (120 ml) milk

FRUIT TOPPING

2 cups (about 250 g) peaches, fresh or frozen

1 cup (about 100 g) blackberries, fresh or frozen

½ cup (100 g) granulated sugar

A small squeeze of lemon

A small grating of nutmeg (optional)

2 teaspoons Cointreau or other fruit liqueur (optional)

Ice Cream (see Master Recipe: Ice Cream, page 300) or Custard Sauce (page 118) for serving

1. Preheat the oven to 350°F (175°C). While the oven is preheating, place the butter in an 8-inch (20 cm) square baking dish and place it in the oven to melt.

2. Sift the flour, baking powder, and sugar into a medium bowl and mix with a whisk or spoon to combine well.

3. Add the milk and mix again. Don't overmix. Set aside.

4. In a small saucepan, heat the peaches, sugar, lemon, and the nutmeg and liqueur, if using, until warmed. Gently spoon the fruit mixture over the batter.

5. Remove the baking dish from the oven and, with a large spoon, place plops of the batter mixture on top of the melted butter, mounding slightly in the center. Be careful not to mix the melted butter into the batter.

6. Bake for 40 to 45 minutes or until the batter has crept through the fruit and has turned golden brown.

7. Remove from the oven. Serve hot or warm with Ice Cream or Custard Sauce.

VARIATIONS

Rhuberry Cobbler

Omit the peaches and use a mix of strawberry and rhubarb to total about 3 cups.

Classic Cream Pies

Creamy

Chiffon Pies

Layered Pies

Pies

Classic Cream Pies

How to Make a Cream Pie

1.
Bake a crust.

2.
Make pastry cream.

3.
Spoon cream into crust.

4.
Chill.

5.
Top.

6.
Don't rush!

Classic Cream Pies

Pastry creams, meringues, and custards are three staples that every pie maker will want to learn. With them we can mix and match layers and textures. We'll be learning about all three in this section.

The filling for a basic cream pie is made with a combination of eggs, milk, and sugar, a flavoring of choice, and then it's cooked on a stove top to make a pastry cream. Once the pastry cream has cooled, it is turned into a pre-baked crust and topped with whipped cream or meringue. It can then be embellished with fresh fruit, coconut, candied citrus peel, or a fruit glacé. Our first step will be to learn how to make and flavor a basic pastry cream, adjust ingredients to fit different-size pie pans, and make our first cream pie. Then, with the techniques we learned, we'll up our game to make the Luscious Pastry Cream (page 190) used for the Nanabanana Cream Pie (page 189), one of my very favorite cream pies ever.

We'll learn to make meringue, a must-know in every pie maker's bag of tricks (see Hints for Making Meringue, page 198). Tucked in this section, we'll learn to make a fruit glacé (see Master Recipe: Fruit Glacé, page 192), which is a fancy way to say fruit sauce topping. Before we leave the kitchen counter, we'll head over to the oven for a Mango Lime Pie (page 208) that uses sweetened condensed milk and a variation of Key lime pie that has been in my family for decades (see Helen's Key Lime Pie, page 209).

Master Recipe: Pastry Cream

Makes cream for one 9-inch (23 cm) shallow pie (use the smaller ingredient amounts)

Makes cream for one 9-inch (23 cm) deep-dish pie or one 10-inch (25 cm) tart (use the larger ingredient amounts)

This is a versatile filling that can be flavored in many ways. Vanilla makes a great canvas to feature fresh fruit, but almond, rum, and coconut, or orange, lemon, and coffee extracts are just a few of the directions where it can go. Add sparingly and taste. Be sure to bring the pastry cream to a full boil for 2 minutes while whisking vigorously to inactivate the enzyme in the egg yolk that can turn it into soup.

4 to 6 egg yolks

1 to 1⅓ tablespoons vanilla extract or other flavor (see the variations that follow)

¾ to 1¼ cups (150 to 170 g) granulated sugar

¼ to ⅓ cup (30 to 40 g) cornstarch

2 to 3 cups (500 to 710 g) half-and-half or whole milk or canned coconut milk (I use Thai Kitchen Organic Coconut Milk)

2 to 3 tablespoons (28 to 42 g) butter, cut in pats

1. Place the egg yolks in a medium bowl. Add the vanilla extract and whisk into the yolks for a minute or so until the eggs are smooth. It's fine to do this with a fork. Set aside.

2. In a medium heavy saucepan, place the sugar and cornstarch, and mix together with a whisk.

3. With a whisk in hand, turn the heat to medium under the saucepan and slowly and steadily pour the half-and-half into the dry ingredients while whisking constantly. I whisk in a figure-eight pattern. Keep whisking until the mixture thickens and you see it begin to bubble.

4. Remove the saucepan from the heat and pour ½ cup of the hot mixture into the eggs in the bowl to temper them. Whisk together in the bowl until it looks blended in. This won't take long.

5. Return the hot egg mixture to the sauce-pan, place it back on the burner, and turn the heat back on to medium. Bring to a boil and continue to whisk in a figure eight constantly and vigorously for 2 minutes, while the pastry cream plop, plop, plops. Remove from the heat. The pastry cream will be thick and coat the back of a spoon.

6. Turn the hot mixture into a bowl and let sit for 5 minutes. Whisk in the butter pats.

7. Cover with wax paper to prevent a skin from forming as it cools. Chill in the fridge for at least 2 hours. Whisk a bit before using.

How to Chill in a Hurry

If you are in a hurry to use your pastry cream, set the bowl into a larger bowl of ice and water, or spread it out on a sheet pan. Be sure to cover.

A FEW VARIATIONS

These are just a few flavor ideas of extracts and liqueurs for you to try. Use the smaller amounts for a 9-inch (23 cm) shallow pie pan.

Orange Pastry Cream

Substitute 1 to 2 tablespoons (15 to 30 ml) Cointreau or orange liqueur, or ¾ to 1 teaspoon orange extract, for the vanilla extract.

Elderflower Pastry Cream

Substitute 2 to 3 tablespoons (30 to 45 ml) D'arbo Elderflower Syrup for the vanilla extract.

Black Currant Pastry Cream

Substitute 2 to 3 tablespoons (30 to 45 ml) crème de cassis or other black currant liqueur or syrup for the vanilla extract.

Spiced Pastry Cream

1. Omit the vanilla.

2. Mix in with the sugar:

   • A small pinch of salt
   • 2 to 2½ teaspoons ground ginger
   • ½ to 1 teaspoon cinnamon
   • A few gratings of nutmeg

NOTE: Good-quality heavyweight saucepans will distribute heat evenly. I have 1-quart (1 L), 2-quart (2 L), and 3.5-quart (3.5 L) sizes that I use for making fillings and custards. My whisk can reach the corners more easily when the saucepans have rounded and sloping sides.

Chocolate Hazelnut Cream Pie

Makes one 9-inch (23 cm) deep-dish pie

I had seen the cocoa hazelnut spread on store shelves, but it wasn't until I was in my 60s that I finally bought a jar and tasted it. I loved it immediately, so much so that I confess to having dipped directly into the jar with a spoon for a treat when no one was around. Then I learned everybody does this, and I didn't feel so bad. This very easy-to-make pie, with a filling that requires no cooking, is topped with sweetened whipped cream, roasted hazelnuts, and raspberries, and is one that will be welcomed by Nutella fans of all ages.

1 recipe Press-In Crumb Crust (see Press-In Crumb Crust recipes, pages 72–77)

1 cup (240 ml) heavy whipping cream

¼ cup (50 g) granulated sugar

1 teaspoon vanilla extract

1 cup (225 g) cream cheese, at room temperature

1½ cups (371 g) chocolate hazelnut spread (such as Nutella)

2 tablespoons hazelnut meal (optional)

1 tablespoon granulated sugar (optional)

1 recipe Chantilly Cream (see Master Recipe: Whipped Cream chart, page 183)

1 cup (about 6 oz, 175 g) raspberries, or more if you like

¼ cup (40 g) hazelnuts, roasted and chopped (see How to Roast Hazelnuts, Pecans, or Walnuts, page 314)

1. Make, pre-bake, and set aside the crust to cool.

2. In the bowl of a stand mixer, place the whipping cream, sugar, and vanilla and whisk on high until medium stiff peaks have formed and set aside. This can also be done with a handheld electric mixer and a deep bowl.

3. In the clean bowl of a stand mixer, place the cream cheese and beat at high speed for 2 minutes, stopping to scrape down the sides of the bowl occasionally.

4. Add the chocolate hazelnut spread and beat at high speed for 2 more minutes.

5. Add the sweetened whipped cream and mix on low with the flat blade of the stand mixer until just combined. This can also be done with a rubber spatula.

6. Turn the mixture into the cooled cookie crumb crust and spread out evenly. Set in the fridge for a minimum of 4 to 6 hours, but overnight is best.

7. Mix the optional hazelnut meal and sugar together and sprinkle evenly on top of the well-chilled filling.

8. Make the Chantilly Cream and spread or pipe evenly over the top of the pie.

9. Arrange the raspberries on top of the Chantilly Cream.

10. Sprinkle the roasted hazelnuts evenly over the top.

How to Make Whipped Cream

Making billowy and light whipped cream to top a cream pie is a basic for any pie maker. Buy the heaviest cream you can find. The one I use has a 40 percent fat content. Sweeten either with confectioners' sugar or granulated sugar. I mix a bit of cornstarch into the granulated sugar to act as a stabilizer so that it holds its shape when piped or swirled on top, which is especially useful when a pie will be refrigerated and served later. If serving a whipped topped dessert right away, or with spooned-on plops of whipped cream, you can leave the cornstarch out.

Heavy cream whips more rapidly when our equipment is chilled well. Place the beaters and bowl in the freezer so they will be frosty cold when we are ready to use them.

Although I do make whipped cream in a stand mixer, I prefer using a handheld electric beater so I can see, and more importantly feel, the cream as it thickens. With handheld beaters, I can stop before the cream becomes over-whipped and grainy. If it is a small amount to be whipped, you can do it by hand with a wire whisk. One trick to whip by hand more quickly is to hold and swirl the bowl to the left, while whisking to the right. It does feel a bit like patting your head and rubbing your tummy at the same time, until you get the hang of it.

If whipping with electric beaters or a stand mixer, begin by mixing on low speed for a minute. Increase the speed up a notch or two for another minute. You will start to see some bubbles on top of the cream. Then increase the speed to high and sprinkle in the sugar over the whipping cream in the bowl. This is also called raining in the sugar.

If you want a plop of cream on top of a dessert, whip until it thickens and you begin to see a trail of ripples in the cream. Continue whipping to the soft peak stage, which is when it falls into soft curves on the beaters as you lift them out. For cream that is easy to pipe, continue on a bit longer, until the cream holds stiffer peaks. Do stop before the whipped cream gets grainy or to the butter stage.

If you do over-whip the cream, all is not lost as there is a fix. Pour more cream in, a tablespoon at a time, and whisk by hand, until it loosens up. Be sure to scrape down the sides, too. Finish by returning to your hand-held electric beater and whipping until it is just right.

I use many different extracts, syrups, and sometimes liqueurs to flavor whipped cream. Vanilla flavored whipped cream is also called Chantilly cream. I have included a few variations for you, but have fun experimenting with others. It's also fine to simply sweeten with sugar and leave out any extra flavoring.

You can spread and smooth the whipped cream on the top of a pie using an offset elbow spatula, a flexible spatula, or a spoon. To pipe the cream, use a pastry bag, or cut off a very small tip of a quart-size plastic zip-lock plastic bag. The hole should be just large enough to tuck whatever tip will be used to pipe. Pipping tips come in metal or plastic, and the starter set I purchased years ago still works well for the top of my pies. Open the bag and fold the sides down. Use a flexible spatula to put the whipped cream inside. Unfold the sides, close and seal the bag, and twist it around at the top. It will look sort of like the shape of a turnip. Squeeze gently and pipe pleasing patterns. My piping skills are pretty basic, but I get better each time I try, and you will, too.

Master Recipe: Whipped Cream

Makes 2 cups whipped cream

I find that one-half to three-quarters of this recipe is enough to pipe around the edge of a pie. This recipe makes a generous 2 cups, but for smaller amounts, reduce the amounts by one-quarter or one-half.

2 tablespoons to ⅜ cup (25 to 75 g) granulated sugar or confectioners' sugar

½ teaspoon cornstarch if using granulated sugar

1 cup (240 ml) heavy whipping cream, well chilled

Flavor extract of choice (see chart)

1. Chill a medium-size deep bowl and electric mixer beaters in the freezer.

2. If using granulated sugar, mix it with the cornstarch in a small bowl to combine, and set aside. If using confectioners' sugar, take a fork and break up any clumps, or sift through a small sieve strainer into a bowl.

3. Pour the whipping cream in the chilled bowl.

4. Mix the cream with an electric mixer on low for a minute. Increase to medium and mix for another minute. You'll see lots of bubbles on top.

5. Increase the speed to high and rain (sprinkle) in the sugar, a tablespoon at a time. Continue whipping for another 2 to 3 minutes until soft peaks form.

6. Add the flavor extract and mix a few seconds more to combine.

WHIPPED CREAM	HEAVY WHIPPING CREAM, WELL CHILLED	GRANULATED SUGAR PLUS CORNSTARCH TO STABILIZE OR CONFECTIONERS' SUGAR	FLAVORING AND EXTRAS
Basic Sweetened	1 cup (240 ml)	¼ cup (50 g) sugar plus ½ teaspoon cornstarch or 2 tablespoons	none
Chantilly Cream	1 cup (240 ml)	¼ cup (50 g) sugar plus ½ teaspoon cornstarch or ¼ cup (40 g)	1 teaspoon vanilla extract
Elderflower Whipped Cream	1 cup (240 ml)	2 tablespoons sugar plus ¼ teaspoon cornstarch or 2 tablespoons	2 tablespoons elderflower syrup or 3 tablespoons St-Germain liqueur
Raspberry Orange Whipped Cream	1 cup (240 ml)	⅜ cup (75 g) sugar plus ½ teaspoon cornstarch or ⅜ cup (60 g)	1 teaspoon orange extract plus 2 teaspoons raspberry fruit powder (see How to Make Fruit Powder, page 309)
Lemony Whipped Cream	1 cup (240 ml)	¼ cup (40 g) sugar plus ½ teaspoon cornstarch or ¼ cup (40 g)	1 teaspoon lemon juice, 1 tablespoon limoncello, or the lemony syrup saved from making candied lemon peel (see Candied Citrus Peels, page 313)
Rum Whip	1 cup (240 ml)	¼ cup (50 g) sugar plus ½ teaspoon cornstarch or ¼ cup (40 g)	1 tablespoon light rum or ½ teaspoon rum extract
Coconut Whipped Cream	1 cup (240 ml)	¼ cup (40 g) sugar plus ½ teaspoon cornstarch or ¼ cup (40 g)	1 teaspoon coconut extract
Orange Whipped Cream	1 cup (240 ml)	⅜ cup (75 g) sugar plus ½ teaspoon cornstarch or ⅜ cup (60 g)	1 teaspoon orange extract
Ginger Whipped Cream	1 cup (240 ml)	⅜ cup (75 g) sugar plus ½ teaspoon cornstarch or ⅜ cup (60 g)	2 tablespoons ginger liqueur
Coffee Whipped Cream	1 cup (240 ml)	⅜ cup (75 g) sugar plus ½ teaspoon cornstarch or ⅜ cup (60 g)	2 teaspoons coffee extract
Orange Blossom Whipped Cream	1 cup (240 ml)	5 tablespoons kumquat-flavored sugar saved from Candied Kumquats (see page 264) or ¼ cup (40 g) sugar plus ½ teaspoon cornstarch or ¼ cup (40 g)	1 tablespoon Starwest Botanicals Orange Blossom Flower Water or other orange blossom water
Boozy Whip	1 cup (240 ml)	¼ cup (50 g) sugar plus ½ teaspoon cornstarch or ¼ cup (40 g)	1 tablespoon whiskey or bourbon

Elderflower Cream Pie

Makes one 9-inch (23 cm)
deep-dish pie

To me, the light and delicate flavor of elderflower is evocative of early morning on a summer's day. These flowers, in my area of the country, bloom just around the time of summer solstice. One year on the solstice, I picked nearly 3 pounds of umbrels covered with the tiny white elderflowers that I then used to make cordial, syrup, and liqueur. Elderflower syrup is also commercially available, and D'arbo Elderflower Syrup is a good option to flavor this pastry cream that fills an almond meal crust.

1 recipe Almond Flour Crust (see Hazelnut Meal or Almond Flour Crust, page 76)

1 recipe Elderflower Pastry Cream (see Master Recipe: Pastry Cream variations, page 179)

1 recipe Elderflower Whipped Cream (see Master Recipe: Whipped Cream chart, page 183)

A few fresh viola or borage blossoms

1. Make, pre-bake, and set aside the crust to cool.

2. Make the Elderflower Pastry Cream and let it cool completely.

3. Whisk the cooled pastry cream a bit, turn into the pre-baked crust, and spread it out evenly using a spatula. Place in the fridge while you make the Elderflower Whipped Cream.

4. Top with Elderflower Whipped Cream and carefully place some fresh viola blossoms on top.

Triple Ginger Cream Pie

Makes one 9-inch (23 cm) shallow pie

This pie was created as a special surprise for a friend who loves ginger. It has multiple layers of ginger flavoring—a gingersnap crust on the bottom, ginger-flavored pastry cream in the middle, and on the top, a big mound of ginger-flavored whipped cream plus a finely diced candied ginger garnish. If there is a ginger lover in your house, this is the pie to make.

1 recipe Gingersnap Crumb Crust (see Master Recipe: Press-In Crumb Crust variation, page 73)

1 recipe Spiced Pastry Cream (see Master Recipe: Pastry Cream variations, page 179)

Ginger Whipped Cream (see Master Recipe: Whipped Cream chart, page 183)

2 tablespoons finely diced candied ginger for topping

1. Make, pre-bake, and set aside the crust to cool.

2. Fill the cooled crust with the cooled Spiced Pastry Cream.

3. Place big spoonfuls of the Ginger Whipped Cream on top of the pastry cream and spread around evenly, taking care to mound a bit higher in the middle.

4. Let set in the fridge for 4 to 6 hours, but overnight is best.

5. Sprinkle the candied ginger evenly on top and serve.

Vanilla Cream Pie

Makes one 9-inch (23 cm) shallow pie

Even though my mom made pudding from a box, I learned to make it from scratch. It takes just about the same amount of time, and most of that is spent waiting for the pudding to cool. I use whole milk, half-and-half, or a mix of the two if that is what I have on hand. This old-fashioned favorite is a template that can be flavored in so many different ways from bottom to top. You can make it with a single blind-baked Roll-Out Dough or any press-in crust. This is an easy pie to substitute orange or rum extract for vanilla. You can also add a layer of fresh berries or sliced bananas, a sprinkling of nuts, and piped or spread Chantilly Cream on top.

½ recipe Roll-Out Dough (see Roll-Out Dough recipes, 38–58; and How to Blind Bake a Crust, page 69) or 1 recipe Press-In Crumb Crust (see Press-In Crumb Crust recipes, pages 72–77)

1 recipe Pastry Cream (see Master Recipe: Pastry Cream, page 178)

½ cup (50 g) chopped nuts (optional) for garnish

1 cup (100 to 135 g) fresh berries (optional) for garnish

2 sliced bananas (optional) for garnish

½ to ¾ recipe Chantilly Cream (see Master Recipe: Whipped Cream chart, page 183) for garnish

1. Make, pre-bake, and set aside the crust to cool.

2. Make and chill the Pastry Cream. Whisk the chilled Pastry Cream a bit and turn it into the prepared crust.

3. Garnish with optional nuts or fruit, and pipe some Chantilly Cream around the edge.

Nanabanana Cream Pie

Makes one 9-inch (23 cm)
deep-dish pie

I humbly say to you, this is the best banana cream pie I have ever eaten. Honestly, I believe I could have stood at the kitchen counter, spoon in hand, devouring much of what I had just created the first time I made it. Instead, with "everything in moderation" foremost in my mind, I headed out in my neighborhood and shared it, until the plate was almost empty. There was a bit of cool creamy filling in the bottom of the pan when I came home, and I am not ashamed to say that I took the spoon and finished all of it off. I did stop before I could lick the plate clean, but I definitely thought about it. A peanut butter cookie crumb crust is just right for this pie. Halve or quarter the recipe for a smaller version.

1 recipe Press-In Crumb Crust, using peanut butter cookies (see Master Recipe: Press-In Crumb Crust, page 72)

1 recipe Luscious Pastry Cream (recipe follows)

3 to 5 ripe but not mushy bananas, sliced in ½-inch- (1.3 cm) thick moons

1 to 2 tablespoons demerara sugar (optional)

½ recipe Chantilly Cream (see Master Recipe: Whipped Cream chart, page 183) for serving

1. Make, pre-bake, and set aside the crust to cool.

2. While the crust is baking and cooling, make the Luscious Pastry Cream and let cool.

3. Place a layer of banana slices inside the bottom of the cooled pie shell; keep some slices to layer on top.

4. Evenly spread the Luscious Pastry Cream over the bananas.

5. Arrange the set-aside banana slices over the top of the filling in whatever pattern you like.

6. Sprinkle the optional sugar over the top and lightly run a blowtorch over it.

7. Serve with a dollop of Chantilly Cream.

Luscious Pastry Cream

8 egg yolks

1 tablespoon vanilla extract

½ teaspoon banana extract (optional, for even more banana flavor)

1½ cups (300 g) granulated sugar

½ cup (70 g) cornstarch

1 quart (950 ml) half-and-half

½ cup (120 ml) heavy whipping cream

1. Place the egg yolks in a medium bowl. Add the vanilla extract and banana extract, if using, and whisk into the yolks for a minute or so until the eggs are smooth. It's fine to do this with a fork. Set aside.

2. In a medium heavy saucepan, place the sugar and cornstarch, and mix together with a whisk.

3. With a whisk in hand, turn the heat to medium under the saucepan and slowly and steadily pour the half-and-half into the dry ingredients while whisking constantly. I whisk in a figure-eight pattern. Keep whisking until the mixture thickens and you see it begin to bubble.

4. Remove the saucepan from the heat and pour ½ cup of the hot mixture into the eggs in the bowl to temper them. Whisk together in the bowl until it looks blended in. This won't take long.

5. Return the hot egg mixture to the saucepan, place it back on the burner, and turn the heat back on to medium. Bring to a boil and continue to whisk in a figure eight constantly and vigorously for 2 minutes, while the Pastry Cream plop, plop, plops. Remove from the heat. The Pastry Cream will be thick and coat the bake of a spoon.

6. Turn the hot mixture into a bowl and let sit for 5 minutes. Whisk in the butter pats.

7. Cover with wax paper to prevent a skin from forming as it cools. Chill in the fridge for at least 2 hours. Whisk a bit before using.

8. Whip the heavy cream until it forms soft peaks and fold into the cooled Pastry Cream until it is evenly distributed.

Thoughts on Enjoying Bananas

I opened one of those video ads that pop up on social media that masquerade as an informative piece but turn out to be an infomercial selling something. This one was purported to be a quick weight loss product and included information on foods to avoid in order to reduce belly fat. Of course, it quickly morphed into hype about some snake-oil miracle product to buy. As much as I'd like to look like I did when I was twenty, or even fifty, I have come to the resigned conclusion that belly fat is a normal part of life . . . along with looking in the mirror and seeing that gravity is no longer my friend. I remember those oh so righteous thoughts of my younger years when I would see women in swimming pool changing rooms . . .

I will never . . . no never . . . let my body get like that.

But one morning you wake up—ta-da!—there you are wearing your mom's body, wondering how the heck did that happen! Now I just chuckle when I see myself in the mirror.

So back to that infomercial I got sucked into for a moment. A food that "they" say to avoid is banana. Really? As a child, I was very happy to avoid most all fruits and vegetables, but the fruit that came in a yellow jacket was one my mom knew I would eat. She gave them to me often, sliced on cereal both hot and cold, in peanut butter sandwiches, in banana bread, on ice cream, and, of course, out of hand. Bananas were cheap, filling, and delicious.

In my late 20s, during a post-divorce trip to Maui (hey, I didn't have a honeymoon, so the least I could have was an "it's-over-moon"), I stopped at fruit stands and found banana varieties I never knew existed. There were big bananas, little bananas, apple bananas, red bananas, blue bananas, ice cream bananas, bananas with variegated peel, ones that looked like praying hands, and another that doesn't look like a banana at all but more like a fig. Did you know that there are over a thousand banana varieties? The yellow one, that most all of us eat, is the Cavendish.

I learned that bananas help us feel happier, as they contain tryptophan that the body converts into serotonin, which is known to promote relaxation and improve moods. So, along with no longer sweating the small stuff like belly fat, I'm all for eating bananas that will keep me calm, centered, and relaxed—especially in a cream pie.

Master Recipe: Fruit Glacé

Makes enough to top one pie

Now, we'll learn to make a simple fruit glacé (pronounced glah-zeh). This is a simple and elegant way to add extra flavor to your pie. It can be used in many ways: as a topping for a cool cream, as an addition to a Pie-Let (page 124), as a drizzle over Fruitful Crostatas (page 134), as an element in a Pie Deconstructed (page 304), and as a topping for an Ice Cream Pie (page 302). It can also be used on some of the pies to follow, like Summer Breeze Blueberry Orange Peach Pie (page 194) and Red Goose Pie (page 195). This versatile topping takes less than 10 minutes to make, plus 5 minutes to cool.

½ to 1 cup (120 to 240 ml) liquid (see chart that follows)

A small pinch of salt

½ teaspoon fresh-squeezed lemon juice

3 tablespoons to 1 cup (37 to 200 g) granulated sugar (see chart)

1 to 3 tablespoon cornstarch (see chart)

2 to 3 cups (about 10 to 15 oz; 250 to 375 g) fruit (see chart)

1. Stir together the liquid, salt, lemon juice, sugar, and cornstarch in a medium saucepan set over medium heat, cooking until the sugar has dissolved. Stir constantly.

2. Add 1 cup of the fruit and bring to a boil, while continuing to stir.

3. Add the remaining 1 to 2 cups fruit and cook for another minute, while stirring.

4. Remove from the heat and let cool for 5 minutes.

FRUIT GLACÉ	FRUIT	LIQUID	SALT	LEMON JUICE	GRANULATED SUGAR	CORNSTARCH
Berry (Blueberry, Blackberry, Raspberry, Strawberry, or a combination)	2–3 cups (250–375 g) about 10–15 ounces berries	½ cup (120 ml) lemonade, orange juice, fruit juice, or water	a small pinch	½ teaspoon fresh-squeezed lemon juice	3 tablespoons	1 tablespoon cornstarch
Red Goose (Green Gooseberries and Red Currants)	2–3 cups (250 to 375 g) 10–15 ounces green gooseberries plus ½ cup (65 g) red currants	½ cup (120 ml) lemonade, orange juice, fruit juice, or water	a small pinch	½ teaspoon fresh-squeezed lemon juice	¼ cup (50 g)	1 tablespoon cornstarch
Pineapple	One 8-ounce (227 g) can crushed pineapple, drained and liquid reserved. Add all the pineapple in Step 2.	Add water to the pineapple juice to make 1 cup (240 ml) total liquid			1 cup (200 g)	3 tablespoons cornstarch
Mango	2 cups sliced or chopped	½ cup (120 ml) lemonade, orange juice, fruit juice, or water	a small pinch	½ teaspoon fresh-squeezed lemon juice	1 cup (200 g)	1 tablespoon cornstarch

Summer Breeze Blueberry Orange Peach Pie

Makes one 9-inch (23 cm) shallow or deep-dish pie

Each year, I host an annual Bring Your Own Lawn Chair Potluck. Just like it sounds, family, neighbors, friends on the Olympic Peninsula, and out-of-towners, too, show up with chairs, and also with dishes full of deliciousness to share. The potluck goes until the sun goes down, and then we start up a campfire in the big firepit made from the top of an old metal water tank that Duncan repurposed, and we roast marshmallows and make s'mores. I first made this as a test pie for the potluck in 2018 and set it on the dessert table thinking I'd come back in a bit and take a small taste. By the time I got back to the table, all that was left were a few crumbs in the pie plate. Everyone who tasted the pie thought it was a summertime winner. I hope you and your friends do, too.

1 recipe Gingersnap Crumb Crust (see Master Recipe: Press-In Crumb Crust variations, page 73)

1 recipe Orange Pastry Cream (see Master Recipe: Pastry Cream variations, page 179)

1 recipe Blueberry Glacé (see Master Recipe: Fruit Glacé chart, page 192)

2 ripe freestone peaches

1. Make, pre-bake, and set aside the crust to cool.

2. Make the Orange Pastry Cream and when it is cooled, whisk it a bit, turn into the baked crust, and spread it out evenly using a spatula. Place in the fridge while you make the Blueberry Glacé.

3. Make the Blueberry Glacé, and when cool, pour over the Orange Pastry Cream and spread it out evenly using a spatula.

4. Cut the peaches in half, twist, and remove the pits. Place the cut side of the peaches on a flat cutting surface, and slice into ¼-inch (6 mm) half-moon slices.

5. Arrange the peach slices on top of the Blueberry Glacé, slightly overlapping the slices.

Red Goose Pie

Makes one 9-inch (23 cm) shallow or deep-dish pie

This cream pie features three layers using red currants, gooseberries, and elderflowers. Make the layers in stages as they fit into your schedule, then assemble. Before serving, top with whipped cream flavored with elderflower syrup and piped in a pretty pattern. If you have some edible flowers in your garden such as violas, you might place a few on top, too.

1 recipe Vanilla Macadamia Nut Crust (see Master Recipe: Press-In Crumb Crust variations, page 73)

1 recipe Orange Pastry Cream (see Master Recipe: Pastry Cream chart, page 179)

1 recipe Red Goose Glacé (see Master Recipe: Fruit Glacé chart, page 192)

½ to ¾ recipe Elderflower Whipped Cream (see Master Recipe: Whipped Cream chart, page 183)

1. Make, pre-bake, and set aside the crust to cool.

2. Make the Orange Pastry Cream, cover with wax paper, and let chill in the fridge while you make the Red Goose Glacé.

3. Make the Red Goose Glacé and let cool.

4. Whisk the cooled Pastry Cream a bit, turn into the pre-baked crust, and spread it out evenly using a spatula. Place in the fridge while you make and cool the glacé.

5. Pour the glacé over the top and spread around evenly with a spatula. Save any extra in the fridge and enjoy with ice cream.

6. Make the Elderflower Whipped Cream and pipe on top of the glacé.

Mango Cream Pie

Makes one 9-inch (23 cm)
deep-dish pie

Another easy-to-make summertime treat is this pie, which features peeled and sliced mango strips that are placed on top of a pastry cream in concentric circles to look like open petals of a flower. If you like, cover the pastry cream with a fruit glacé of choice before topping with the freshly cut mango slices.

1 recipe Press-In Crumb Crust (see Press-In Crumb Crust recipes, pages 72–77) or ½ recipe Roll-Out Dough (see Roll-Out Dough recipes, pages 38–58; and How to Blind Bake a Crust, page 69)

1 recipe Pastry Cream (see Master Recipe: Pastry Cream, page 178)

1 recipe Mango Glacé (optional; see Master Recipe: Fruit Glacé chart, page 192)

3 ripe mangos, peeled and sliced into long strips (see Note)

Several small sprigs of mint for garnish

1. Make, pre-bake, and set aside the crust to cool.

2. Make the Pastry Cream, cover with wax paper, and let chill in the fridge.

3. Whisk the cooled Pastry Ceeam a bit, turn into the baked crust, and spread it out evenly using a spatula. Place in the fridge.

4. Make the optional Mango Glacé and set aside to cool.

5. Peel the mangos and, with a sharp knife, carefully cut the mango away from the pit lengthwise into long strips. Slice the strips into long thin slices.

6. Take the filled pie shell out of the fridge and top the Pastry Cream with the optional Mango Glacé.

7. Place a first row of mango strips all the way around the interior edge of the pie plate so they form a circle on top of the Pastry Cream.

8. Continue placing additional slices, making circles one row at a time, until you get to the center. Save the smaller pieces for the last circle made from about three slices.

9. Garnish with sprigs of fresh mint.

NOTE: To prepare the mango, cut the mango using a sharp knife on a cutting mat, or use a mango slicer. Slice off about ½ inch (1.25 cm) of both the bottom and top of the mango. Stand the mango up on one of the cut ends. Slice down the sides of the mango in long strips, just under the skin, until all the skin is removed. Starting at the top, cut down through the flesh, avoiding the large, long pit in the center.

Hints for Making Meringue

- Older egg whites may take less time to whip up, but they may not gain as much volume.

- Whites from fresh eggs are more stable and gain more volume.

- When separating the white from the yolk, don't get even the tiniest speck of yolk into it. If one slips in, there's really no solution other than to start over. Any bit of yolk, even the slightest amount, can ruin a meringue.

- Have a small bowl for separating out each egg white one at a time, and a larger bowl into which you will combine all the egg whites. This extra precaution can save time and frustration if, when separating the last of five eggs into a common bowl, the yolk breaks or falls into already separated and pristine egg whites.

- Separate the eggs while cold, and let the whites warm up to room temperature.

- Egg whites beaten at room temperature will increase to a greater volume.

- Use a squeaky-clean dry glass, metal, or copper bowl. If you are really fanatical, wipe out the bowl, the whisk, or beater blades with a cut lemon or vinegar to remove all the grease, rinse with water, and dry. Plastic bowls are not a good choice as they can hold grease.

- Whip the egg whites first at a low or medium speed until soft peaks form, then raise the speed, and add the sugar so it can dissolve.

- Either granulated sugar or superfine (castor) sugar may be used. Make your own castor sugar by processing a cup of granulated sugar in the food processor for 30 seconds.

- Sugar that is added when the whites form stiff peaks is likely not to dissolve fully and will form liquid drops on top of the meringue as the pie sets.

- Over-beating will break down egg whites. Although they may look fluffy when first topping the pie, they will later shrink into very tough and unattractive continents on top of the pie. To demonstrate what works at a session on making meringue at Pie Camp, I once put very cold egg whites (that had previously been frozen) into the bowl of my stand mixer, turned it on high, dumped in all the sugar at once, and beat, beat, beat until the whites were well past a stiff peak stage. While I was spreading it onto the top of a lemon meringue pie, the meringue was already collapsing, and a few hours later we had little white shrunken nuggets.

- Weeping meringues are not pretty. Sprinkle a layer of finely ground cookie crumbs or breadcrumbs on top of the filling before adding the meringue. This will help to absorb some of the extra moisture.

- Place meringue on a hot filling.

- Rather than placing the meringue in the middle and spreading to the edge, first spread some of the meringue around edge of the crust, making sure there are no gaps. Add more and work toward the middle.

- Meringues really should be eaten on the day they are made, and preferably within six hours, so if you are entering meringue-topped pie in a contest, you'll want to check the timing so the judges see and taste it at its peak.

- If you are traveling for Thanksgiving holidays or a special event and want to present a meringue-topped pie, consider making it where you will be. A meringue, made the day before it is to be served, will lose some of its loft and may weep if the sugar has not dissolved.

- You may have heard to never make a meringue on a rainy day, as sugar will absorb moisture from the air, weighing down the billowy peaks. But as I live in a coastal town in the rainy northwest of Washington State, this would preclude me from making meringues often. Truthfully, I haven't found rain to be an issue. On the other hand, I do avoid making meringues in a hot and steamy kitchen.

- Meringue powders work well to top a pie, and also as an ingredient in chiffon pie, which we will be learning about soon. Be sure to follow the directions on the container.

Now let's make a meringue to top our pies.

Master Recipe: Meringue

Makes enough to top one pie

This is the meringue I learned to make from my grandmother, and the directions are simple. Put egg whites in a squeaky-clean bowl, beat with an electric handheld beater or a stand mixer with a whisk attachment, while sprinkling in sugar, until medium stiff peaks form. The word that she used for sprinkling in sugar was "raining."

½ teaspoon cream of tartar

¼ cup plus 2 tablespoons (75 g) granulated sugar or superfine sugar

5 egg whites

½ teaspoon vanilla extract (optional)

1. Mix the cream of tartar and sugar together and set aside.

2. In a squeaky-clean bowl, place the egg whites and optional vanilla extract and, with an electric handheld beater or a stand mixer, beat them on low for a minute. Increase the speed to medium and continue to beat until you see soft peaks when you lift the beaters.

3. Sprinkle 2 tablespoons of the sugar mixture and continue to beat on medium.

4. Turn the beater to high, add the remainder of the sugar mixture, 2 tablespoons at a time, and mix until stiff peaks are formed. Lift the beaters out.

5. With a flexible rubber spatula, turn the meringue onto the top of the pie near the edges to set a seal, and lightly and evenly spread it toward the center. Make sure the meringue reaches all the way to the edge of the crust and that there are no gaps. Use the backside edge of a spoon to make some peaks and valleys.

6. To brown the meringue, place in a pre-heated 375°F (190°C) oven for 6 minutes, or use a blowtorch.

Vanilla Meringue Pie

Makes one 9-inch (23 cm) shallow pie

A recipe for "meringue" was first published in France in 1691, but it was probably not the light topping that we think of today. That light meringue was invented in 1720 by a Swiss pastry chef and was later brought to France. Here, you can change up the Vanilla Cream Pie by pouring the hot filling into a pre-baked crust and top with a light and fluffy meringue.

1 recipe Press-In Crumb Crust (see Press-In Crumb Crust recipes, pages 72–77)

1 recipe Pastry Cream (see Master Recipe: Pastry Cream, page 178)

1 recipe Meringue (see Master Recipe: Meringue, page 200)

1. Make, pre-bake, and set aside the crust to cool.

2. Preheat the oven to 375°F (190°C).

3. Make the Pastry Cream and pour while still hot into the pre-baked crust.

4. Make a meringue of your choice and spread on top of the hot filling.

5. Pop the pie into the preheated oven for 6 minutes, until the peaks of the meringue are slightly browned.

6. Let cool before serving.

About That Blowtorch

Although Julia Child is credited with saying, "Every woman should have a blowtorch," it was actually Chef Mary Bergin who said it on a segment of *Baking with Julia* (PBS) when she was demonstrating how to make her Chocolate Bundt Cake with Crème Brûlée and Chambord Raspberries. If you use one to lightly brown a meringue, do remember to toast Julia, and Chef Mary, with a "Bon Appétit!"

Take Your Time Ginger Lime Pie

Makes one 9-inch (23 cm) shallow pie

One afternoon, when hurriedly making a lime variation of a lemon meringue pie, I misread my scribbled out notes and added an extra ¼ cup (60 ml) water. (Note to self: Work on penmanship.) It seemed a little runny when I finished cooking it, but there was no time start over. So I topped it with a meringue and hoped for the best, figuring that I could always call it lime posset in a gingersnap crumb crust. When it was time to serve it for dessert, the extra water had indeed made the curd softer than usual, but I was surprised to find that it still held some shape. The leftovers went in the fridge, and, lo and behold, the next morning I had filling that was holding its shape perfectly. I now call it the Take Your Time Ginger Lime Pie. As a rule, I don't suggest you add an extra ¼ cup (60 ml) water when making curd, but if an extra tablespoon or two do find their way into the pot, you may find that with some extra time it will set up just fine. Top with a full meringue or meringue dollops.

1 recipe Gingersnap Crumb Crust (see Master Recipe: Press-In Crumb Crust variations, page 73)

4 egg yolks, fork beaten

1 cup (200 g) granulated sugar

⅓ cup (45 g) cornstarch

A small pinch of salt

1¼ cups (300 ml) warm water

2 tablespoons (28 g) butter

Zest of 1 lime

½ cup (120 ml) lime juice (about 6 limes)

1 recipe Meringue (see Master Recipe: Meringue, page 200)

1 to 2 tablespoons candied ginger

1. Make, pre-bake, and set aside the crust to cool.

2. Place the fork-beaten egg yolks in a medium bowl.

3. In a saucepan, combine the sugar, cornstarch, and salt.

4. Add the water and, while constantly stirring with a whisk, bring the mixture to a boil. Reduce the heat and cook for 2 more minutes while continuing to whisk. Don't be afraid to whisk vigorously as it gets thicker.

5. Take about ½ cup of the hot mixture and stir it into the egg yolks. Return this mixture to the saucepan and cook at a full boil, while stirring constantly for 2 minutes more, until the mixture is thick.

6. Stir in the butter, lime zest, and lime juice, and cook for another minute.

7. Immediately pour into the pre-baked piecrust.

8. Make the Meringue and top the pie with it, choosing one of the two methods that follows.

9. Cut the candied ginger in slices and place on top of the pie.

TO MAKE A FULL MERINGUE TOP

1. Preheat the oven to 375°F (190°C).

2. Spread the Meringue on top of the hot lime filling, starting at the edges first, and then adding to the middle. Make sure the Meringue reaches all the way to the edge of the crust and is snuggly on top of the filling without any gaps. With the back of a spoon pull up some soft peaks.

3. Bake for 6 minutes, or until the peaks are a golden brown.

TO MAKE MERINGUE DOLLOPS

1. Using half the Meringue, pipe dollops on top and give them a quick once over with a blow-torch.

VARIATIONS

Orange Meringue Pie
Adding the juice of one lemon will brighten up the smooth orange flavor.

1. Make with a single blind-baked Roll-Out Dough crust (see Roll-Out Dough recipes, pages 38–58; and How to Blind Bake a Crust, page 69) or Press-In Crumb Crust, using vanilla wafers (see Master Recipe: Press-In Crumb Crust, page 72).

2. Replace the lime zest with orange zest.

3. Add the juice of 1 lemon to the orange juice so that the citrus juice totals ½ cup (120 ml).

Lemon-Lime-Orange Meringue Pie
This curd features three citrus flavors. If you are a citrus fan, be sure to try Mrs. T's Three Citrus Pie, too (page 289).

1. Make with a single blind-baked Roll-Out Dough crust (see Roll-Out Dough recipes, pages 38–58; and How to Blind Bake a Crust, page 69) or Press-In Crumb Crust, using vanilla wafers (see Master Recipe: Press-In Crumb Crust, page 72).

2. Use equal parts lemon, lime, and orange zest to make a total of about 2 teaspoons.

3. Use equal parts lemon, lime, and orange juice to total ½ cup (60 ml).

Meyer Lemon Sour Cream Pie

Makes one 9-inch (23 cm) shallow pie

My cousin Patty's husband loves lemon pies. When the two of them drove four and a half hours to our hometown of Santa Barbara so we could meet up one year, it was just good manners to make a lemon meringue pie as a welcome, and then this sour cream version for them to take for the journey home. Although other lemons can be used, I like it best with thinner-skinned Meyer lemons, which are not quite as tart, too.

1 recipe Press-In Crumb Crust, using graham crackers or lemon wafers or a combination of both (see Master Recipe: Press-In Crumb Crust, page 72)

3 egg yolks

1 cup (200 g) granulated sugar

A pinch of salt

¼ cup (30 g) cornstarch

1 cup (120 ml) half-and-half

½ cup (60 ml) fresh-squeezed Meyer lemon juice

Zest of 2 Meyer lemons

2 tablespoons (28 g) butter

¾ cup (90 ml) sour cream

1 recipe Lemony Whipped Cream (see Master Recipe: Whipped Cream chart, page 182)

1 tablespoon candied lemon or orange peel (optional) for garnish

1. Make, pre-bake, and set aside the crust to cool.

2. In a small bowl, fork beat the egg yolks and set aside.

3. In a medium saucepan, place the sugar, salt, and cornstarch and mix to combine with a fork or whisk.

4. Whisk in the half-and-half and lemon juice until well combined.

5. Turn the heat to medium and bring to a boil, while stirring with a whisk or fork. Let boil for 2 minutes while continuing to stir. It will start to get thick so be sure to keep stirring. Remove from the heat.

6. Take ¼ cup (60 ml) of the hot mixture and mix it into the egg yolks with a fork or whisk. Return the egg yolk mixture to the saucepan.

7. Turn the heat back to medium, bring to a full boil, and cook for another 2 minutes, while stirring constantly. It will be thick, but keep stirring. Remove from the heat.

8. Add the lemon zest and butter, and stir until the butter is melted. Set aside to cool to room temperature.

9. When cool, add the sour cream and stir well to incorporate evenly.

10. Pour into the waiting cooled pie shell.

11. Make the Lemony Whipped Cream and spread it on top of the pie, or pipe in a pleasing pattern. Garnish with optional candied lemon peel and, if you saved the extra lemon sugar when you made the candied peel, sprinkle a bit of it on top, too.

Mango Lime Pie

Makes one 9-inch (23 cm) shallow pie

The sound of Caribbean steel drums would be just the right soundtrack for this simple riff on a Key lime pie. This filling, made with egg yolks, sweetened condensed milk, mango puree, and lime juice, is turned into a pre-baked graham cracker crust that will have an additional bake in the oven. When it cools we'll top it with Coconut Whipped Cream. Serve with an ice-cold mojito.

1 recipe Press-In Crumb Crust, using graham crackers (see Master Recipe: Press-In Crumb Crust, page 72)

4 egg yolks

One 14-ounce (396 g) can sweetened condensed milk

1 ripe mango, peeled, pit removed, chopped, and pureed (frozen and thawed mangos are fine, too)

1 teaspoon lime zest

3 tablespoons lime juice

1 recipe Coconut Whipped Cream (see Master Recipe: Whipped Cream chart, page 183)

Toasted shredded sweetened coconut (optional; see How to Toast Coconut, page 263) for topping

Chopped macademia nuts for topping

1. Make, pre-bake, and set aside the crust to cool.

2. Preheat the oven to 325°F (165°C).

3. Place the egg yolks in a medium bowl and, with a handheld mixer, beat on high for 3 minutes. The mixture will increase in volume and become pale and thick.

4. Add the sweetened condensed milk and mix again on medium-high for 2 more minutes.

5. Add the mango puree, lime zest, and lime juice, and stir until well blended.

6. Turn the mango-lime filling into the baked graham cracker crust.

7. Bake for 25 to 30 minutes. Remove from the oven and let cool completely.

8. Top the pie with the Coconut Whipped Cream, optional toasted coconut, and macadamia nuts.

What Lime to Use?

It takes approximately 20 tiny Key limes to make just one Key lime pie, and I rarely see Key limes in the markets where I live. I've heard that Mexican limes are the same, but those don't frequently show up either. Since these precious limes are hard to come by, look for Nellie & Joe's Key West Lime Juice, or just use whatever limes are available in your produce section. And if you do see authentic Key limes or Mexican limes, buy them and make a Key lime pie!

Helen's Key Lime Pie

Makes one 9-inch (23 cm) shallow pie

This recipe comes from a family recipe box and uses heavy whipping cream instead of canned sweetened condensed milk, which makes a lighter filling than what's in the Mango Lime Pie (opposite). Its crispy graham cracker crust and billowy light filling has become a regular on my table, and it just might become one on yours, too. The filling can be topped with a meringue, piped or spread over the top and toasted lightly with a blowtorch, and finished with some candied lime peel. Or it can be served just as is.

CRUST

1¼ cups (170 g) finely ground graham crackers

3 tablespoons granulated sugar

A pinch of salt

4 tablespoons (60 g) butter, melted

FILLING

4 egg yolks

½ cup (100 g) granulated sugar

Zest of two limes

⅓ cup (80 ml) lime juice

1½ cups (360 ml) heavy whipping cream

OPTIONAL TOPPINGS

½ recipe Meringue (see Master Recipe: Meringue, page 200)

Candied lime peel (see Candied Citrus Peels, page 313)

TO MAKE THE CRUST

1. Place the graham cracker crumbs, sugar, salt, and melted butter in a bowl and mix to combine.

2. Press into a 9-inch (23 cm) shallow pie pan.

3. Preheat the oven to 375°F (190°C) and bake for 10 to 12 minutes.

4. Remove from the oven and let cool completely before filling.

TO MAKE THE FILLING AND TOP

1. Combine the egg yolks, sugar, lime zest, and lime juice, and place in the top of a double boiler.

2. Turn the burner to high and cook, while stirring in a figure-eight pattern, for about 10 minutes, until the mixture thickens.

3. Remove from the heat immediately and turn into a medium bowl. Cover with wax paper and completely cool to room temperature.

4. Pour the whipping cream in a separate medium bowl. Whip on medium-high until the peaks hold their shape but are not stiff.

5. Lightly fold the whipped cream into the lime curd in three additions.

6. Turn into the cooled graham cracker crust and let set in fridge for 4 to 6 hours. Overnight is fine, too.

7. Top with optional Meringue, candied lime peel, or both.

Key Lime Pie with Blueberry Glacé

Makes one 9-inch (23 cm) shallow pie

Blueberry glacé, plus a liberal amount of whipped cream, make a wonderful contrast in flavor and color for a classic Key lime pie. Blueberries can range in size from small like a pea to the almost cherry-sized giants pictured opposite. I like a graham cracker crust with this pie, but it's very good with a chocolate cookie crumb crust, too. This pie is best prepared, baked, and cooled a day ahead or at least four hours before serving.

1 recipe Press-In Crumb Crust, using graham crackers or chocolate cookie crumbs (see Master Recipe: Press-In Crumb Crust, page 72)

3 egg yolks, fork beaten

One 14-ounce (397 g) can sweetened condensed milk

1 teaspoon lime zest

⅓ cup (80 ml) lime juice (Nellie & Joe's Key West Lime Juice, or freshly squeezed)

1 recipe Blueberry Glacé (see Master Recipe: Fruit Glacé chart, page 192)

1 recipe Chantilly Cream (see Master Recipe: Whipped Cream chart, page 183)

1. Make, pre-bake, and set aside the crust to cool for at least 4 hours, but preferably a full day.

2. Preheat the oven to 325°F (165°C).

3. In a medium bowl, place the egg yolks, condensed milk, lime zest, and lime juice, and mix with a fork or a whisk until well blended.

4. Pour the mixture into the prepared cookie crumb crust and bake for 25 to 30 minutes. Be careful not to overbake. Remove from the oven and let cool.

5. Make the Blueberry Glacé and let cool.

6. Make the Chantilly Cream.

7. Top the pie with the Blueberry Glacé and pipe the Chantilly Cream around the edges. Any extra whipped cream can be served on the side.

Chiffon Pies

Chiffon Pies

Monroe Boston Strause, who was known as the Pie King in the early 20th century, is credited with creating chiffon pie back in 1926. My treasured copy of his book, *Pie Marches On*, contains chiffon pie fillings made with lemon, cranberry, cherry, berry, strawberry, almond, banana, chocolate, vanilla, and more. Our family gobbled up the pumpkin, lemon meringue, and apple pies that my grandmother put on the table for our family picnics, dinners, and holiday celebrations, but I don't recall her ever making a chiffon pie, so I went on a quest to learn about them.

The texture of a chiffon pie is creamy and light. It is made with a stove-top custard or pudding-like batter that always uses gelatin. Some batters are thickened with egg yolks, and others with a combination of milk or half-and-half and flour. When the batter cools, whipped cream, stiffly beaten egg whites, or a combination of both, are gently folded in. Then it is turned into a pre-baked crust and topped with more whipped cream. Once I learned how easy they are, I began making chiffon pies in a variety of different flavors to celebrate every season. You can, too.

We'll have three master recipes:

- Fruit Mousse Chiffon Pie (see Master Recipe: Fruit Mousse Chiffon Pie, page 214).
- Chocolate Mousse Chiffon Pie (See Master Recipe: Chocolate Mousse Chiffon Pie, page 222).
- Classic Citrus Chiffon Pie (see Master Recipe: Classic Citrus Chiffon Pie, page 226).

You'll also find a few special chiffon recipes including a Sweet Potato or Pumpkin Chiffon Pie (page 230), Pumpkin Orange Chiffon Pie (page 233), Snowy Day Coconut Rum Chiffon Pie (page 235), and an Eggnog Chiffon Pie (page 236).

Pre-Bake the Crust

All our chiffon pies will start with a pre-baked crust, which can be made either with a Roll-Out Dough (see Roll-Out Dough recipes, pages 38–58; and How to Blind Bake a Crust, page 69) or a Press-In Crust (see Press-In Crust recipes, pages 72–77). I do love the ease of a Press-In Crust, because it bakes so quickly. Be sure to do this step first, so it will be fully cooled and ready for your filling.

A few crust options that are particularly nice with fruit chiffon pies are crumb crusts made with lemon wafers, a Coconut Almond Oat Crust (page 75), or a nut meal crust made with hazelnuts or almonds (see Hazelnut Meal or Almond Flour Crust, page 76).

What Is Gelatin?

Gelatin is an animal-based product made from cartilage and bone. It is famously used in Jell-O. It is also used in chiffon pie to solidify the filling. There are vegetarian options, such as unflavored vegan gel or agar-agar, which need to be boiled separately in water before adding. If you use an option other than animal-based gelatin, it may be a hit or miss substitution with a recipe that requires some adjustment until you get it just right.

Master Recipe: Fruit Mousse Chiffon Pie

Makes one 9-inch (23 cm)
deep-dish pie

Our master recipe for a fruit mousse chiffon pie will use whipped cream to lighten the custard batter. We can use a variety of fruits that are smooshed or pureed as smooth as possible.

1 recipe Press-In Crumb Crust (see Press-In Crumb Crust recipes, pages 72–77) or ½ recipe Roll-Out Dough (see Roll-Out Dough recipes, pages 38–58; and How to Blind Bake a Crust, page 69)

Approximately 1 quart fruit, enough to make a generous 2-plus cups when pureed or smooshed smooth; reserve a few whole pieces for placing on top

¾ cup (150 g) granulated sugar

2½ teaspoons (7 g; 1 envelope) unflavored gelatin

⅓ cup (80 ml) water

3 egg yolks, fork beaten

1 teaspoon to 2½ tablespoons fresh-squeezed lemon juice, liqueur of choice, or other flavor extract or seasoning

A tiny pinch of salt

¾ cup (180 ml) heavy whipping cream

1 recipe Whipped Cream (See Master Recipe: Whipped Cream, page 182)

1. Make, pre-bake, and set aside the crust to cool.

2. Place the fruit in a blender or food processor, puree until smooth, and set aside. You can also smoosh as smooth as possible with a potato masher or fork.

3. Place the sugar and gelatin in a medium saucepan and mix with a whisk or fork.

4. Stir in the water, egg yolks, lemon juice, and salt.

5. Turn the heat to medium and stir constantly in a figure-eight pattern, until the mixture comes to a boil. Remove from the heat.

6. Turn into a medium-large bowl and stir in the pureed fruit.

7. Place the bowl in the fridge and let chill for about an hour. Stir about halfway through the chill so that the fruit solids are mixed through the filling and not all settling on the bottom.

8. Pour the whipping cream into a deep metal bowl that has been chilling in the freezer. Beat the cream with an electric hand mixer or a stand mixer, until it makes stiff peaks.

9. Remove the fruit gelatin mixture from the fridge and lightly fold in the whipped cream, taking care not to overmix. You may see some streaks in it but try to get it as homogenous looking as possible.

10. Return the bowl to the fridge and chill for about 30 minutes.

11. Turn the chilled mixture into the pre-baked pie shell. Place in the fridge and let set for 3 to 4 hours, although overnight is best.

12. Make the Whipped Cream and pipe it on top in a pleasing pattern, or spread it evenly all over the top of the chilled pie. Place a few pieces of whole fruit on top of the pie.

On Smooshing or Pureeing Fruit

A blender or food processor will quickly turn solid fruit into a smooth puree, but you can also smoosh the fruit by hand. When smooshing berries or slices of peeled stone fruit with a fork or a potato masher, smoosh, smoosh, smoosh to make them as smoooooth as possible. Some solid pieces will remain when using a fork or potato masher, so once added to the filling, you'll want to gently mix it several times during its chill period to make sure those solid pieces are well distributed through the mix and not all settled onto the bottom.

Peach Mousse Chiffon Pie

Makes one 9-inch (23 cm)
deep-dish pie

In my opinion, a perfectly ripe peach is a thing of beauty and a little taste of heaven. Years ago, I visited an Asian Art Museum and saw beautiful, centuries-old, painted panels of peaches. From reading the curator notes placed next to them, I learned that peaches are considered to have magical properties in Asia, where they confer immortality upon mere mortals after being consumed. I'd settle for a long life with family, good health, and happiness, and many peach pies to share. This is especially good with a press-in crust using gingersnaps.

1 recipe Press-In Crumb Crust (see Press-In Crumb Crust recipes, pages 72–77)

6 large freestone peaches (about 2½ lb; 1.1 kg); reserve one to slice and place on top of the finished pie

¾ cup (150 g) granulated sugar

2½ teaspoons (7 g; 1 envelope) unflavored gelatin

⅓ cup (80 ml) water

3 egg yolks, fork beaten

2½ tablespoons fresh-squeezed lemon juice or orange liqueur

A tiny pinch of salt

¾ cup (180 ml) heavy whipping cream

1 recipe Orange Whipped Cream (see Master Recipe: Whipped Cream chart, page 183)

1. Make, pre-bake, and set aside the crust to cool.

2. Peel and pit 5 of the peaches (see How to Peel a Ripe Peach, page 251)

3. Place the peeled peaches in a blender or food processor, puree until smooth, and set aside. You can also smoosh the peaches to be as smooth as possible with a potato masher or fork.

4. Place the sugar and gelatin in a medium saucepan and mix with a whisk or fork.

5. Stir in the water, egg yolks, lemon juice, and salt.

6. Turn the heat to medium and stir constantly in a figure-eight pattern, until the mixture comes to a boil. Remove from the heat.

7. Turn into a medium-large bowl and stir in the pureed fruit.

8. Place the bowl in the fridge and let chill for about an hour. Stir about halfway through the chill so that the fruit solids are mixed through the filling and not all settling on the bottom.

9. Pour the whipping cream into a deep metal bowl that has been chilling in the freezer. Beat the cream with an electric hand mixer or a stand mixer, until it makes stiff peaks.

10. Remove the fruit gelatin mixture from the fridge and lightly fold in the whipped cream, taking care not to overmix. You may see some streaks in it but try to get it as homogenous looking as possible.

11. Return the bowl to the fridge and chill for about 30 minutes.

12. Turn the chilled mixture into the prebaked pie shell. Place in the fridge and let set for 3 to 4 hours, although overnight is best.

13. Make the Orange Whipped Cream and pipe it on top in a pleasing pattern, or spread it evenly all over the top of the chilled pie. Place slices of the reserved peach on top of the pie.

VARIATIONS

Apricot Mousse Chiffon Pie

16 to 20 fresh sweet apricots (about 2½ lb; 1.1 kg); save some of the prettiest apricots to place on top of the finished pie

1. Peel, pit, and puree almost all of the apricots.

2. Top with Orange Whipped Cream and top with slices of the remaining apricots.

Nectarine Mousse Chiffon Pie

6 ripe nectarines (about 2½ lb; 1.1 kg); reserve one to slice and place on top of the finished pie

1. Peel, pit, and puree 5 of the nectarines.

2. Top with Orange Whipped Cream and top with slices of the remaining nectarines.

Blackberry Ginger Peach Mousse Chiffon Pie

4 large freestone peaches (about 800 g); save a few slices to place on top of the finished pie

1 pint blackberries (about 200 g); save some of the prettiest blackberries to place on top of the finished pie

1 recipe Ginger Whipped Cream (see Master Recipe: Whipped Cream chart, page 183)

1 tablespoon candied ginger, thinly sliced

1. Peel and pit the peaches (see How to Peel a Ripe Peach, page 251) and puree with the blackberries.

2. Top with Ginger Whipped Cream and top with the remaining peach slices, blackberries, and candied ginger.

Sunset Mousse Chiffon Pie

Makes one 9-inch (23 cm)
deep-dish pie

Summer sunset. Two words that bring to my mind the alpine glow on the Olympic Mountains—the red, pink, and orange reflected on the clouds on beautiful long summer evenings at my home. This pie is my attempt to capture some of that color using ripe fruits of the season.

---

1 recipe Press-In Crumb Crust (see Press-In Crumb Crust recipes, pages 72–77)

5 ripe peaches (1 kg); save a few slices to place on top of the finished pie

1 pint raspberries (240 g); save some of the prettiest raspberries to place on top of the finished pie

2½ teaspoons (7 g; 1 envelope) unflavored gelatin

⅓ cup (80 ml) water

3 egg yolks, fork beaten

2½ tablespoons fresh-squeezed lemon juice or orange liqueur

A tiny pinch of salt

¾ cup (180 ml) heavy whipping cream

1 recipe Raspberry Orange Whipped Cream (see Master Recipe: Whipped Cream chart, page 183)

1. Make, pre-bake, and set aside the crust to cool.

2. Peel and pit the peaches (see How to Peel a Ripe Peach, page 251) and puree with the raspberries. You can also smoosh the fruit to be as smooth as possible with a potato masher or fork.

3. Place the sugar and gelatin in a medium saucepan and mix with a whisk or fork.

4. Stir in the water, yolks, lemon juice, and salt.

5. Turn the heat to medium and stir constantly in a figure-eight pattern, until the mixture comes to a boil. Remove from the heat.

6. Turn into a medium-large bowl and stir in the pureed fruit.

7. Place the bowl in the fridge and let chill for about an hour. Stir about halfway through the chill so that the fruit solids are mixed through the filling and not all settling on the bottom.

8. Pour the whipping cream into a deep metal bowl that has been chilling in the freezer. Beat the cream with an electric hand mixer or a stand mixer, until it makes stiff peaks.

9. Remove the fruit gelatin mixture from the fridge and lightly fold in the whipped cream, taking care not to overmix. You may see some streaks in it but try to get it as homogenous looking as possible.

10. Return the bowl to the fridge and chill for about 30 minutes.

11. Turn the chilled mixture into the prebaked pie shell. Place in the fridge and let set for 3 to 4 hours, although overnight is best.

12. Make the Raspberry Orange Whipped Cream and pipe it or spread it evenly on top of the chilled pie. Place the reserved peach slices and raspberries on top.

Persimmon Mousse Chiffon Pie

Persimmons can be found during their short season in winter, and this pie is a wonderful way to feature them. Carefully peel the persimmons using a sharp knife.

Makes one 9-inch (23 cm)
deep-dish pie

1 recipe Press-In Crumb Crust (see Press-In Crumb Crust recipes, pages 72–77)

4 ripe Hachiya persimmons

¾ cup (150 g) granulated sugar

2½ teaspoons (7 g; 1 envelope) unflavored gelatin

⅓ cup (80 ml) water

3 egg yolks, fork beaten

1 teaspoon vanilla extract

A tiny pinch of salt

¾ cup (180 ml) heavy whipping cream

1 recipe Chantilly Cream (see Master Recipe: Whipped Cream chart, page 183)

1. Make, pre-bake, and set aside the crust to cool.

2. Peel the persimmons.

3. Place the peeled persimmons in a blender or food processor, puree until smooth, and set aside. You can also smoosh the persimmons to be as smooth as possible with a potato masher or fork.

4. Place the sugar and gelatin in a medium saucepan and mix with a whisk or fork.

5. Stir in the water, egg yolks, vanilla, and salt.

6. Turn the heat to medium and stir constantly in a figure-eight pattern, until the mixture comes to a boil. Remove from the heat.

7. Turn into a medium-large bowl and stir in the pureed fruit.

8. Place the bowl in the fridge and let chill for about an hour. Stir about halfway through the chill so that the fruit solids are mixed through the filling and not all settling on the bottom.

9. Pour the whipping cream into a deep metal bowl that has been chilling in the freezer. Beat the cream with an electric hand mixer or a stand mixer, until it makes stiff peaks.

10. Remove the fruit gelatin mixture from the fridge and lightly fold in the whipped cream, taking care not to overmix. You may see some streaks in it but try to get it as homogenous looking as possible.

11. Return the bowl to the fridge and chill for about 30 minutes.

12. Turn the chilled mixture into the prebaked pie shell. Place in the fridge and let set for 3 to 4 hours, although overnight is best.

13. Make the Chantilly Cream and pipe it on top in a pleasing pattern, or spread it evenly all over the top of the chilled pie.

Strawberry Heaven Mousse Chiffon Pie

Makes one 9-inch (23 cm) deep-dish pie

One year, friends gathered at Pie Cottage for a potluck on the Strawberry Moon—the full moon in June. I really didn't realize it was a Strawberry Moon until I was already deep into making the pie. Coincidence? Maybe. When I set this pie on the table, it was eaten up very quickly. Always a good sign. One friend even said, "This is so good it makes me want to cry!"

1 recipe Press-In Crumb Crust (see Press-In Crumb Crust recipes, pages 72–77)

1 quart strawberries, or enough to make 2-plus cups of finely smooshed strawberries

¾ cup (150 g) granulated sugar

2½ teaspoons (7 g; 1 envelope) unflavored gelatin

⅓ cup (80 ml) water

3 egg yolks, fork beaten

2½ tablespoons fresh-squeezed lemon juice, orange liqueur, or a combination of both

A tiny pinch of salt

¾ cup (180 ml) heavy whipping cream

1 recipe Whipped Cream or Orange Whipped Cream (see Master Recipe: Whipped Cream, page 182)

1. Make, pre-bake, and set aside the crust to cool.

2. Puree the strawberries in a blender or food processor, or smoosh them with a potato masher or fork, and set aside.

3. Place the sugar and gelatin in a medium saucepan and mix with a whisk or a fork.

4. Stir in the water, egg yolks, lemon juice, and salt.

5. Turn the heat to medium and stir in a figure-eight pattern, until the mixture comes to a boil. Remove from the heat.

6. Turn into a medium-large bowl and stir in the smooshed strawberries.

7. Place the bowl in the fridge and let chill for about an hour. Stir about halfway through the chill so that the fruit solids are mixed through the filling.

8. Pour the whipping cream into a deep metal bowl that has been chilling in the freezer. Beat with an electric hand mixer or a stand mixer, until the cream makes stiff peaks.

9. Remove the strawberry gelatin mixture from the fridge and lightly fold in the whipped cream, taking care not to overmix. You may see some streaks in it but try to get it as homogenous looking as possible.

10. Return the bowl to the fridge and chill for about 30 minutes.

11. Turn the chilled mixture into the pre-baked pie shell. Place in the fridge and let set for 3 to 4 hours, although overnight is best.

12. Make the Whipped Cream and pipe on top in a pleasing pattern, or spread it evenly all over the top of the chilled pie.

Master Recipe: Chocolate Mousse Chiffon Pie

Makes one 9-inch (23 cm) deep-dish pie

This recipe requires a hot chocolate mixture to be added to egg yolks. To keep the yolks from curdling from the heat, you will add a small amount of the hot chocolate mixture to the yolks and stir quickly and thoroughly—this process is called tempering. Once the yolks have been exposed to the warm mixture, you can add them to the saucepan with the rest of the chocolate mixture to cook for one more minute while stirring. Once cool, the whipped cream will be folded in and—voilà—you'll have the technique for making a chocolate mousse chiffon, which can be adapted and flavored in many ways.

1 recipe Press-In Crumb Crust, using graham crackers or cookie crumbs (see Master Recipe: Press-In Crumb Crust, page 72), or Hazelnut Meal Crust (see Hazelnut Meal or Almond Flour Crust, page 76), or ½ recipe Roll-Out Dough (see Roll-Out Dough recipes, pages 38–58; and How to Blind Bake a Crust, page 69)

3 egg yolks

½ cup (120 ml) water

2½ teaspoons (7 g; 1 envelope) unflavored gelatin

4 ounces (113 g) 100% dark chocolate for baking

¼ cup plus 3 tablespoons (87 g) granulated sugar

A tiny pinch of salt

⅔ cup (160 ml) half-and-half

¼ cup (60 ml) crème de cacao

1 tablespoon (14 g) butter

¾ cup (180 ml) heavy whipping cream

1 recipe Chantilly Cream (see Master Recipe: Whipped Cream chart, page 183)

1 Make, pre-bake, and set aside the crust to cool.

2 Place the yolks in a small bowl, fork beat, and set aside.

3 Place the water and gelatin in a medium saucepan. Turn the heat to low and stir with a whisk until gelatin is dissolved.

4 Add the chocolate, sugar, salt, half-and-half, and crème de cacao. Raise the heat to medium-low and cook until the chocolate is melted, while stirring constantly in a figure-eight pattern with a whisk. When it reaches a boil, remove from the heat.

5 Take ¼ cup of the hot mixture and stir it into the fork-beaten egg yolks. Return the egg and chocolate mixture to the saucepan and cook over medium heat for 1 minute more, while constantly stirring in a figure-eight pattern as it bubbles. Remove from the heat and stir in the butter.

6 Turn into a medium bowl and set on the counter to cool to room temperature and partially set.

7 Pour the whipping cream into a deep metal bowl that has been chilling in the freezer. Beat in a stand mixer or in a bowl with a hand mixer until the cream makes stiff peaks. Set aside. Fold gently into the chocolate mixture.

8 Turn the mixture into the pre-baked pie shell. Place in the fridge and let set for 3 to 4 hours, although overnight is best.

9 Make the Chantilly Cream and pipe it on top in a pleasing pattern, or spread it evenly all over the top of the chilled pie.

Chocolate Raspberry Mousse Chiffon Pie

1. Add a small grating of nutmeg.

2. Substitute raspberry liqueur for the crème de cacao.

3. Pipe or spread Whipped Cream (see Master Recipe: Whipped Cream, page 182) around the edge of the pie.

4. Place fresh ripe raspberries in the middle.

Chocolate Ginger Mousse Chiffon Pie

1. Substitute ginger liqueur for the crème de cacao.

2. Chop ½ cup (85 g) candied ginger into small pieces and fold into the filling.

3. Top with Ginger Whipped Cream (see Master Recipe: Whipped Cream chart, page 183).

Chocolate Coconut Pistachio Mousse Chiffon Pie

1. Add a small grating of nutmeg.

2. Sprinkle ¼ cup (30 g) chopped pistachios and ¼ cup (30 g) toasted shredded sweetened coconut on top.

Spicy Hot Chocolate Chiffon Mousse Pie

1. Add ½ to ¾ teaspoon ground chipotle pepper and ½ teaspoon cinnamon.

Mocha Mousse Chiffon Pie

1. Replace the crème de cacao with ¼ cup plus 2 tablespoons (90 ml) of cooled strong coffee.

2. Top with Coffee Whipped Cream (see Master Recipe: Whipped Cream chart, page 183).

Double Chocolate Banana Mousse Chiffon Pie

1. In Step 4, increase the sugar to ½ cup (100 g).

2. Slice 2 bananas and arrange a single layer in the pre-baked pie shell.

3. At the end of Step 7, gently fold in ½ cup (85 g) semi-sweet chocolate chips.

4. Turn the chocolate mixture on top of the bananas. Let chill for at least 3 hours in the fridge.

5. Top with Whipped Cream (see Master Recipe: Whipped Cream, page 182).

Rocky Road Chiffon Pie

I remember when my dad would bring home rocky road candy from the See's Candies store downtown, and then set the big white bag high up on a pantry shelf. Maybe he thought I hadn't seen him, but after he left the kitchen, and when I thought no one was looking, I would climb up the three risers of the pull-down metal step stool, open the bag and break off a tiny piece, and then do my best to return the bag to the exact spot where he had placed it. It wouldn't surprise me at all if he knew all along what I had been up to. In fact, I like to think that my youthful shenanigans might have brought a smile to his face and a twinkle to his bright blue eyes, which I wish I could see just one more time.

Use the recipe for Master Recipe: Chocolate Mousse Chiffon Pie (page 222) with these variations:

- In Step 4, increase the sugar to ½ cup (100 g).
- In Step 7, gently mix in 1 cup (60 g) mini marshmallows and ¾ cup (90 g) roughly chopped almonds.

Master Recipe: Classic Citrus Chiffon Pie

Makes one 9-inch (23 cm) deep-dish pie

Although classic citrus chiffon pies can be made any time of the year, it is especially nice to make them during the winter when lemons, and oranges are in season. The process is easy. We'll make a curd on the stovetop, let it cool in the fridge, and fold in whipped cream and stiffly beaten egg whites to lighten our filling.

1 recipe Press-In Crumb Crust (see Press-In Crumb Crust recipes, pages 72–77)

⅔ cup (132 g) granulated sugar

2½ teaspoons (7 g; 1 envelope) unflavored gelatin

½ cup (120 ml) water

4 eggs, yolks and whites separated

1 teaspoon citrus zest

½ cup (120 ml) fresh-squeezed citrus juice

⅛ teaspoon salt

¾ cup (180 ml) heavy whipping cream

1 recipe Whipped Cream, basic or flavored (optional; see Master Recipe: Whipped Cream, page 182)

Candied Citrus Peels (page 313) for garnish

1. Make, pre-bake, and set aside the crust to cool.

2. Place ⅓ cup (66 g) of the sugar and gelatin in a medium saucepan and mix with a whisk or a fork.

3. In a medium bowl, fork beat the egg yolks with the water, zest, juice, and salt.

4. Stir the wet ingredients into the dry ingredients in the saucepan.

5. Turn the heat to medium and stir constantly in the shape of a figure-eight, until the mixture comes just about to a boil and thickens. This will take about 5 minutes. Remove from the heat when you see the first bubble.

6. Using a flexible spatula, turn the mixture into a medium bowl, and let cool in the fridge for about 20 minutes. Stir with a spoon every 5 minutes or so.

7. Pour the whipping cream into a deep metal bowl that has been chilling in the freezer. Beat the cream with an electric hand mixer or with a stand mixer until the cream makes stiff peaks. Gently fold into the cooled citrus mixture.

8. In a squeaky-clean bowl, whip the egg whites, gradually adding the remaining ⅓ cup (66 g) sugar, using an electric handheld beater or a stand mixer on medium, until stiff, and gently fold into the citrus mixture.

9. Using a flexible spatula, turn the citrus mixture into the crust. Place in the fridge and let set for 3 to 4 hours, although overnight is best.

10. Make the optional Whipped Cream and spread or pipe on top and garnish with Candied Citrus Peel.

How to Freeze a Chiffon Pie

- Make the pie according to the recipe. Double wrap, label, date, and freeze for up to 1 month.
- Thaw the unwrapped pie at room temperature for 3 hours, or overnight in the fridge.

Lemon Chiffon Mousse Pie

Makes one 9-inch (23 cm) deep-dish pie

I use a lot of lemons in my baking and I especially love to use Meyer lemons when I can get them. They are a smaller lemon with bright yellow skin, just a hint of orange, and a flavor that is a bit mellower. Don't worry if you can't find Meyers in your store, regular lemons will do just fine, too. You can also make an Orange Chiffon Pie by replacing the lemon juice with orange juice (keeping a tablespoon or two of lemon juice to brighten up the flavor), and replace the lemon zest with orange zest.

1 recipe Press-In Crumb Crust (see Press-In Crumb Crust recipes, pages 72–77)

⅔ cup (132 g) granulated sugar

2 teaspoons (7 g; 1 envelope) unflavored gelatin

½ cup (120 ml) water

4 eggs, yolks and whites separated

1 teaspoon lemon zest

½ cup (120 ml) fresh-squeezed lemon juice

⅛ teaspoon salt

¾ cup (180 ml) heavy whipping cream

1 recipe Lemon Whipped Cream (optional; see Master Recipe: Whipped Cream chart, page 183)

Candied Citrus Peels (page 313) for garnish

1. Make, pre-bake, and set aside the crust to cool.

2. Place ⅓ cup (66 g) of the sugar and gelatin in a medium saucepan and mix with a whisk or a fork.

3. In a medium bowl, fork beat the egg yolks with the water, zest, juice, and salt.

4. Stir the wet ingredients into the dry ingredients in the saucepan.

5. Turn the heat to medium and stir constantly in the shape of a figure eight, until the mixture comes just about to a boil and thickens. This will take about 5 minutes. Remove from the heat when you see the first bubble.

6. Using a flexible spatula, turn the mixture into a medium bowl, and let cool in the fridge for about 20 minutes. Stir with a spoon every 5 minutes or so.

7. Pour the whipping cream into a deep metal bowl that has been chilling in the freezer. Beat the cream with an electric hand mixer or a stand mixer until the cream makes stiff peaks. Gently fold into the cooled citrus mixture.

8. In a squeaky-clean bowl, whip the egg whites, gradually adding the remaining ⅓ cup (66 g) sugar, using an electric handheld beater or a stand mixer on medium, until stiff, and gently fold into the citrus mixture.

9. Using a flexible spatula, turn the citrus mixture into the crust. Place in the fridge and let set for 3 to 4 hours, although overnight is best.

10. Make the optional Lemon Whipped Cream and spread or pipe on top and garnish with Candied Citrus Peel.

Sweet Potato or Pumpkin Chiffon Pie

Makes one 9-inch (23 cm)
deep-dish pie

My friend Shannon makes a light and delicious pumpkin chiffon pie for Thanksgiving each year, and she graciously shared it with me when I saw her one day. As soon as I got home, I started in, but I had no pumpkin puree on hand. I'm not about to let one little thing like that stop me from making pie, so I substituted a can of pureed sweet potato that was peeking out at me from the back of a pantry shelf, adjusted the seasoning to my taste, and added a tasty splash of orange liqueur. Both pureed sweet potato and pumpkin are heavy, so to make this chiffon pie light, we will use both beaten egg whites and whipped cream. Serve chilled and topped with a scoop of your favorite ice cream or whipped cream flavored with the liqueur of your choice. If you happen to have a slice left on the morning after Thanksgiving, it is excellent with a cup of coffee. Rum or bourbon adds a nice kick . . . to the coffee and the pie.

1 recipe Press-In Crumb Crust, using graham crackers, chocolate cookies, or gingersnaps (see Master Recipe: Press-In Crumb Crust, page 72)

¾ cup (150 g) firmly packed brown sugar

2½ teaspoons (7 g; 1 envelope) unflavored gelatin

½ teaspoon salt

1 teaspoon cinnamon

¼ teaspoon freshly ground nutmeg

1 teaspoon ground ginger

A pinch of ground clove

3 egg yolks

¾ cup (180 ml) half-and-half, milk, or canned unsweetened coconut milk (I use Thai Kitchen Organic Coconut Milk)

1 tablespoon orange liqueur, rum, or bourbon (optional)

1¼ cups (about 300 g) canned pureed sweet potato or pumpkin

3 egg whites

⅓ cup (66 g) granulated sugar

1 recipe Whipped Cream, flavored as you like (see Master Recipe: Whipped Cream chart, page 183)

1. Make, pre-bake, and set aside the crust to cool.

2. Place the brown sugar, gelatin, salt, cinnamon, nutmeg, ginger, and clove in a saucepan and mix with a whisk or a fork.

3. In a bowl, mix together the egg yolks, half-and-half or milk, and optional liqueur. Stir into the brown sugar mixture and let stand for a few minutes.

4. Turn the heat to medium and stir in a figure-eight pattern until it comes to a boil. Remove from the heat.

5. Stir in the sweet potato or pumpkin puree.

6. Place in the fridge and let chill for about an hour.

7. In a stand mixer or in a bowl with a hand mixer, beat the egg whites until soft peaks form. Rain (sprinkle) the sugar over the egg whites while continuing to beat until stiff peaks form.

8. Remove the sweet potato mixture from the fridge and lightly fold in the egg whites, taking care not to overmix. You may see some streaks, but try to get it as homogenous looking as possible.

9. Turn the chilled mixture into the pre-baked pie shell. Place in the fridge and let set for 3 to 4 hours, although overnight is best.

10. Make the Whipped Cream and pipe on top in a pleasing pattern, or spread it evenly all over the top of the chilled pie.

Pumpkin Orange Chiffon Pie

The flavors of pumpkin and orange blend together well, and it doesn't need to be Thanksgiving to make this pie because it is good any time of the year. The candied orange rounds that crown the top make it a showstopper, too.

Makes one 9-inch (23 cm) deep-dish pie

1 recipe Press-In Crumb Crust, using graham crackers or gingersnaps (see Master Recipe: Press-In Crumb Crust, page 72)

¾ cup (150 g) firmly packed brown sugar

2½ teaspoons (7 g; 1 envelope) unflavored gelatin

½ teaspoon salt

1 teaspoon cinnamon

¼ teaspoon freshly ground nutmeg

1 teaspoon ground ginger

A pinch of ground clove

3 egg yolks

½ cup (120 ml) half-and-half, milk, or canned unsweetened coconut milk (I use Thai Kitchen Organic Coconut Milk)

1 tablespoon grated orange zest

¼ cup (60 ml) fresh-squeezed orange juice

1¼ cups (about 300 g) canned pumpkin puree

3 egg whites

⅓ cup (66 g) granulated sugar

Candied orange rounds (see Candied Citrus Rounds, page 310)

1. Make, pre-bake, and set aside the crust to cool.

2. Place the brown sugar, gelatin, salt, cinnamon, nutmeg, ginger, and clove in a saucepan and mix with a whisk or a fork.

3. In a bowl, mix together the egg yolks, half-and-half, orange zest, and orange juice. Stir into the brown sugar mixture and let stand for a few minutes.

4. Turn the heat to medium and stir until it comes to a boil. Remove from the heat.

5. Stir in the pumpkin puree.

6. Place in the fridge and let chill for about an hour.

7. In a stand mixer or in a bowl with a hand mixer, beat the egg whites until soft peaks form. Rain (sprinkle) sugar over the egg whites while continuing to beat until stiff peaks form.

8. Remove the pumpkin mixture from the fridge and lightly fold in the egg whites, taking care not to overmix. You may see some streaks in it but try to get it as homogenous looking as possible.

9. Turn the chilled mixture into the pre-baked pie shell. Place in the fridge and let set for 3 to 4 hours, although overnight is best.

10. Top with candied orange rounds.

Snowy Day Coconut Rum Chiffon Pie

This fluffy white pie reminds me of the soft deep snowdrifts after big winter snows at Pie Cottage. The filling is flavored with vanilla and almond, and it's topped with a rum-laced whip. For an extra kick, add some rum to the filling in addition to the extracts.

Makes one 9-inch (23 cm)
deep-dish pie

---

1 recipe Press-In Crumb Crust, using chocolate cookies (see Master Recipe: Press-In Crumb Crust, page 72)

1½ cups plus 2 tablespoons (325 g) granulated sugar

¼ cup (35 g) flour

2½ teaspoons (7 g; 1 envelope) unflavored gelatin

½ teaspoon salt

1¾ cups (420 ml) half-and-half

1 teaspoon vanilla extract

¾ teaspoon almond extract

2 tablespoons light rum or 1 teaspoon rum extract

1 cup (110 g) shredded sweetened coconut, plus ¼ cup (28 g) more to sprinkle on top

3 egg whites

¼ teaspoon cream of tartar

½ cup (120 ml) whipping cream

1 recipe Rum Whip (see Master Recipe: Whipped Cream chart, page 183)

Toasted coconut flakes (optional; see How to Toast Coconut, page 263) for topping

1. Make, pre-bake, and set aside the crust to cool.

2. Place 1¼ cups (250 g) of the sugar, flour,

gelatin, and salt in a medium saucepan and mix with a whisk or a fork.

3. Whisk in the half-and-half gradually.

4. Turn the heat to medium and stir in a figure-eight pattern, until it comes to a boil. Let it boil for 1 minute, while stirring. Remove from the heat and pour into a large bowl.

5. Stir in the vanilla and almond extracts, rum, and 1 cup coconut. Let cool.

6. In a stand mixer or bowl with a hand mixer, beat the egg whites until soft peaks form. Add the cream of tartar, and rain (sprinkle) the remaining ¼ cup plus 2 tablespoons sugar (75 g) over the egg whites while continuing to beat until stiff peaks form. Set aside.

7. Pour the whipping cream into a deep metal bowl that has been chilling in the freezer. Beat in a stand mixer or in a bowl with a hand mixer, until the cream makes stiff peaks. Set aside.

8. Fold the beaten egg whites into the cooled filling. Then carefully fold in the whipping cream.

9. Turn the filling into the pre-baked pie shell and sprinkle with ¼ cup coconut. Place in the fridge and let set for 3 to 4 hours, although overnight is best.

10. Make the Rum Whip and spread or pipe it over the top in a pleasing pattern. Top with optional toasted coconut flakes before serving.

Eggnog Chiffon Pie

Makes one 9-inch (23 cm) shallow pie

From the time he was a little boy, my son Duncan has always loved eggnog, and as he was growing up, I found that it was really easy to adapt recipes to include the eggnog flavor. The nice thing about eggnog pie is that you don't have to wait until the winter holidays arrive to enjoy it. Vanilla and whiskey in the filling and freshly grated nutmeg sprinkled over the top give that special holiday feeling at any time of the year.

½ recipe Roll-Out Dough (see Roll-Out Dough recipes, pages 38–58;; and How to Blind Bake a Crust, page 69) or 1 recipe Press-In Crumb Crust (see Press-In Crumb Crust recipes, pages 72–77)

¾ cup (150 g) granulated sugar

2 tablespoons flour

2½ teaspoons (7 g; 1 envelope) unflavored gelatin

¼ teaspoon salt

1 cup (240 ml) half-and-half

½ teaspoon vanilla extract

2 tablespoons whiskey

2 egg whites

⅛ teaspoon cream of tartar

⅓ cup whipping cream

1 recipe Boozy Whip (see Master Recipe: Whipped Cream chart, page 183)

Freshly grated nutmeg for topping

1. Make, pre-bake, and set aside the crust to cool.

2. Place sugar, flour, gelatin, and salt in a medium saucepan and mix with a whisk or a fork.

3. Whisk in the half-and-half gradually.

4. Turn the heat to medium and stir in a figure-eight pattern, until it comes to a boil. Let it boil for 1 minute, while stirring. Remove from the heat and pour into a large bowl.

5. Stir in the whiskey. Let cool.

6. In a stand mixer or bowl with a hand mixer, beat the egg whites until soft peaks form. Add the cream of tartar while continuing to beat until stiff peaks form. Set aside.

7. Pour the whipping cream into a deep metal bowl that has been chilling in the freezer. Beat in a stand mixer or in a bowl with a hand mixer, until the cream makes stiff peaks. Set aside.

8. Fold the beaten egg whites into the cooled filling.

9. Carefully fold the whipped cream into the filling.

10. Turn the filling into the pre-baked pie shell. Place in the fridge and let set for 3 to 4 hours, although overnight is best.

11. Make the Boozy Whip and pipe it around the edge in a pleasing pattern, or spread over the top of the pie. Sprinkle the top with grated nutmeg.

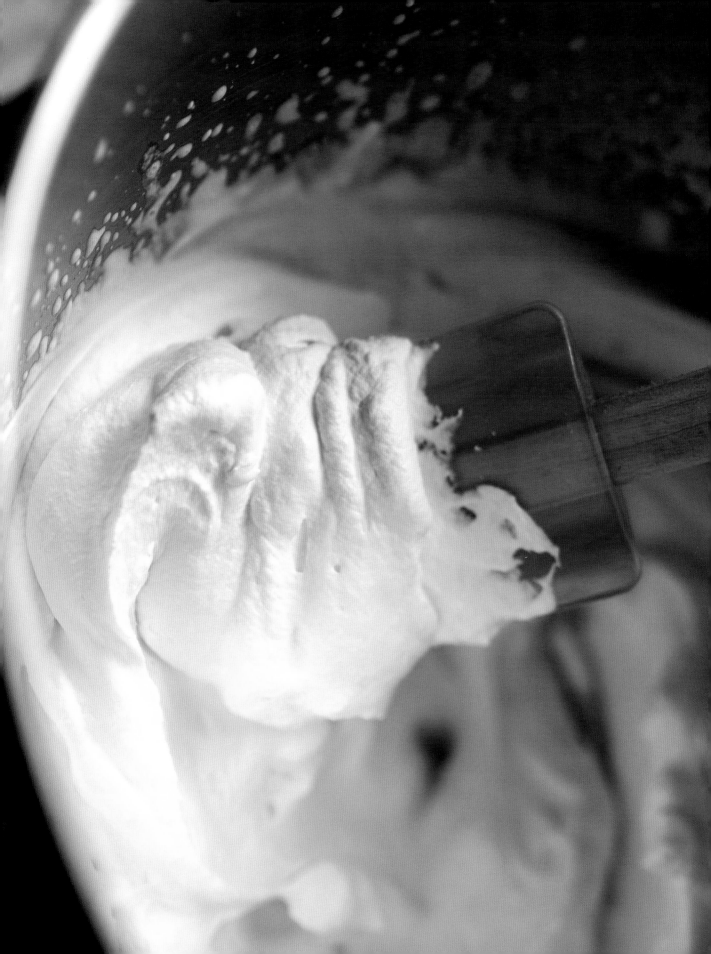

Layered Pies

Layered Pies

Multilayers of filling and toppings piled in a single pre-baked crust are called layered pies. Rich chocolate, hazelnut, peanut butter, fruit, crumble toppings, sweetened mascarpone or cream cheese, and pastry creams are all part of a mix and match creative pie-making session.

Pie feels like a metaphorical foundation that holds my life together. Dough, when placed in a pie pan, is both pliable and strong, supporting the many layers of my life: family, friends, lovers long since gone, times I wish I could relive again, and others I'm relieved to have gotten through in one piece. These layers—some sweet, some smooth, some rocky, and some precipitous—are what have added depth and texture to my life.

Baking holds a strong place in the lives of many that I meet and perhaps in yours, too. More than once, I have seen heads nodding in passionate agreement when I tell them of how often I go to the kitchen to bake when there are no words to express what is inside of me. Like Jenna in the movie *Waitress*, I ground and cen-ter myself at the baking counter, finding calm in the simple act of rolling out my feelings in the dough and creating layers of expressive filling combinations. This process gives my feelings a tangible way to come together and I feel better.

When, as a world, we were asked to shelter in place during the COVID-19 virus in 2020, I turned to my kitchen to feed my family. I was worried about our future. Using my hands to provide nourishment got me through many days of uncertainty and, as long I could smell a pie baking, I knew I was okay.

Our master recipe will use techniques we have already mastered, and variations are only limited by your taste and imagination.

A few things to think about before we start:

- A deep-dish pie pan can hold more layers than a shallow pie pan.
- If you are using a juicy fruit layer, place it on top of a pastry cream so the juice doesn't seep into the bottom crust.
- If any of your layers are made with dairy or eggs, be sure to store any leftovers in the fridge.

Master Recipe: Layered Pie

Makes one 9-inch (23 cm) deep-dish or shallow pie

These mix-and-match pies remind me of the flip books we had when I was growing up, with eyes, noses, and mouths that made funny faces when lined up. Multiple layers are a great way to play with pairings of flavors and textures, and any combo is fair game. Here are the simple steps to make a layered pie.

1 recipe Press-In Crumb Crust (see Press-In Crumb Crust recipes, pages 72–77) or ½ recipe Roll-Out Dough (see Roll-Out Dough recipes, pages 38–58; and How to Blind Bake a Crust, page 69)

1 or 2 fillings such as Pastry Cream (see Master Recipe: Pastry Cream, page 182) or Stove-Top Fruit Filling (page 306)

Fresh fruit (optional)

1 recipe Fruit Glacé (optional; see Master Recipe: Fruit Glacé, page 192)

1 recipe Whipped Cream (optional; see Master Recipe: Whipped Cream, page 182)

Nuts, coconut, chocolate bits or shavings, candied citrus, etc.

1. Make, pre-bake, and set aside the crust to cool.

2. Fill with a layer of Pastry Cream or Stove-Top Fruit Filling.

3. Top with one or two more layers of choice.

Easy as pie, right?

Mom's Peanut Butter Chocolate Pie

Makes one 9-inch (23 cm)
deep-dish pie

This pie is in homage of my mom's love of Reese's Peanut Butter Cups. She would buy a package of the bite-size candies, stow them away in the corner cabinet above the kitchen counter, and ration out one, or maybe two at the most, as a special treat. When I made and served this pie after dinner one night to willing tasters, it received rave reviews. The pie is very rich, so like my mom's peanut butter cups, you may need to ration yourself on this one, too.

CRUST

1 recipe Press-In Crumb Crust, using equal parts graham crackers and chocolate sandwich cookies (see Master Recipe: Press-In Crumb Crust, page 72)

PEANUT BUTTER LAYER

4 ounces (116 g) cream cheese, room temperature

¼ teaspoon salt

½ teaspoon vanilla extract

½ cup (80 g) confectioners' sugar

½ cup (130 g) peanut butter, smooth or chunky

½ cup (120 ml) heavy cream

CHOCOLATE LAYER

3 eggs yolks

½ cup (120 ml) water

2½ teaspoons (7 g; 1 envelope) unflavored gelatin

4 ounces (113g) dark chocolate for baking (at least 85%)

¼ cup (50 g) granulated sugar

A pinch of salt

⅔ cup (160 ml) half-and-half

1 tablespoon (14 g) butter

CHANTILLY CREAM LAYER

½ recipe Chantilly Cream (see Master Recipe: Whipped Cream chart, page 183)

OPTIONAL GARNISH

Chocolate-covered coffee beans or cocoa nibs

CONTINUED

1. Make, pre-bake, and set aside the crust to cool.

2. Make the peanut butter layer (see below) and place in the cooled pie shell.

3. Make and cool the chocolate layer (see below). Spread over the top of the peanut butter layer.

4. Place the pie in the fridge and let set for 3 to 4 hours, although overnight is best.

5. Before serving, make the Chantilly Cream layer and pipe in a pleasing pattern, or spread evenly over the top of the chilled pie.

6. Top with the optional garnish of chocolate-covered coffee beans.

TO MAKE THE PEANUT BUTTER LAYER

1. Place the room temperature cream cheese in a deep medium bowl and whip with an electric hand mixer on high for a full minute.

2. Add the salt, vanilla extract, confectioners' sugar, and peanut butter, and beat to combine well.

3. Pour the heavy whipping cream into the bowl of a stand mixer and beat with the whisk attachment until the whipping cream makes stiff peaks. You can also use a chilled deep metal bowl and handheld electric beater.

4. Fold the whipped cream into the peanut butter mixture.

TO MAKE THE CHOCOLATE LAYER

1. Place the yolks in a small bowl, fork beat, and set aside.

2. Place the water and gelatin in a medium saucepan. Turn the heat to low and stir with a whisk until the gelatin is dissolved.

3. Add the chocolate, sugar, salt, and half-and-half. Raise the heat to medium-low and cook until the chocolate is melted, while stirring constantly with a whisk in a figure-eight pattern. Add the butter and stir to combine. When it comes to a boil, remove from the heat.

4. Take ¼ cup of the hot mixture and stir it into the fork-beaten egg yolks. Return the egg and chocolate to the saucepan and cook over medium heat for 1 minute more, while constantly stirring in a figure-eight pattern as it bubbles. Remove from the heat and stir in the butter.

5. Turn into a medium bowl, set aside on the counter to cool to room temperature and partially set.

TO MAKE THE CHANTILLY CREAM LAYER

1. Make the Chantilly Cream.

VARIATIONS

Banana Peanut Butter Chocolate Pie

Add ¼ to ½ cup roughly chopped roasted and salted peanuts on top of the peanut butter layer, followed by a layer of sliced bananas.

Black Bottom Pie

Makes one 9-inch (23 cm)
deep-dish pie

Silky, smooth, rich, luscious, decadent, cool, and creamy are all words to describe this delicious layering of cookie crumbs, two pastry creams (one chocolate and one rum flavored), all topped with rum-spiked whipped cream. This pie began to appear toward the turn into the 20th century, was featured in "Pie King" Monroe Boston Strause's book Pie Marches On (1939), and was lauded by author and cook Marjorie Kinnan Rawlings in Cross Creek Cookery (1942) with words that just might say it best—"I think this is the most delicious pie I have ever eaten." There is plenty of room for variation, starting on the bottom with your choice of cookie crumb crust or a single blind-baked pie dough crust. I've included some filling variations for you to enjoy, too.

CRUST

1 recipe Press-In Crumb Crust, using graham crackers or cookie crumbs (see Master Recipe: Press-In Crumb Crust, page 72)

CUSTARD

4 egg yolks

½ cup (100 g) granulated sugar

1 tablespoon gelatin

1½ tablespoons cornstarch

¼ teaspoon salt

2 cups (480 ml) milk

CHOCOLATE LAYER

2 ounces (56 g) unsweetened baking chocolate

1 tablespoon (14 g) butter

1 teaspoon vanilla extract

½ of the custard (above)

RUM CUSTARD LAYER

1 tablespoon dark rum

½ of the custard (left)

4 egg whites

¼ teaspoon cream of tartar

½ cup (100 g) granulated sugar

RUM WHIP LAYER

1 recipe Rum Whip (see Master Recipe: Whipped Cream chart, page 183)

GARNISH

Semi-sweet chocolate shavings

CONTINUED

THE GAME PLAN

1. Make, pre-bake, and set aside the crust to cool.

2. Make the custard and combine half of it with the melted chocolate mixture to create the chocolate layer (see below) and place in the cookie crumb crust. Set aside to cool.

3. Make and cool the rum custard layer with the remaining custard. Let cool and spread over the top of the chocolate layer.

4. Place the pie in the fridge and chill for at least 6 hour, although overnight is best.

5. Before serving, make the Rum Whip layer and pipe in a pleasing pattern, or spread evenly over the top of the chilled pie.

6. Top with the chocolate shavings.

TO MAKE THE CUSTARD

1. Fork beat the yolks in a bowl and set aside.

2. In a medium saucepan, place ½ cup (100 g) of the sugar, gelatin, cornstarch, and salt, and whisk to combine.

3. Whisk the milk into the dry ingredients in the saucepan. Turn the heat to medium and continue to whisk in a figure-eight pattern until the mixture starts to bubble around the edges.

4. Take ¼ cup of the hot mixture and whisk into the fork-beaten eggs to temper them.

5. Add the tempered egg yolks back into the milk mixture and continue to whisk constantly in a figure-eight pattern until the mixture thickens, you see a few bubbles, and it can coat the back of a spoon. This will take about 2 minutes. Remove from the heat.

TO MAKE THE CHOCOLATE LAYER

1. Melt the baking chocolate (see How to Melt Chocolate, page 315). Stir in the butter and let it melt. Stir in the vanilla. Set aside.

2. Place a generous cup of the hot custard into a small bowl.

3. Add the melted chocolate mixture and stir to combine.

TO MAKE THE RUM CUSTARD LAYER

1. In a medium bowl, place the remaining custard and stir in the rum. Let cool to room temperature, stirring occasionally so it does not set completely.

2. In a squeaky-clean bowl, whip the egg whites with an electric handheld beater or a stand mixer on medium, until they are frothy but not stiff.

3. Add the cream of tartar and ¼ cup (50 g) sugar. Whip on medium until soft peaks form.

4. Turn the beater to high, add another ¼ cup (50 g) sugar. Whip until stiff peaks form. Lift the beaters out.

5. Gently fold the whipped egg whites into the cooled rum custard in three additions.

TO MAKE THE RUM WHIP LAYER

1. When the pie is chilled and ready to serve, make the Rum Whip.

Black Bottom Banana Pie

Peel and slice 2 to 3 bananas on top of the chocolate layer and top with the Rum Whip. Instead of slicing, you can also coil the bananas around on top of the chocolate layer so that when the pie is sliced, you will see a round cross-section of banana.

Black Bottom Macadamia Pie

Sprinkle 1 cup (150 g) chopped macadamia nuts on top of the black bottom custard layer.

Black Bottom Rum Coconut Pie

1. Sprinkle 1 cup (110 g) shredded sweetened coconut on top of the chocolate layer.

2. Top the pie with an additional ½ cup (55 g) shredded sweetened coconut sprinkled over the Rum Whip.

Black Bottom Peppermint Pie

1. Substitute ½ teaspoon peppermint extract for the rum when making the rum–egg white custard.

2. Omit all the rum and substitute ¼ teaspoon peppermint in the rum–egg white custard, and ¼ teaspoon peppermint extract in the Rum Whip.

Judy's Oatmeal Crust Cheesecake Pie

Makes one 9-inch (23 cm)
deep-dish pie

Judy told me about a quick four-layer pie she used to make when she was baking for a restaurant in Massachusetts. The press-in oatmeal crust is similar to what is used for a crumble or crisp top; the filling uses premade preserves of your choice; the topping is sweetened whipped cream cheese. I first made it with blueberries and served it on movie night for my family. It was even more delicious for breakfast the next day. Judy says that fresh or frozen fruit is not gloppy enough for the filling, so be sure to use preserves.

OATMEAL CRUST

1 cup (145 g) flour

1 cup (110 g) rolled oats

⅔ cup (133 g) firmly packed brown sugar

½ teaspoon aluminum-free baking powder

12 tablespoons (1½ sticks; 178 g) butter, softened

PRESERVE TOPPING

12 ounces (340 g) preserves of choice: raspberry, blueberry, peach, apricot

CREAM CHEESE TOPPING

½ cup (80 g) confectioners' sugar

3 tablespoons milk or half-and-half

1½ teaspoons vanilla extract

8 ounces (227 g) cream cheese, softened

1 cup (240 ml) heavy whipping cream

1. Preheat the oven to 350°F (175°C).

2. In a medium bowl, combine the flour, rolled oats, brown sugar, baking powder, and butter until crumbly and well blended.

3. Reserve 1 cup of the pastry mixture. Pat the rest into the bottom and sides of the pie pan.

4. Stir the preserves to loosen, then gently spread them over the bottom of the oatmeal crust but not the sides.

5. Sprinkle the remaining oat crust mixture over the preserves and press down lightly.

6. Bake for 25 minutes, until golden brown. Remove from the oven and let cool.

7. In a medium bowl that has been chilled, combine the confectioners' sugar, milk, vanilla, and cream cheese, and blend until very smooth.

8. Beat the heavy cream to soft peaks and lightly fold into the cream cheese mixture until fluffy and combined.

9. Place the cream cheese mixture on top of the cooled piecrust and refrigerate at least 30 minutes, and preferably longer, before serving.

Layered Peach Mascarpone Pie

Makes one 9-inch (23 cm) shallow pie

The combination of mascarpone and peach in an almond flour crust is lovely on a summer evening when peaches are ripe and the scent of honeysuckle is in the air. If you like, prepare the crust, filling, and fruit topping separately, as they fit into your schedule, and place them in the fridge. You can finish the pie, and then place it back in the fridge for an hour before serving. Be sure to place slices of a perfectly ripe peach on top, too.

CRUST

1 recipe Almond Flour Crust (see Hazelnut Meal or Almond Flour Crust, page 76)

MASCARPONE FILLING

8 ounces (227 g) mascarpone cheese

4 ounces (115 g) plain Greek yogurt (I use Kirkland Signature Nonfat Plain Greek Yogurt)

⅔ cup (90 g) confectioners' sugar

1 tablespoon orange liqueur (such as Cointreau), or 2 teaspoons orange extract

FRUIT TOPPING

4 large peaches (2 lbs, 1 kg); save one unpeeled peach to slice and place on top of the pie before serving

¼ cup (60 ml) water

1 tablespoon cornstarch

½ cup (100 g) granulated sugar

WHIPPED TOPPING

1 recipe Chantilly Cream (see Master Recipe: Whipped Cream chart, page 183)

TO MAKE THE CRUST

1. Make, pre-bake, and set the crust in the fridge to cool.

TO MAKE THE MASCARPONE FILLING

1. In a medium bowl, add the mascarpone, yogurt, confectioners' sugar, and orange liqueur.

2. Whip on high with a handheld mixer until well combined. Scrape down the sides with a rubber spatula once, and mix again.

3. Chill until ready to use.

TO MAKE THE FRUIT TOPPING

1. Peel and pit three of the peaches and cut them into ½-inch (6 mm) pieces (see How to Peel a Ripe Peach, opposite).

2. In a small bowl, mix the water and cornstarch together with a fork or small whisk. Place the mixture in a saucepan and add the sugar.

3. Add the peaches and turn up the heat to medium, stirring gently. When the mixture comes to a boil, continue to cook for a minute or two longer. It should look a little glossy and not quite so opaque.

4. Remove from the heat and turn into a bowl. Let cool completely. Refrigerate until needed.

TO ASSEMBLE

1. With a spatula, turn the cheese mixture into the baked and chilled Almond Flour Crust and spread around lightly and evenly.

2. Add the cooked and cooled peach mixture next and place in the fridge until ready to serve.

3. Before serving, make the Chantilly Cream and pipe around the edge on top of the pie.

4. Slice the remaining peach and arrange the slices on top of the pie. You can also serve dollops of whipped topping on individually cut pieces and place a peach slice on top.

How to Peel a Ripe Peach

For those times when a recipe calls for a peeled peach, here's how to do it. Try one peach first. If the skin does not come off easily at all, try Steps 3 and 4 one more time. If all else fails, take a knife, cut the skin off, and discard. Be sure to use freestone peaches as the pit of cling peaches must be cut or pried out, which can damage the flesh.

EQUIPMENT NEEDED

Saucepan

Slotted spoon

Bowl filled with ice water, a.k.a. an ice water bath

Knife

1. Fill a medium saucepan with water and bring to a rolling boil.

2. With a knife, score the smooth end, opposite the stem end, of each peach with an X just so it breaks the skin.

3. With a slotted spoon, lower the scored peaches into the boiling water. Lift out with peaches with the spoon after 40 to 60 seconds and place into the ice water bath.

4. Remove a peach from the ice water. Hopefully, the skin should now be loose enough to slip off starting at the corners of the X. If there are a few places where the skin remains, remove with a knife. Discard the skin.

5. Cut the peach in half, and twist the halves in opposite directions to open. Remove the pit inside with your fingers and discard.

What Is It about Sweet Potato Pie?

Everybody seems to have an idea of what a sweet potato pie should be like . . . well, maybe except a Northwesterner. Sweet potato pie is a custard pie similar to pumpkin. Old recipes that I researched are really more like a list of ingredients:

- Cooked and mashed sweet potatoes
- Sweetener
- Seasonings
- Egg
- Milk, of some sort

Plus, I found measuring terms like knob, dash, and one for a ½ teaspoon called a scruple. They may sound quaint to us today, but I do love the image of a knife tip measurement, and I use it in recipes and teaching.

If you are thinking of using canned yams, aficionados of this pie will be the first to tell you that a yam is a yam, and not a sweet potato. Sweet potatoes are actually roots, and the plant itself is related to the morning glory. The sweet potato flourishes in more tropical climates, but there are varieties that do grow in northern gardens, and one of these days maybe I'll try growing one. For now we'll use what is available in the produce section at the local grocer.

Speaking of which, I learned that sweet potatoes are not all alike. I'm not talking about color, because a purple sweet potato can be as sweet as an orange Garnet, the variety that is generally found at the grocery store. White varieties are noted as being dryer and having more starch. Orange flesh potatoes are moister. Size matters here, and in this case, small is best; the flesh will be sweeter, smoother, and less stringy and fibrous.

Our first step will be to prepare the sweet potatoes for our filling.

How to Prepare Sweet Potatoes

You'll need about 2 pounds of sweet potatoes, a bit less than 1 kilogram. If they are too big to fit in your pot, cut them down to a size that will be able to fit in it. Boil the roots well in unsalted water, until they are good and soft. If a sharp knife doesn't go through all the way easily, then boil them some more until it does. Remove them from the pot with a slotted spoon, or you can partially cover the pot with its lid and carefully pour the hot water down the drain of the sink. I like to cool and save my cooking water and pour it into my garden or compost. I figure that it has some extra nutrients for my veggies.

Next, you'll slip their jackets off. Look for a flap of skin that is loose, and pull or gently tug it off. You can also take a sharp paring knife, or even kitchen shears, and make a lengthwise cut through the cooked skin layer, and then peel it off. The skin goes in my compost, too. Once you've done that, get them into a bowl and get your potato masher out. If you don't have one, the back of a fork will do nicely. An immersion blender would probably do the trick here, too, but do consider getting yourself a potato masher as they're quite fun to use and very low tech. Smoosh the potatoes smooth, and then smoosh them some more. Use the back of a fork to fine-tune the mash as small as you can. Finally, get out the electric beater or immersion blender and whip the mash to increase its volume with some extra air. I know that's a lot of mashing, but for a smooth filling you'll be happy you did it, although I did talk to one pie eater who remembered her Great Aunt Vita's sweet potato pie as being chunky.

Now our sweet potatoes are ready to become the filling for pie.

Pineapple-Coconut Sweet Potato Pie

Makes one 9-inch (23 cm)
deep-dish pie

This version of sweet potato pie is not so sweet that it will knock you off your feet. Great Aunt Vita's niece told me that I got the spicing just right, and that she liked it even better than the one she grew up eating. Once baked and cooled, top with layers of pineapple glacé and whipped cream, and sprinkle over coconut flakes and candied pecans. Another option is to serve the pie with some or none of the layers and sprinkles. For a colorful surprise, try making the filling with purple sweet potatoes.

½ recipe Roll-Out Dough (see Roll-Out Dough recipes, pages 38–58)

2 pounds (1 kg) sweet potatoes, unpeeled (enough to make about 2 cups cooked)

1½ teaspoons cinnamon

¾ teaspoon ground allspice

½ teaspoon ground ginger

½ teaspoon freshly ground nutmeg

A pinch of ground cloves

½ teaspoon salt

¼ teaspoon aluminum-free baking powder

1 tablespoon all-purpose flour or gluten-free flour

1 cup (200 g) granulated sugar

2 large eggs

1 cup (240 ml) evaporated milk or half-and-half

½ teaspoon vanilla extract

3 tablespoons (42 g) butter, melted

¼ cup (50 g) brown sugar

1 recipe Pineapple Glacé (see Master Recipe: Fruit Glacé chart, page 192)

1 recipe Chantilly Cream (see Master Recipe: Whipped Cream chart, page 183)

1 cup shredded sweetened coconut

A few candied pecans

1. Roll out the pie dough, place in the pie pan, and crimp or flute the edges (see How to Crimp, Flute, and Edge the Crust, page 59). Set in the fridge while you make the filling.

2. In a medium saucepan, cover the unpeeled sweet potatoes with unsalted boiling water, cover, and cook at a medium boil until you can easily get a knife all the way through the root. This may take 30 minutes, but larger potatoes will take more time. Remove the potatoes from the pot with a slotted spoon. Peel as soon as they are cool enough to handle.

3. While you are waiting for the potatoes to cool, place the cinnamon, allspice, ginger, nutmeg, cloves, salt, baking powder, flour, and sugar in a bowl and mix with a fork until the spices are evenly distributed through the dry mix.

4. Place the potatoes in a bowl and mash with a potato masher or large fork, until they are as smooth as possible. Beat for a minute or two with a hand mixer or immersion blender to incorporate more air into the mashed sweet potatoes.

5. Add the eggs one at time, whisking after each addition to incorporate.

6. Add the sugar-spice mixture and whisk until evenly distributed.

7.   Add the evaporated milk, vanilla, and 2 tablespoons of the melted butter and whisk again until smooth.

8.   Preheat the oven to 400°F (200°C). Brush the inside of pie shell with the remaining 1 tablespoon melted butter, and evenly sprinkle the brown sugar on top. Bake for 12 minutes. Turn down the oven to 350°F (175°C).

9.   Pour the filling into the hot par-baked pie shell.

10.   Return the filled pie pan to the oven and bake about 55 minutes, or until the edges around the pie are puffed-up and a toothpick or skewer comes out clean when inserted into the middle. Set aside to cool.

11.   Make the Pineapple Glacé and Chantilly Cream.

12.   When the pie is cooled, spread a layer of Pineapple Glacé over the filling, and pipe the Chantilly Cream around the edges or spread over the top.

13.   Sprinkle the coconut and candied pecans on top.

Coconuts

"Watch for falling coconuts!" Those are the words I saw as I walked down the steps into an open-air restaurant on my first trip to the Virgin Islands. I chuckled and took a picture of it because that's definitely not a warning you see every day . . . at least not for me. If a coconut had fallen down while I was there, I like to think that I would have asked if a trade might be possible: one very local coconut for one Pineapple-Coconut Sweet Potato Pie.

Hurry Up Pie

Makes one 9-inch (23 cm)
deep-dish pie

When I had just one hour to make an entire pie from crust to filling before heading out the door to a potluck, this is the pie I made from ingredients I had on hand. As soon as my oven was preheated, I placed a Coconut Almond Oat Crust inside to pre-bake. Then I immediately moved on to making an Orange Pastry Cream, followed by a layer of Blueberry Glacé topped the Pastry Cream—although a jar of blueberry preserves would work, as well. Then I topped it with sliced peaches. Extras to consider would be some Chantilly Cream piped around the edges, and if there's any extra Coconut Almond Oat Crust, sprinkle it over the top, as well.

1 recipe Coconut Almond Oat Crust (page 75) or another Press-In Crumb Crust (see Press-In Crumb Crust recipes, pages 72–77), or ½ recipe Roll-Out Dough (see Roll-Out Dough recipes, pages 38–58; and How to Blind Bake a Crust, page 69)

1 recipe Orange Pastry Cream or other flavor option (see Master Recipe: Pastry Cream variations, page 178)

1 to 2 peaches (200 to 400 g), sliced, or 1 cup berries (about 100 to 135 g; you can use blueberries, blackberries, raspberries, or strawberries), or other fresh fruit, sliced or chopped

2 to 3 teaspoons Cointreau or orange liqueur, or another liqueur you like (optional; more for the glacé, if desired)

1 recipe Blueberry Glacé (see Master Recipe: Fruit Glacé chart, page 192) or a 12-ounce jar blueberry preserves

1 recipe Chantilly Cream or other flavor option (optional; see Master Recipe: Whipped Cream chart, page 183) for topping

1 to 2 tablespoons shredded sweetened coconut (optional) for garnish

1 to 2 teaspoons lemon sugar (optional; see Candied Citrus Peels, page 313) for garnish

1. Make, pre-bake, and set aside the crust to cool. Save a few tablespoons of crumbs to sprinkle over the top of the finished pie.

2. Make the Orange Pastry Cream. If you want to cool your cream faster, see page 179 for tips. Be sure to cover in any case.

3. Slice the peaches, set on a plate, and sprinkle a little orange liqueur over them, if using. If using berries, place them in a small bowl and pour the optional orange liqueur over them. Stir around to mix a bit so they are coated.

4. Make the Blueberry Glacé. You can also just open a jar of blueberry preserves and stir them around a bit so they are spreadable. Add a little extra orange liqueur in them, too.

5. Turn the cooled Pastry Cream into the cooled crust and spread it around evenly with a spatula.

6. Spread the Blueberry Glacé or preserves on top.

7. Arrange the peach slices on top of the Blueberry Glacé, or if using berries or other fruit, spoon them on top.

8. You can add additional toppings by piping Chantilly Cream around the edge, or garnish with shredded coconut, and lemon sugar.

Montgomery Pie

Makes one 9-inch (23 cm) shallow pie

There are a number of stories about how this pie got its name, and it's hard to know the accuracy of any of them. The one I like best says it originated in Montgomery County, Pennsylvania, a county named for General Richard Montgomery, who fought in the American Revolutionary War. The closest thing that I can compare it to is Shoofly Pie (page 269), as both pies separate into layers when baked. Shoofly Pie is denser, and it features a distinctively molasses flavor. Although some recipes call for the Montgomery Pie to be made with molasses, I find that its lemony flavor really shines through when made with a mixture of dark and light corn syrup or Lyle's Golden Syrup. This unusual pie had me wondering if it was going to turn out okay when I was first making it, as the bottom layer was very liquid and the top layer was nothing more than plops of batter. After cooling completely, I cut into it, and I found a layer of lemon-like custard, a shallow cake-like topping, and a very thin crispy golden brown layer topping it all. Because there is so much moisture in the filling, a totally crispy crust is missing when baked, but it isn't completely raw either, and it cuts well.

DOUGH

½ recipe Roll-Out Dough (see Roll-Out Dough recipes, pages 38–58)

FILLING LAYER

½ cup (120 ml) mixture of light and dark corn syrup, or Lyle's Golden Syrup

½ cup (100 g) granulated sugar

1 egg

⅞ cup (205 ml) water

1 tablespoon lemon zest

3 to 4 tablespoons fresh-squeezed lemon juice

TOPPING LAYER

¾ cup (150 g) granulated sugar

4 tablespoons (½ stick; 56 g) butter, softened

1 egg

¼ cup (60 ml) milk or half-and-half

½ teaspoon aluminum-free baking powder

1 cup (145 g) flour

CONTINUED

1. Preheat the oven to 350°F (175°C).

2. Roll out the pie dough, lay in the pan, and crimp or flute edges (see How to Crimp, Flute, and Edge the Crust, page 59). Cover with plastic wrap and place in the fridge while you make the filling and topping.

3. To make the filling, place the light and dark corn syrup mixture, sugar, egg, water, lemon zest, and lemon juice in the bowl of a stand mixer. Mix for a minute or two on medium speed, until well blended. Set aside. You can also use an electric hand mixer.

4. To make the topping, place the sugar, butter, egg, milk, baking powder, and flour in the bowl of a stand mixer. Mix at medium speed for 2 to 3 minutes, until well blended. You can also use an electric hand mixer.

5. Remove the dough-filled pie pan from the fridge and pour in the filling. Yes, it will be very liquidy, and you will now be wondering if this can possibly be right.

6. Scoop the topping onto the top of the filling as best you can. Don't worry about spreading it around, as it will do that on its own as it bakes.

7. Carefully place in the oven and bake for 50 minutes.

8. Remove from the oven and let cool completely before slicing.

NOTE: If you like a molasses flavor, substitute molasses for the corn syrups.

Coconut Mascarpone Cream Pie

Makes one 9-inch (23 cm)
deep-dish pie

Most coconut cream pies have two classic layers: a flavored pastry cream topped with a sweetened whipped cream. One day, I stood in front of my open fridge, pondering what I might do to give a slightly different spin on this classic. I decided to add a third layer! I found some mascarpone cheese, which I decided to lighten, sweeten, and flavor by folding in whipped cream, confectioners' sugar, vanilla and coconut extracts, plus a generous cup of shredded sweetened coconut. After I spread this over a pre-baked Vanilla Macadamia Nut Crust, the two classic layers were added, and the pie was set in the fridge to chill. The flavor and texture gave me the variation I hoped for, and I hope you will enjoy it, too.

---

1 recipe Vanilla Macadamia Nut Crust (see Master Recipe: Press-In Crumb Crust variations, page 73) or other Press-In Crumb Crust (see Press-In Crumb Crust recipes, pages 72–77)

4 egg yolks

1 tablespoon plus 1 teaspoon vanilla extract

1 teaspoon coconut extract

1 cup (200 g) granulated sugar

¼ cup (30 g) cornstarch

A small pinch of salt

2½ cups (600 ml) half-and-half

8 ounces (227 g) mascarpone

¼ cup (60 ml) heavy whipping cream

¼ cup (40 g) confectioners' sugar

1 cup (100 g) shredded sweetened coconut

Double recipe Chantilly Cream (see Master Recipe: Whipped Cream chart, page 183)

¼ cup (25 g) toasted shredded sweetened coconut (see How to Toast Coconut, opposite) for topping

1. Make, pre-bake, and set aside the crust to cool.

2. Place the egg yolks in a medium bowl. Add 1 tablespoon vanilla extract and ½ teaspoon coconut extract, and whisk with a fork for a minute or so until the eggs are smooth. Set aside.

3. Place the sugar, cornstarch, and salt in a medium saucepan and mix together with a whisk or fork.

4. With a whisk in hand, turn the heat to medium under the saucepan and pour the half-and-half slowly and steadily into the dry ingredients, while whisking constantly in a figure-eight pattern. Keep whisking until the mixture thickens and begins to bubble.

5. Remove the pan from the heat momentarily and pour about ⅓ cup of the hot mixture into the eggs in the bowl. Whisk them together in the bowl until it looks blended in. This won't take long.

6. Pour the hot egg mixture from the bowl into the saucepan and return it to the stove top. Turn the heat back to medium and whisk the mixture constantly in a figure-eight pattern, until you bring it to a full boil for at least 1 minute. It will be thick and coat the bake of a spoon. Remove the pan from the heat.

7. Turn the hot mixture into a bowl and cover with wax paper to prevent a skin from forming as it cools. Chill in the fridge for at least 2 hours.

8. In a medium bowl, place the mascarpone cheese. Beat with a hand mixer on high for a minute or two. Add the whipping cream and the confectioners' sugar, and beat another minute. Add the 1 cup (100 g) untoasted coconut and beat just long enough to mix evenly through the mascarpone mixture.

9. With a spatula, evenly spread the coconut-mascarpone mixture on top of the cooled piecrust.

10. Remove the cooled pastry cream from the fridge. Remove the wax paper and give the pastry cream a few turns of a spoon to mix.

11. With a spoon or spatula, evenly spread the pastry cream on top of the coconut-mascarpone layer.

12. Make the double recipe of Chantilly Cream. Place big spoonfuls of the whipped cream on top of the coconut-mascarpone mixture and spread around evenly, taking care to mound a bit higher in the middle.

13. Let the pie set in the fridge for 4 to 6 hours or overnight.

14. Sprinkle the ¼ cup cooled toasted coconut on top of the whipped cream and serve.

NOTE: This pie can also be made with a Coconut Almond Oat Crust (page 75) or any blind-baked crust (see Roll-Out Dough recipes, pages 38–58; and How to Blind Bake a Crust, page 69).

How to Toast Coconut

This crunchy texture is a nice addition on a pie top.

1. Preheat the oven to 325°F (165°C).

2. Sprinkle shredded sweetened coconut on a sheet pan that has been lined with parchment paper or a sheet pan liner. Shake to spread the coconut out evenly.

3. Toast for 9 minutes. It's okay to shake the pan a bit, and also turn the pan around if it is toasting unevenly. If it needs a little longer, keep it in the oven for a few minutes more. The goal is that most all of the coconut will be toasted to a golden color.

4. Remove the pan from the oven and immediately turn the coconut onto a plate to cool. If it stays on the hot pan longer, it will continue to cook and can get too dark, or worse yet, burn.

5. It is ready for use when cool. Store any extra in an airtight container.

Kumquat Cream Pie

Makes one 9-inch (23 cm) deep-dish pie

On a chilly February day, I received a box of kumquats from my long-time friend Farmer Al Courchesne, of Frog Hollow Farm. Never having made anything with kumquats before, I was excited to see what I could create with the precious fruits that arrived at my door. Wanting to use every part of the tiny fruits, I saved the sugar syrup that was left after simmering the kumquat peels and piths, and any extra sugar that was left from the candying process to use in the Kumquat Cream Puree and also the Orange Blossom Whipped Cream. The steps in this recipe do take extra effort and time, but when the pie is ready for tasting, you'll be happy to have eked out every last bit of flavor from the tiny citrus fruits. You'll need a little over 1 pound (450 g) kumquats for this recipe.

CANDIED KUMQUATS

2½ ounces (75 g) kumquats

2½ cups (500 g) granulated sugar

1 cup (240 ml) water

CRUST

1 recipe Almond Flour Crust (see Hazelnut Meal or Almond Flour Crust, page 76) or Press-In Crumb Crust, using graham crackers sweetened, if possible, with kumquat or orange sugar (see Master Recipe: Press-In Crumb Crust, page 72)

KUMQUAT CREAM PUREE

Juice of 2 oranges, to make about ¼ cup (60 ml)

16 to 17 ounces (about 400 g) kumquats

2 cups (440 g) mascarpone cheese

6 tablespoons kumquat syrup reserved from making candied kumquats

½ teaspoon salt

1 cup (240 ml) heavy whipping cream

¼ cup (50 g) kumquat sugar reserved from making candied kumquats

2 tablespoons orange blossom water

TOPPINGS

1 recipe Orange Blossom Whipped Cream (see Master Recipe: Whipped Cream chart, page 183)

6 tablespoons shredded sweetened coconut

1 to 2 tablespoons finely chopped lightly salted pistachios

1 to 2 tablespoons candied kumquat peel

1 tablespoon candied kumquat pith

TO MAKE THE CANDIED KUMQUATS

1. With a vegetable peeler, peel 2½ ounces (75 g) of kumquats, and reserve the peel.

2. With a sharp paring knife cut the peeled kumquats in half around the equator. Set aside.

3. Carefully remove the seeds with a knife tip and discard.

4. Fill a small saucepan with water, add the peeled kumquat halves, and bring to a boil for 5 minutes. Pour off the water.

5. Repeat Step 4.

6. With a slotted spoon, remove the kumquats and set aside.

7. Place 2 cups (400 g) of the sugar into the saucepan and add the water. Turn the heat to medium-high and bring to a boil while whisking. When the sugar has dissolved, put in the reserved kumquat peels. Turn the heat down to medium-low. Simmer the peels for about 10 to 15 minutes until they become somewhat translucent. Remove from the heat, carefully remove the peels with a fork or tongs, and set on a plate to cool. Reserve and cool the kumquat sugar syrup in a lidded jar. You will have a generous 2 cups which will be used later, and any extra can be stored in the fridge.

8. Place ½ cup (100 g) of the sugar in a medium bowl and add the cooled kumquat peels. Toss with your fingers or a fork until the peels are well coated with sugar. Shake off any extra kumquat sugar and set aside. Toss the peeled kumquat halves in the sugar, and set aside. Reserve as much as sugar possible for use in the Kumquat Cream Puree and Orange Blossom Whipped Cream.

TO MAKE THE CRUST

1. Make, pre-bake, and set aside the crust to cool.

TO MAKE THE KUMQUAT CREAM PUREE

1. Place ¼ cup of the orange juice in a blender or Vitamix. Add 16 to 17 ounces (400 g) whole unpeeled kumquats and puree until smooth. Be sure to add the orange juice first as this makes the pureeing easier. Turn the puree into a bowl and, with a fork or spoon, stir around a bit to locate and remove any stray seeds you may have missed. Set aside.

2. In the bowl of a stand mixer, place the mascarpone cheese. With the flat paddle attachment, beat on medium, stopping to scrape down the sides with a rubber spatula. Mix again on high. This can also be done with a bowl and hand mixer.

3. Add the kumquat puree and mix again.

4. Add 6 tablespoons of the reserved kumquat syrup, salt, heavy whipping cream, the reserved kumquat sugar, and the orange blossom water and mix on high until smooth, stopping to scrape down the sides with a rubber spatula, and mixing again.

5. Turn the whipped Kumquat Cream Puree into the cooled crust, spreading evenly. Set in the fridge to chill for at least 4 hours.

TO ASSMEBLE AND TOP

1. Before serving, make the Orange Blossom Whipped Cream and spread or pipe the whipped cream in a pleasing pattern on top of the pie. This can also be made and placed on top of the Kumquat Cream Puree before it goes into the fridge to chill.

2. Before serving, evenly sprinkle the pistachios and Candied Kumquats on top.

Kitchen
Cupbo

CHAPTER FIVE

ard Pies

Kitchen Cupboard Pies

Once you get to be known as a pie maker, you will start to be asked the same question that is regularly posed to me: "Will you bring a pie?" I take it as a compliment that my pie making has progressed to the point where I can usually say yes without fretting about how to make dough, the amount of thickener to add, and the time needed for a fruit filling to set up when it comes out of the oven, which, if you are wondering, is as long as possible.

Sugar, butter, flour, eggs, cookies, nuts, and maple syrup left over from a pancake breakfast, spices like cinnamon, ginger, and nutmeg, a flavor extract, or pour of rum, bourbon, or whiskey: When we look on the shelves in our kitchen cupboards and in the fridge, chances are we already have everything needed to make the pies in this section. These are simple pies. They have been called Depression Era Pies, Desperation Pies, but I call them Kitchen Cupboard Pies. Although you may have to go out for a pint of buttermilk, which my grandmother usually had in her fridge, with the basics on hand we can whip up something in a jiffy.

Most often these pies will use a 9-inch (23 cm) shallow pie pan, which is closer to the size pie pans were back then, and will have three easy steps:

1. Make and roll out a single disc of dough (see Roll-Out Dough recipes, pages 38–58) and place it in the pie pan.

2. With a hand mixer, whisk, or even a fork, mix together eggs, sugar, butter, and milk.

3. Pour the filling into the dough-filled pie pan and bake open faced, most often for less than an hour. What could be easier than that?!

One of the best things about these pies is that they can be made plain, or they can be dressed up with spices or extracts and topped with whipped cream or a meringue, both of which we have already learned to make.

A helpful hint when baking this style of pie is to place a sheet pan on the lowest oven rack during the preheat so it gets good and hot. Just before baking, place a sheet pan liner or piece of parchment paper on the preheated sheet pan in case of any spill, carefully set the pie on top, and bake. That hot pan will give the bottom crust a good set.

Now let's try out some kitchen cupboard pies.

Shoofly Pie

Makes one 9-inch (23 cm) shallow pie

In her influential book from 1960, *How America Eats*, Clementine Paddleford described three versions of Shoofly Pie: one that results in "a dry pie . . . good for dunking"; "a gooey type with a truly wet bottom"; and "a real cake type." The pie is finished with a crumb mixture on top, or, for the cake type, mixed in with the filling. This version is the wet version, made with a combination of molasses, light corn syrup, and a bit of vanilla. I like it served with a freshly brewed cup of very strong coffee. If you are feeling especially decadent, serve it with a drizzle of chocolate sauce and some Chantilly Cream.

½ recipe Roll-Out Dough (see Roll-Out Dough recipes, pages 38–58)

1¼ cups (180 g) flour

½ cup brown sugar

½ teaspoon cinnamon

½ teaspoon ginger

⅛ teaspoon salt

6 tablespoons (85 g) butter, cold and cut into ½-inch (1.25 cm) pieces

¾ teaspoon baking soda

¾ cup (180 ml) boiling water

½ cup (120 ml) unsulphured molasses

½ cup (120 ml) light corn syrup

1 teaspoon vanilla extract

1 egg, beaten

Chocolate sauce, store-bought (optional), or Chantilly Cream (optional; see Master Recipe: Whipped Cream chart, page 183) for serving

1. Preheat the oven to 400°F (205°C).

2. Roll out the pie dough, place in the pan, and crimp or flute the edges (see How to Crimp, Flute, and Edge the Crust, page 59). Cover with plastic wrap and place in the fridge while you make the filling.

3. In a medium bowl, place the flour, brown sugar, cinnamon, ginger, and salt, and mix well with a fork or fingers.

4. Add the butter pieces into the flour mix and smoosh them with your fingers until they are flattened and well blended. This can also be done by pulsing the flour and butter in a food processor. Set aside.

5. In another medium bowl, place the baking soda, and pour over the boiling water.

6. Add the molasses, corn syrup, and vanilla, and mix well with a fork or a whisk.

7. Add the beaten egg and mix well with a fork or a whisk.

8. Pour the molasses mixture into the unbaked pie shell.

9. Sprinkle the flour mixture evenly over the top of the liquid mixture. Don't pat it down.

10. Bake for 15 minutes. Turn down the oven to 350°F (175°C) and bake for 25 minutes more, for a total of 40 minutes.

11. Remove from the oven. Let cool completely. Serve with an optional drizzle of chocolate sauce or Chantilly Cream.

Maple Walnut Pie

Makes one 9-inch (23 cm) shallow pie

I did not grow up in Vermont's Northeast Kingdom where sugar maples give up their sap in the wintertime, and there are sugaring parties with doughnuts aplenty. The amber liquid that we poured out of the brown Aunt Jemima bottle with the yellow metal cap onto our pancakes was made from corn syrup and artificial flavoring, and it had no maple syrup in it whatsoever. I'm not sure if it was at a friend's house when I tasted pure maple syrup for the first time, or if I decided to splurge and buy a bottle for myself. Whichever it was is really no matter, because after tasting the delicious flavor of the real thing, there was no turning back. I use Grade A Amber Color or, when I can get it, Grade A Dark Color, as it adds even more flavor to this old-time and simple-to-make pie. It is very good served with ice cream on top of a slice.

½ recipe Roll-Out Dough (see Roll-Out Dough recipes, pages 38–58; and see How to Blind Bake a Crust, page 69)

3 eggs, room temperature

⅛ teaspoon salt

¼ cup (50 g) sugar, either brown or granulated

3 tablespoons (42 g) butter, melted

1 cup (240 ml) maple syrup

1 cup (115 g) chopped walnuts

1. Make, pre-bake, and set aside the crust to cool.

2. Preheat the oven to 350°F (175°C).

3. Beat the eggs with the salt until well mixed, but not frothy.

4. Add the sugar, melted butter, and maple syrup and mix again—again taking care not to mix until frothy.

5. Place the walnuts evenly in the pre-baked piecrust. Pour the filling over the walnuts.

6. Bake for 35 to 40 minutes, or until the filling is set. The filling will puff up a bit when baking. Remove from the oven and let cool. The filling will relax back down as it cools.

7. Serve at room temperature. It will store well in the fridge for up to 5 days.

NOTE: Before serving a chilled custard pie, set it on the counter for 15 minutes so you can taste its full flavor.

Transparent Pie

Makes one 9-inch (23 cm) shallow pie

The most basic of ingredients—sugar, eggs, butter, and milk or half-and-half— makes a filling that, simply put, is delicious. It is good both with and without a meringue. If there are any pieces left over, enjoy one with a steaming hot cup of coffee in the morning.

½ recipe Roll-Out Dough (see Roll-Out Dough recipes, pages 38–58)

5 egg yolks

1¼ cups (250 g) granulated sugar

12 tablespoons (1½ sticks; 180 g) butter, softened

¼ cup (60 ml) milk or half-and-half

Zest of 1 lemon

1 recipe Meringue (see Master Recipe: Meringue, page 200)

1. Roll out the pie dough, place in the pan, and crimp or flute edges (see How to Crimp, Flute, and Edge the Crust, page 59). Cover with plastic wrap and place in the fridge while you make the filling.

2. Place a sheet pan on the lowest oven rack and preheat the oven to 350°F (175°C).

3. In a medium bowl, place the egg yolks and sugar, and beat with an electric hand mixer or stand mixer, until light in color.

4. Add the softened butter and beat well.

5. Add the milk and lemon zest, and mix again.

6. Pour the filling into the unbaked dough.

7. Place a sheet pan liner or piece of parchment paper on the preheated sheet pan, place the pie on it, and bake on the lowest rack for 35 to 40 minutes. The filling should not jiggle, and the top of the pie will be a lovely golden brown when done.

8. During the last part of the bake, make the Meringue.

9. Remove the pie from the oven and spread Meringue over the top of the pie while it is still hot, making little peaks and valleys with the back of a spoon.

10. Return the pie to the oven for 6 to 7 minutes to brown the Meringue slightly.

11. Let cool and serve.

NOTE: Meringues are best eaten within 4 to 6 hours.

Sugar Cream Pie

Makes one 9-inch (23 cm) shallow pie

Also known as Hoosier Pie, this is Indiana's state pie. It's a simple homey kind of pie with a satisfyingly smooth texture. You can either oven bake a filling in a rolled-out pie dough or cook the filling on the stove top and turn it into a waiting blind-baked crust. We'll learn to make it both ways. The filling of this eggless pie uses half-and-half or whole milk, and is thickened with flour. Season simply with a bit of vanilla and some freshly ground nutmeg sprinkled over the top. Serve with a big bowl of whipped cream.

⅔ cup (100 g) flour

1¾ cups (350 g) granulated sugar

A tiny pinch of salt

2½ cups (600 ml) half-and-half or whole milk

1 teaspoon vanilla extract

3 tablespoons (42 g) butter, melted

½ recipe Roll-Out Dough (see Roll-Out Dough recipes, pages 38–58; and How to Blind Bake a Crust, page 69)

Freshly grated nutmeg for topping

1 recipe Whipped Cream (optional; see Master Recipe: Whipped Cream, page 183) for serving

TO MAKE A STOVE TOP FILLING

1. Make, pre-bake, and set aside the crust to cool.

2. In a medium saucepan, mix the flour, sugar, and salt with a whisk or fork until well combined.

3. In a small bowl, combine the half-and-half and vanilla.

4. Mix the wet ingredients into the dry ingredients until it looks smooth.

5. Turn the heat to medium-high, add the melted butter, and whisk for about 5 minutes until thick.

6. Remove from the heat and spoon into the pre-baked pie shell.

7. Sprinkle some nutmeg over the top and cool. Serve with a big bowl of Whipped Cream, if desired.

NOTE: For either method, you can use gluten-free flour, or you can replace the flour with 5 tablespoons of cornstarch for a sturdier filling.

TO MAKE AN OVEN-BAKED PIE

1. Roll out the pie dough, place in the pan, and crimp or flute edges (see How to Crimp, Flute, and Edge the Crust, page 59). Cover with plastic wrap and place in fridge while you make the filling.

2. Place a sheet pan on the lowest oven rack, and preheat the oven to 425°F (220°C).

3. In a medium bowl, mix the flour, sugar, and salt with a whisk or fork until well combined.

4. In a smaller bowl, combine the half-and-half and vanilla.

5. Mix the wet ingredients into the dry ingredients until it looks smooth.

6. Whisk in the melted butter.

7. Roll out the dough and place it in the pie pan. Turn the mixture into the unbaked pie shell and sprinkle with freshly ground nutmeg.

8. Place a sheet pan liner or piece of parchment paper on the preheated sheet pan and place the pie on it. Bake for 10 minutes, and then turn down the oven to 350°F (175°C) and bake for another 30 minutes. The pie will finish setting up as it cools.

9. Remove from the oven, let cool, then place in the fridge to chill for 2 to 4 hours or overnight.

10. Top with freshly grated nutmeg and serve with a bowl of Whipped Cream.

VARIATIONS

Sugar Cream and Spice Pie

Add to the sugar:

1 tablespoon ground ginger

½ teaspoon freshly ground nutmeg

1 teaspoon cinnamon

A pinch of ground clove (optional)

¼ teaspoon salt

Elderflower Sugar Cream Pie

Replace the vanilla with 6 tablespoons (90 ml) D'arbo Elderflower Syrup. Yes, I know that sounds like a lot, but elderflower is a delicate flavor and it really does need it all.

Top the cooled pie with:

1 recipe Elderflower Whipped Cream (see Master Recipe: Whipped Cream chart, page 183)

Zest of 1 small lemon

The Good Doctor's Whiskey Raisin Pie

Makes one 9-inch (23 cm) shallow pie

I met Patricia at a community gathering and we quickly found pie to be a common interest for us both. She raved about a special pie made by her uncle, a doctor from the Deep South who was born in the early 1900s. She graciously shared his recipe with me, and I agree that it's a keeper. The good doctor's recipe says that in the fridge "it will keep for days or a week or so," but it's so good it will be finished up long before then. Start this pie the night before by soaking the raisins in good bourbon whiskey. The bourbon whiskey is not cooked or baked out of the filling, so this is definitely a 21-plus pie.

1 cup golden raisins

About ⅓ cup (80 ml) good bourbon whiskey

½ recipe Roll-Out Dough (see Roll-Out Dough recipes, pages 38–58; and How to Blind Bake a Crust, page 69)

A scant ¼ cup (58 ml) water

2½ teaspoons (7 g; 1 envelope) unflavored gelatin

¾ cup (150 g) granulated sugar

2 tablespoons cornstarch

1¼ cups (300 ml) milk or half-and-half

2 eggs, beaten

1 tablespoon (14 g) butter

½ teaspoon vanilla extract

1 cup (240 ml) heavy whipping cream

A small grating of nutmeg

1 recipe Chantilly Cream (optional; see Master Recipe: Whipped Cream chart, page 183) for serving

1. Place the raisins in a small bowl and pour the bourbon over the top to cover. Cover with wrap so the fruit flies don't discover it, and let it sit overnight.

2. Make, pre-bake, and set aside the crust to cool.

3. Place the water in a small bowl or cup and sprinkle the gelatin over it. Set aside.

4. In a medium saucepan, mix together the sugar and cornstarch.

5. Whisk in the milk and eggs until blended.

6. Turn the heat to medium-high and bring the mixture to a boil. Let boil for 1 minute, while stirring constantly in a figure-eight pattern. Remove from the heat.

7. Add the butter and gelatin, and stir until the gelatin dissolves.

8. Set aside to cool, stirring several times so it doesn't gel completely.

9. When cool, stir in the bourbon-raisin mixture and vanilla.

10. Whip the cream until stiff peaks form and fold into the filling.

11. Spoon the filling evenly into the baked pastry shell. Sprinkle over a little freshly grated nutmeg. Let chill in the fridge for 2 to 4 hours until set. Overnight is fine, too.

12. Serve with an optional dollop of Chantilly Cream on the side if you like.

Orange Spice Carrot Pie

Makes one 9-inch (23 cm) shallow pie

Inspired by my very favorite carrot cake recipe that uses cooked carrots, I made a pie version with a pound of rainbow-colored carrots that were in my fridge. While they were cooking, I set out jars of spices that I thought might be nice additions to the filling. Calling my mom's potato masher into service, I then smooshed the cooked carrots as smooth as possible, added coconut milk, eggs, and sugar, and began to add spices—a bit of this, a bit of that—tasting as I went. The final addition was a dash of orange extract. The baked-up pie is a great alternative to a pumpkin pie.

½ recipe Roll-Out Dough (see Roll-Out Dough recipes, pages 38–58)

1 pound (450 g) carrots, trimmed, peeled, and cut into 1-inch (2.5 cm) pieces

3 eggs

1 cup (240 ml) canned lite coconut milk, evaporated milk, or half-and-half

½ cup (100g) granulated sugar

½ cup (100g) brown sugar

½ teaspoon salt

1 teaspoon cinnamon

1 teaspoon ground ginger

¼ teaspoon freshly ground nutmeg

¼ teaspoon ground allspice

A pinch of ground clove

½ teaspoon orange extract

Candied orange peel or rounds (optional; pages 310 and 313) for garnish

1. Roll out the pie dough, place in the pan, and crimp or flute edges (see How to Crimp, Flute, and Edge the Crust, page 59). Cover with plastic wrap and place in fridge while you make the filling.

2. In a medium saucepan, place the cut carrots and cover with water. Turn the heat to medium-high and cook until the carrots are tender. Skim off any foam and discard. Remove from the heat, drain, and puree with a potato masher until as smooth as possible. Set aside.

3. Place a sheet pan on the lowest oven rack, and preheat the oven to 425°F (220°C).

4. Whisk the eggs in a medium bowl or in a stand mixer, until they are light-colored and fluffy. Add the carrot puree, coconut milk, granulated and brown sugars, salt, cinnamon, ginger, nutmeg, allspice, clove, and orange extract. Mix until all the ingredients are thoroughly combined. Turn the filling into the pan.

5. Place a sheet pan liner or piece of parchment paper on the preheated sheet pan and place the pie on it. Immediately turn down the oven to 350°F (175°C). Bake for 45 to 50 minutes. The pie will not be totally set, but will firm up as it cools.

6. Remove the pie from the oven and set on a rack to cool completely.

7. Garnish with optional candied orange peels or rounds.

Honey Walnut Orange Pie

Makes one 9-inch (23 cm) tart or shallow pie

The idea for this recipe came to me in a dream, and when I woke up I couldn't wait to make it. I took it as a very good omen when "Cook with Honey," a Judy Collins song I remembered from my early 20s, began to stream on the internet radio just as I was adding in a cup of orange blossom honey, which I had been saving for a special occasion. The combination of the music and special honey made this pie seem magical. Defrost the delicate phyllo dough in the fridge overnight, and use a light touch when handling.

1 cup (240 ml) honey, orange blossom if possible (see Note)

1 tablespoon flour

12 tablespoons (1½ sticks; 168 g) butter, melted

2 eggs, fork beaten

¾ teaspoon vanilla extract

1 teaspoon orange blossom water (optional)

Zest of 1 orange

1 teaspoon cardamom

⅛ teaspoon salt

2 cups (240 g) finely chopped walnuts

1 pound (453 g) phyllo dough, defrosted

1. Preheat the oven to 350°F (175°C).

2. In a medium bowl, place the honey, flour, 1 tablespoon of the melted butter, fork-beaten eggs, vanilla, orange blossom water, orange zest, cardamom, salt, and 1½ cups (180 g) of the chopped walnuts. Mix together until combined and set aside.

3. Butter the pan with some of the melted butter.

4. Carefully and gently lay one sheet of phyllo dough over the buttered plate. The edges will hang over the rim of the pan. Lightly brush with butter.

5. Repeat with three more sheets of phyllo dough, brushing lightly with butter after each sheet is added.

6. Lightly press the buttered sheets of phyllo down into the pan.

7. Pour in the walnut honey orange filling, using a rubber or silicone spatula to get the entire delicious filling into the pan.

8. As if they were all one, roll tightly the edges of the phyllo dough sheets that are hanging over the rim of the pan, an inch or so toward the center of the pan, so they form a coil touching the inner edges of the pan.

CONTINUED

9. Brush another sheet of phyllo dough with butter and carefully roll it up into one long rope. Lay the rope in a coil on top of the filling. Repeat this step six or seven times more until the entire top of the filling is topped with buttered and rolled sheets of phyllo dough in concentric circles.

10. If you like, take an additional buttered sheet of phyllo dough, lightly scrunch it up and place it in the middle of the pie, tucking it down just a bit into the center of the coils.

11. Sprinkle the remaining ½ cup of walnuts over the top of the pie.

12. Brush any remaining butter over the top of the pie.

13. Bake for 50 minutes until golden brown. Cool for at least one hour before cutting.

NOTE: Orange blossom honey has a mild and light citrus flavor. Clover honey, which is also mild tasting, can be substituted.

Phyllo Dough Tips

"Phyllo" is the Greek word for "leaf," which is an apt description of the tissue-thin dough sheets used in Mediterranean baking that can be found in the freezer section at the grocery store. As it is more fragile than pie dough, a little extra care is needed when working with it. Defrost the dough slowly in the fridge. The sheets can dry out quickly, so keep them covered with plastic wrap and a damp kitchen towel on top to keep them moist. Brush each layer with melted butter before adding another layer. When working with this fragile dough, I say the words "light light light . . . butter butter butter" as I lift and brush each layer. Be patient as you go. The end result is worth the effort.

Vinegar Pie Two Ways

Makes one 9-inch (23 cm) shallow pie

A vinegar pie does sound kind of weird, but when you make one you'll find that it is delicious. This is another easy old-time recipe that uses the simplest of ingredients—butter, sugar, eggs, sour or whipping cream, flour, and, yes, vinegar. When made with apple cider vinegar, the pie tastes like lemon, which is a great place to start. But if you are feeling bold, swap out that apple cider vinegar for one that is flavored. A few of the vinegars on my shelf are apple, blueberry, fig, mango, pear, pomegranate, quince, raspberry, and balsamic. Pick one and give it a try.

As mentioned in the name of the recipe, there are two ways to make the filling for this pie. If you want to use a pre-made cookie, nut meal, or graham cracker crumb crust, then you'll want to precook the filling on the stove, as in option one. Option two is to mix all the filling ingredients together, pour into an unbaked pie shell, and bake. The pies are great topped with whipped cream, too.

I. Stove-Top Vinegar Pie

½ recipe Roll-Out Dough (see Roll-Out Dough recipes, pages 38–58; and How to Blind Bake a Crust, page 69) or 1 recipe Press-In Crumb Crust (see Press-In Crumb Crust recipes, pages 72–77)

3 eggs

1 cup (200 g) granulated sugar

A pinch of salt

3 tablespoons cornstarch

1 cup (240 ml) water

¼ cup (60 ml) apple cider vinegar (Bragg's or another artisan apple cider vinegar) or flavored vinegar of your choice

1. Make, pre-bake, and set aside the crust to cool.

2. In a medium bowl, place the eggs, ¼ cup (50 g) of the sugar, and salt, and whisk until well mixed. Set aside.

3. In a medium saucepan, place the cornstarch and the remaining ¾ cup (150 g) sugar, and whisk to combine. Whisk in the water and vinegar, and mix well.

4. Turn the heat to medium-high and bring to a boil while whisking constantly in a figure-eight pattern. Remove from the heat.

5. Whisk about ¼ cup of the hot mixture to the eggs.

6. Return the egg mixture to the saucepan and cook over medium-high heat, while whisking in a figure-eight pattern, until it thickens and coats the back of a spoon.

7. Turn into a bowl, cover with wax paper, and let cool. Fold into the pre-baked crust.

II. Baked Vinegar Pie

½ recipe Roll-Out Dough (see Roll-Out Dough recipes, pages 38–58)

8 tablespoons (1 stick; 112 g) butter, softened

¼ cup (35 g) flour

1⅓ cups (265 g) granulated sugar

A pinch of salt

3 eggs

¼ cup (60 ml) apple cider vinegar (Bragg's or another artisan apple cider vinegar) or flavored vinegar of your choice

⅓ cup (80 ml) sour cream or whipping cream

¼ cup (30 g) chopped nuts (optional)

1. Preheat the oven to 325°F (165°C).

2. Roll out the pie dough, place in the pan, and crimp or flute edges (see How to Crimp, Flute, and Edge the Crust, page 59). Cover with plastic wrap and place in fridge while you make the filling.

3. Cream the butter, flour, sugar, and salt in a medium bowl using a hand mixer or stand mixer.

4. Add the eggs one at a time, mixing after each addition.

5. Add the vinegar and sour cream, and mix until blended.

6. Fold in the optional chopped nuts.

7. Place in the chilled pie shell and bake for 50 minutes. Let cool.

Two-Way Buttermilk Pie

Makes one 9-inch (23 cm) shallow pie

Having grown up on an Iowa farm, my grandmother, Geeg, was well acquainted with using whatever ingredients were on hand in the larder. This simple pie uses buttermilk, eggs, butter, and sugar, and can be seasoned two different ways—with lemon or vanilla. You won't want to stop just there. It's a pie that can handle many variations, so use your imagination. I've included a few ideas to get you started, too.

½ recipe Roll-Out Dough (see Roll-Out Dough recipes, pages 38–58)

3 eggs

1 cup (200 g) granulated sugar

2 tablespoons flour or cornmeal

4 tablespoons (½ stick; 56 g) butter, melted

1 teaspoon vanilla extract or ½ teaspoon lemon zest plus 1½ tablespoons fresh-squeezed lemon juice

1½ cups (360 ml) buttermilk

⅛ teaspoon salt

1. Roll out the pie dough, place in the pan, and crimp or flute the edges (see How to Crimp, Flute, and Edge the Crust, page 59). Cover with plastic wrap and place in the fridge while you make the filling.

2. Preheat the oven to 425°F (220°C). Place a sheet pan in the oven to preheat.

3. In a large bowl, whisk the eggs and sugar.

4. Add the flour, melted butter, vanilla or lemon juice and zest, buttermilk, and salt. Mix with a fork or whisk to combine well.

5. Pour into the unbaked chilled pie shell.

6. Set your pie on the preheated sheet pan on the lowest rack for the first 15 minutes of the bake to set the bottom crust.

7. Then lower the temperature to 350°F (175°C), move the sheet pan and pie up to the middle rack, and bake for 30 to 35 minutes more. The filling will poof up and there will be a slight jiggle, not a slosh, in the middle when it is ready to come out of the oven. Let cool.

8. Serve slightly warm or at room temperature. Store any leftovers in the fridge.

VARIATIONS

Extras to Add

½ teaspoon almond extract in addition to the vanilla

1 cup raisins or currants

1 cup dried cherries

1 cup toasted and chopped almonds (see How to Roast Hazelnuts, Pecans, or Walnuts, page 314)

1 cup fresh berries

1 cup shredded sweetened coconut

½ cup toasted shredded sweetened coconut (see How to Toast Coconut, page 263) for garnish

Cranberry Orange Buttermilk Chess Pie

Makes one 9-inch (23 cm) shallow pie

Occasionally, there is so much snow at Pie Cottage that I can be snowed in for a week. One year when snowed in, I created this pie using what I had on hand: a blood orange, frozen cranberries, buttermilk, white cornmeal, eggs, butter, and sugar. I called my over-the-fence neighbor to see if she would enjoy some snowbound dessert. She very happily said yes and, after bundling up, walked over to fetch the piece. I put on the kettle for tea and we had a little catch-up chat. A few minutes later my son showed up, followed by the mailman's knock on the door. Now we had a real impromptu gathering, so I sliced pieces for everyone. When my neighbor was ready to walk back home with her promised slices of pie, I accidentally bumped the pie pan, and the pieces landed upside down on the floor. Neither of us could believe what just had happened. What to do? The very next day I made it again.

½ recipe Roll-Out Dough (see Roll-Out Dough recipes, pages 38–58)

1¼ cups (250 g) granulated sugar

4 tablespoons (½ stick; 56 g) butter, chopped into small ½-inch (1.25 cm) pieces, room temperature

A pinch of salt

¼ cup (40 g) fine cornmeal (white or yellow)

4 eggs

Zest of 1 medium orange (about ½ teaspoon)

Juice of 1 medium orange (about 2½ tablespoons)

1¼ cups (300 ml) buttermilk

1 cup cranberries, chopped slightly in a food processor

1. Preheat the oven to 425°F (220°C).

2. Roll out the pie dough, place in the pan, and crimp or flute edges (see How to Crimp, Flute, and Edge the Crust, page 59). Cover with plastic wrap and place in fridge while you make the filling.

3. In a food processor, insert the steel blade. Add the sugar, butter, salt, and cornmeal, and mix until the batter is smooth-ish. You can also do this with an electric hand beater or stand mixer.

4. Add the eggs, orange zest, and orange juice, and buttermilk, and blend thoroughly.

5. Pour the filling into the pie shell. Sprinkle the chopped cranberries evenly over the top of the filling.

6. Bake for 10 minutes. After 10 minutes, reduce the heat to 350°F (175°C) and continue to bake for 50 minutes.

7. Place the pie on a cooling rack and let cool for at least 2 hours so it can set up before serving.

Heirloom Recipes

When I hear in a passing conversation of a family pie long remembered, you would be absolutely right if you imagine that my immediate response is to ask if there is a recipe to share. "I sure wish I had it, and I may know someone who might still." Then begins a short litany of various generations of family members who had been in the kitchen with grandma so many years ago. If I am lucky, days, weeks, or even months later, an email arrives with the recipe.

While I was making the dough for one of these treasures, a great-granddaughter who had tracked down one of her family recipes for me, stopped in to see how it was going. She was my direct connection to her great-grandmother, and I asked her to hold the dough for a moment. Later that day, when the pie had cooled, she stopped by again for a taste. Her eyes closed as she took a bite, and when she opened them, she told me that it was the taste she remembered from when she was a little girl. Now it is a reclaimed heirloom, not only for my young friend, but as a new addition for my family recipes, too.

Buttermilk Bourbon Pumpkin Pie

This is a riff on the traditional pumpkin pie that is made special with the addition of tangy buttermilk and a splash of bourbon. As with all pumpkin pies, pull it from the oven before it is completely set, when you can see a slight jiggle in the middle.

Makes one 9-inch (23 cm) shallow pie

½ recipe Roll-Out Dough (see Roll-Out Dough recipes, pages 38–58)

3 eggs

One 15-ounce (425 g) can pumpkin puree (about 2 cups)

1 cup (240 ml) buttermilk

⅓ cup (68 g) granulated sugar

½ cup (100 g) brown sugar, packed

½ teaspoon salt

1 teaspoon ground cinnamon

1 teaspoon ground ginger

¼ teaspoon freshly ground nutmeg

A tiny pinch of ground clove

2 tablespoons bourbon whiskey

1. Preheat the oven to 425°F (220°C).

2. Roll out the pie dough, place in the pan, and crimp or flute edges (see How to Crimp, Flute, and Edge the Crust, page 59). Cover with plastic wrap and place in fridge while you make the filling.

3. Whisk the eggs in a medium bowl until they are light-colored and fluffy.

4. Stir in the pumpkin, buttermilk, white and brown sugars, salt, cinnamon, ginger, nutmeg, clove, and bourbon whiskey and mix until the ingredients are thoroughly combined.

5. Pour the filling into the dough-lined pie pan. Place in the hot oven and turn down immediately to 375°F (190°C). Bake for approximately 50 minutes.

6. Remove the pie from the oven and set on a rack to cool completely.

Mrs. T's Three Citrus Pie

Makes one 9-inch (23 cm) shallow pie

This easy no-bake filling requires just a wee bit of time on the stove top, capped off by an overnight chill in the deep freeze. Its inspiration came from the Frozen Lemon Pie made by Bess Truman, the wife of president Harry S. Truman. Her original recipe uses ⅓ cup lemon juice, but I've adapted it to include the flavors of orange and lime, too. She said that this recipe serves four, which, at a quarter of a pie per person, is a very large serving. But on a hot summer day, you and a friend might be tempted to eat the whole thing.

1 recipe Press-In Crumb Crust, using graham crackers (see Master Recipe: Press-In Crumb Crust, page 72)

2 eggs

⅓ cup (80 ml) fresh-squeezed juice from 2 oranges, ½ lemon, and ½ lime

2 teaspoons orange or lemon zest, or a combination of both

½ cup (100 g) granulated sugar

1 cup (240 ml) heavy whipping cream

1. Make, pre-bake, and set aside the crust to cool.

2. Separate the eggs and set the whites aside. Place the yolks in a small saucepan.

3. Beat the egg yolks with a whisk or fork until well combined.

4. Whisk in the citrus juice, citrus zest, and 2 tablespoons of the sugar.

5. Turn the heat to low and cook for a minute or two while whisking constantly in a figure-eight pattern. It won't take long for the mixture to thicken. When it does, immediately remove from the heat and, using a rubber spatula, turn into a medium bowl. Be sure to get all of the yummy mixture from the sides of the saucepan into the bowl, too. Set aside to cool to room temperature.

6. In a stand mixer or with and electric beater, whip the egg whites and 2 more tablespoons of sugar until you have medium stiff peaks. With a rubber spatula, gently fold into the cooled citrus mixture.

7. In a stand mixer or with an electric beater, whip the heavy cream, while raining (sprinkling) over the remaining ¼ cup (50 g) sugar until the peaks hold their shape. With a rubber spatula, gently fold the whipped cream into the citrus–egg white mixture.

8. Pour the filling into the waiting crust and freeze overnight.

VARIATIONS

Orange Freezer Pie

Use 2 teaspoons zest and ⅓ cup fresh-squeezed juice from 2 oranges.

Cool Lime Freezer Pie

Use ¼ cup fresh-squeezed lime juice.

Blum's Coffee Toffee Pie

Makes one 9-inch (23 cm)
deep-dish pie

When I was a little girl, my family would travel to San Francisco to visit close friends of my parents. Seeing the lights of the Golden Gate Bridge at night through the windows of their home near The Presidio always felt magical. When our trips coincided with the winter holidays, my mom dressed me in my very best dress, coat, hat, and shoes, and off we went, my dad, mom, brother, and I, to the City of Paris store to see the beautiful 40-foot-high Christmas tree that nearly touched the glass dome ceiling. Then it was off to Blum's, a mecca for lovers of sweets. My good friend Judy brought all of this back to mind when she said to me that I absolutely must share the recipe for Blum's Coffee Toffee Pie with you. But there's more to the story. Blum's also had a shop in Beverly Hills, quite near Haggarty's department store where my grandmother sold fine dresses. I remember that as a special treat, she would take me there and we would sit at one of the tables, in the pink and white restaurant, and enjoy a bowl of ice cream or a slice of this absolutely delicious pie with its chocolate crust, filling, and topping.

CHOCOLATE DOUGH

1 cup (145 g) flour

8 tablespoons (1 stick; 112 g) butter

¼ cup (50 g) brown sugar

1 ounce (28 g) unsweetened chocolate, grated

1 teaspoon vanilla extract

2 tablespoons milk, more if needed

¾ cup walnuts

Butter to grease the foil

FILLING

8 tablespoons (1 stick; 112 g) butter

¾ cup (150 g) granulated sugar

2 teaspoons powdered instant coffee

1 ounce (28 g) unsweetened chocolate, melted

2 eggs

TOPPING

1½ cups (360 ml) heavy cream, chilled

6 tablespoons confectioners' sugar

1½ tablespoons powdered instant coffee

1 tablespoon unsweetened chocolate, grated

TO MAKE THE CHOCOLATE DOUGH

1. In a medium bowl, place the flour, butter, brown sugar, and grated chocolate, and mix together with your fingers or a pastry blender, until well combined and blended. You can do this with a food processor or stand mixer, too.

2. Add the vanilla, milk, and walnuts, and mix again, until the dough is damp but not sticky and tacky. If it needs a little more milk, dribble in a few drops and mix until it feels like a sturdy cookie dough.

3. Roll out the dough between two pieces of wax paper, although it's perfectly fine to press the dough into the pan and up the sides with your fingers.

4. Prick the dough all over with the tines of a fork and place in the fridge to chill while you preheat the oven to 425°F (220°C).

5. Line the dough with lightly buttered foil, making sure that the foil is well pressed on top of it, and bake for 6 minutes. Remove the foil from the pie shell, return the pie to the oven, and bake for 10 minutes more, or until the shell feels dry. Set aside and let cool.

TO MAKE THE FILLING

1. In a large deep bowl, place the butter and, with a hand-held electric mixer, beat until it is light and fluffy.

2. Gradually add the sugar over the top while continuing to beat.

3. Continue to beat while adding the instant coffee and melted chocolate.

4. Add 1 egg and beat for 5 minutes.

5. Add the remaining egg and beat for another 5 minutes.

6. Turn the filling into the baked and cooled chocolate crust, spreading around evenly. Cover with wax paper and place in the fridge overnight, or at least 6 hours, so it can set up completely.

TO MAKE THE TOPPING

1. In a medium deep mixing bowl, place the cream, confectioners' sugar, and instant coffee and beat on high until stiff.

2. Spread or pipe the topping over the chilled filling.

3. Refrigerate for an additional 2 hours before serving.

Mocha Banana Freezer Pie

Makes one 9-inch (23 cm)
deep-dish pie

This easy no-bake filling is a cool way to enjoy chocolate and coffee. The filling starts with a layer of sliced bananas placed on top of a chocolate cookie crumb crust. If you leave out the bananas, you'll have a Mocha Freezer Pie. Either way is really good.

1 recipe Press-In Crumb Crust, using chocolate cookie crumbs (see Master Recipe: Press-In Crumb Crust, page 72)

2 eggs

⅓ cup (80 ml) espresso or strong dark coffee

1 tablespoon unsweetened cocoa powder

½ cup plus 2 tablespoons (125 g) granulated sugar

1 cup (240 ml) heavy whipping cream

1½ teaspoons vanilla extract, divided

¼ teaspoon coffee extract

2 ripe bananas, sliced in ½-inch full moons

2 tablespoons store-bought chocolate sauce for topping

2 tablespoons finely chopped pistachios (optional) for topping

1. Make, pre-bake, and set aside the crust to cool.

2. Separate the eggs and set the whites aside. Place the yolks in a small saucepan.

3. Lightly mix the egg yolks with a whisk or fork.

4. Whisk in the espresso, cocoa powder, ¼ cup (50 g) of the sugar, and ½ teaspoon of the vanilla.

5. Turn the heat to low and cook for a minute or two while whisking constantly. It won't take long for the mixture to thicken. When it does, immediately remove from the heat and, using a rubber spatula, turn into a medium bowl. Be sure to get all of the yummy mixture from the sides of the saucepan into the bowl, too. Set aside to cool to room temperature.

6. In a stand mixer, or with a handheld electric beater, whip the egg whites with 2 more tablespoons of sugar until you have medium-stiff peaks. With a rubber spatula, gently fold the whipped whites into the cooled coffee-cocoa mixture.

7. In a stand mixer or with a handheld electric beater, add the heavy cream, remaining 1 teaspoon vanilla, and coffee extract. Whip on high while raining (sprinkling) in the remaining ¼ cup (50 g) sugar until the peaks hold their shape. With a rubber spatula, gently fold into the filling.

8. Lay the sliced bananas in the bottom of the cookie crumb crust.

9. Lightly spread the filling over the bananas and freeze overnight.

10. Before serving, drizzle the chocolate sauce and sprinkle the optional chopped pistachios over the top of the pie.

Extras

CHAPTER SIX

Celebration Pies

Baking for a celebration is a gift of service from our hearts and hands. It is a beautiful and creative way to mark both large and small accomplishments, as well as the milestones of life: births and birthdays, music recitals and first dance performances and soccer games, graduations, new jobs, weddings, anniversaries, retirement, and celebrations of life. Even the day-to-day joy of being alive is a celebration with homemade pie.

Celebration pies range from tiny tarts that pack a wallop of flavor and happiness in just two or three bites, to full-sized pies with carefully crafted and decorated tops. Being asked to make one is a great honor. When I begin baking a celebration pie, my thoughts turn to what brings me to this moment. I think of who I am baking for, those who will enjoy it, and how blessed I am to be alive and able to share a simple craft I love so much. Each step, from setting up my mise en place to setting a finished pie on the counter to cool, are all done with care. This is baking with intention, and a way to express love.

Sharing a celebration pie brings joy to both the giver and receiver. When dear friends asked me if I would make pies for the wedding of their daughter, I happily agreed. A salesperson that became a friend asked if I would make two pies for a family reunion, and then returned my pie plates with the stories of the multiple generations who had enjoyed them. When I learned how important a birthday apple pie is at the yearly celebration of young friend's family elder, and that she could not attend, I showed her how to make one and she celebrated virtually with her family so as not to miss the occasion.

Whether we are making multiple pies for a wedding celebration, tiny pies for an afternoon of tea and conversation with a good friend, or simply the joy of another wonderful day, let us bring our hearts and hands to the baking counter, use the skills we've learned, and make pies to celebrate and share.

Ice Cream

A scoop, or two, of ice cream on a piece of freshly baked pie is iconic. The fruit and cream blend together and become pie à la mode . . . a classic. The basic technique for the custard for our ice cream is also used for cream pies (see Chapter 3: Creamy Pies, page 174) and the delicious custard sauce from the Irish Apple Tart with Custard Sauce (page 118). My son Duncan McDermott Graham's teaching debut at Pie Camp was not a session on pie making, but on the vanilla à la mode that tops a perfect slice.

Since he pulled a chair over to the baking counter, climbed up on it, and cradled his toddler's hands around a piece of dough that I pinched off for him to play with, Duncan has been baking with me. Those early days were the beginning of a decades' long baking apprenticeship. By watching, listening, learning, and doing, he is now a great home baker and pie maker. He has learned not only my techniques of pie making, sometimes becoming my second set of hands at Pie Camp, but also how I teach pie making, so it will come as no surprise that he is my favorite Pie Camp Counselor. Now, he solo teaches Pie Camp workshops, and I couldn't be prouder.

At his first teaching session, he showed us how easy it is to make the custard, from cream, sugar, and eggs, that's needed to make ice cream. Once the basics were under our belt, he showed us how we could change the flavor using extracts, cordials, and liqueurs, added after the custard is heated. Once the custard was removed from the stove, he poured it through a fine-sieve strainer, stirred it for 5 to 10 minutes, and then set it in the fridge to finish cooling. He had already pre-made some vanilla custard, so he poured it into a countertop electric ice cream maker. In less than an hour, we were enjoying freshly churned homemade vanilla ice cream. Ice cream is a palette for flavor and texture creativity, too. Fresh fruit, chocolate or butterscotch mini-chips, marshmallows, toasted or candied nuts, crystallized ginger, and even chopped up cookies, brownies, cakes, or gingerbread can be added during the churn.

Now, let's get our chill on.

Rescue and Recycle

When I was a Brownie Scout, we made ice cream in an old-style wooden hand-cranked ice cream maker at one of our troop meetings. Even though it took a long time to make, the anticipation of the frozen treat outweighed the wait. Now I rescue and put back into service ice cream makers I find at yard and estate sales. The price is right and it keeps them out of the landfill, too. Manuals can usually be found online.

How to Make Ice Cream

To make ice cream, we will first learn to make a basic custard using eggs, sugar, heavy cream, milk, and flavor additions. My ice cream maker makes one quart at a time, but you can cut the recipes in half for a pint-size version. The steps will be exactly the same.

A tip before we begin: If your ice cream maker uses a metal bowl that needs to be chilled, set it into the freezer the night before, or at least 12 hours before the ice cream maker is to be turned on. You want to completely freeze the liquid sealed inside the walls of the bowl. You should not hear any sloshing when you shake the bowl.

Here's the game plan:

1. Make a stove top custard in either a heavy sauce pan or a double boiler. The double boiler will take a little longer, but there is less chance of curdling the eggs. If they do curdle, we'll learn how to uncurdle them so the custard can still be used.

2. Turn the custard into a bowl and add your flavoring of choice.

3. Stir for 5 to 10 minutes to cool. Place in the fridge to chill for 2 hours or overnight.

4. Pour the chilled custard into the ice cream maker and churn, following the manufacturer's directions.

5. Toward the end of the churn, while the ice cream is still soft, add extras like fruits, nuts, cookies, cakes, and brownies.

6. That's it!

Master Recipe: Ice Cream

Makes 1 quart

This is the basic recipe for Duncan's Ice Cream, which my family loves.

---

2 cups (240 ml) heavy cream

⅔ cup (133 g) granulated sugar

6 egg yolks

⅓ teaspoon salt

1 cup (120 ml) whole milk

1 tablespoon vanilla extract or other extract of your choice (see chart opposite)

Fruit, nuts, or other extras for variations (see chart)

1. Place the cream, sugar, yolks, and salt in a heavy saucepan, or in the top pan of the double boiler, and combine with a handheld beater or whisk.

2. Heat and stir the custard. If using a saucepan, turn the heat to medium-low. If using a double boiler, set the filled pan over boiling water.

3. With a wooden spoon, stir gently and constantly in a figure-eight pattern for about 6 to 8 minutes, until the mixture begins to thicken and coat the back of the spoon. When you see some steaming, you are really close to the custard being hot enough. This will be about 175°F (80°C) or just a few degrees lower. Remove from the heat.

- If the mixture starts to boil, fix the curdled custard by removing the pan from the heat at once and vigorously mixing the custard with a whisk or an electric handheld beater.

4. Place a medium bowl on the counter and pour the custard through a fine sieve to remove any solids.

5. Add the milk and vanilla and stir gently for 5 to 10 minutes to cool. Cover and place in the fridge to chill for 2 hours or overnight.

6. When the custard is completely chilled, pour into the frozen bowl of the ice cream maker and churn for 25 to 30 minutes, or use the manufacturer's instructions.

7. The ice cream will be soft and creamy. Take a taste and scoop it into a container with a top, like a quart-size yogurt container, and place in the freezer for at least two hours before serving.

Ice Cream Variations

Now let's get creative by adding fresh fruits, flavor extracts or liqueurs, cookies, cake, and brownies from the following chart to the Master Recipe. Then we'll go on to making an Ice Cream Pie (page 302).

ICE CREAM	FLAVORING	ADDITIONS	EXTRA STEPS
Vanilla	1 tablespoon vanilla extract		
Orange	1 tablespoon orange extract		
Coffee	1 tablespoon vanilla extract, 2 tablespoons coffee extract		
Coffee Chip	1 tablespoon vanilla extract, 2 tablespoons coffee extract	Add ½–1 cup mini chocolate chip morsels	Gently fold in with a spoon or add at the end of the churn.
Brownie, Cake, or Gingerbread	1 tablespoon vanilla extract, optional 2 tablespoons coffee extract	1–2 cups chopped leftover brownies, cake, or gingerbread	Break up into small pieces and gently fold in with a spoon or add at the end of the churn.
Peach	1 tablespoon vanilla extract	2 fresh sweet peaches, peeled and finely chopped, ¾ cup sugar, freshly squeezed juice of ½ small lemon, optional 1 teaspoon orange liqueur Note: The pieces of peach will freeze solid in the ice cream, so you will want to cut them in very small pieces.	1. Mix the peaches with the sugar, lemon juice, and optional orange liqueur. 2. Place covered in the fridge and let macerate for 1–2 hours. 3. Drain the juice from the peaches and mix ½ cup into the cooled custard before churning the ice cream. 4. Smoosh the peaches a bit more and add 1 cup to the ice cream toward the end of the churning.
Very Berry	1 tablespoon vanilla extract	1 pint berries (strawberry, raspberry, blueberry, blackberry, or huckleberry), ¾ cup sugar, freshly squeezed juice of ½ small lemon, optional 1 teaspoon orange liqueur	1. Mix together the berries, sugar, lemon juice, and optional orange liqueur. Reserve ⅓ cup berries for Step 4. 2. Place covered in the fridge and let macerate for 1–2 hours. 3. Drain the juice from the berries and mix it into the cooled custard before churning the ice cream. 4. Smoosh the remaining berries so they are relatively smooth and add to the ice cream toward the end of the churning.

Ice Cream Pie

Makes one 9-inch (23 cm)
deep-dish pie

Ice Cream Pie is a mix and match affair where you can let your imagination run wild. It's easy, fun, and oh so cool. If you want to make smaller pint-size pies, use 5-inch pie pans or 4-inch tart pans, size down the cookie crumb or graham cracker crust to one-half or even one-quarter, as well as the ice cream and toppings. Traditional pastry dough can be blind baked in canning lids (see Canning Lid Pies, page 131), filled with ice cream and toppings, and popped into the freezer for another fun dessert. So that you can see the frozen layers when the pie is sliced, be sure to give a good solid freeze to each layer before adding the next layer.

1 recipe Press-In Crumb Crust, using cookie crumbs or graham crackers (Master Recipe: Press-In Crumb Crust, page 72)

2 quarts (about 2 L) Ice Cream (see Master Recipe: Ice Cream, page 300)

1 to 2 cups toppings of your choice (see Toppings for Ice Cream Pies, page 303)

1 cup caramel or chocolate sauce, or 1 recipe Fruit Glacé (see Master Recipe: Fruit Glacé, page 192)

1 recipe Chantilly Cream or other flavor (optional; see Master Recipe: Whipped Cream chart, page 183) for serving

1. Make, pre-bake, and set aside the crust to cool.

2. Set the Ice Cream on the counter to soften up for about 15 minutes.

3. Place scoops of 1 quart of the Ice Cream into the crust. Use a spatula or the backside of a spoon to spread the scoops out evenly.

4. Evenly sprinkle half the topping(s) of your choice over the Ice Cream.

5. Drizzle half the sauce over the topping.

6. Place the pan into the freezer for an hour or longer to firm up the Ice Cream.

7. Repeat Steps 3, 4, and 5 with the remaining quart of Ice Cream, topping(s), and sauce.

8. Place the pie in the freezer for at least 2 hours or overnight, so it will cut well when you serve it.

9. Remove from the freezer 15 to 20 minutes before serving.

10. Slice and serve with an optional dollop of Chantilly Cream.

Toppings for Ice Cream Pies

The main thing here is to have fun creating a cool treat that can be different every time.

CRUNCHY	SOFT	SMOOTH
Granola	Raisins	Fruit glacé
Trail mix	Citrus zest	Lemon curd
Crushed nut brittle	Marshmallow fluff	Fruit conserve
Toasted nuts of all kinds	Mini marshmallows	Hot fudge, caramel, butterscotch sauce
Candy bars, coarsely chopped	Chocolate-covered cherries	Whipped cream
Jimmies, sprinkles, and Red Hots	Shredded sweetened coconut	
Finely ground coffee, espresso beans	Nutella, peanut butter, almond butter	
Chocolate- or yogurt-covered pretzels	Fresh sliced or chopped fruit marinated in liqueur	
Candied, chocolate-covered, and honey-roasted nuts		
Chocolate chips, peanut butter chips, butterscotch chips, white chocolate chips		
Crumbled gingersnaps, graham crackers, lemon or chocolate or vanilla wafers, biscotti, oatmeal, sandwich or sugar cookies		

Pie Deconstructed

Makes 4 to 8 desserts

As much as we joke about there always being room for pie, sometimes ending a meal with a full piece is just too much. So here's a way to enjoy a little serving without having to push away the plate or loosening a belt a notch or two. One disc of dough will be more than enough for four to eight servings. Leftover dough scraps that have been frozen and defrosted can be used also. Use a premade fruit filling, and you have everything you need to make a picture-perfect dessert.

½ recipe Roll-Out Dough (see Roll-Out Dough recipes, pages 38–58)

Sparkling, demerara, or granulated sugar for sprinkling

1 recipe Stove-Top Fruit Filling (see page 306)

1 recipe Ice Cream (see Master Recipe: Ice Cream, page 300) or Chantilly Cream (see Master Recipe: Whipped Cream chart, page 183) for serving

EGG WASH

1 egg white plus 2 teaspoons water, fork beaten (or other wash of your choice; see Washes for the Top, page 90)

1. Make the dough and place in the fridge to chill.

2. Preheat the oven to 400°F (205°C).

3. Place a sheet of parchment paper on a sheet pan.

4. Roll out the pie dough.

5. Cut the dough into pie-shaped wedges, or other shapes of your choice.

6. With a pastry brush, remove any extra flour. Place the cutout shapes on top of the parchment-covered sheet pan.

7. Brush the dough wedges with the egg wash and sprinkle with sugar.

8. Place in the oven and bake for 10 to 12 minutes, or until golden brown on top. Your oven baking time may be different than mine, so be sure to look at about 8 minutes to get an idea of how things are moving along. Take them out of the oven and let cool.

9. When ready to serve, place a baked pie-shaped wedge on a plate. Add a few tablespoons of the premade crostatas filling and a small scoop of Ice Cream or dollop of Chantilly Cream.

Stove-Top Fruit Filling

Makes enough to fill one pre-baked
9-inch (23 cm) shallow piecrust

Fruit filling can be cooked on a stove top, cooled, and then used to fill a blind-baked pie shell (see How to Blind Bake a Crust, page 69) or in a press-in crust like Coconut Almond Oat Crust (page 75) or a Pie Deconstructed (page 304). When making a stove-top fruit filling, we'll use cornstarch as our thickener. Top with Whipped Cream (see Master Recipe: Whipped Cream, page 182), either store-bought or homemade Ice Cream (see Master Recipe: Ice Cream, page 300), or with Custard Sauce (page 118). If you need lots of fruit filling, this basic recipe can be doubled, tripled, or more. It will hold in the fridge for up to three days.

3 tablespoons water

¼ cup (30 g) cornstarch

4 cups fruit (about 1 lb; 500 g), cut, sliced, or chopped

½ to ¾ cup (100 to 150 g) granulated sugar, depending on the sweetness of the fruit

A pinch of salt

A squeeze of lemon

A grating of nutmeg

Zest of 1 orange or a splash of orange or other fruit liqueur

SOME FRUIT FILLING SUGGESTIONS

Rhubarb, cut in ½-inch (1.25 cm) pieces, and strawberries

Peaches and blackberries

Gooseberries and red currants

Strawberries and blueberries

Cherries and berries

Nectarines and raspberries

Apricots and blueberries

1. In a small bowl, place the water and whisk in briskly the cornstarch. Set aside.

2. In a medium saucepan, place the fruit, sugar, salt, lemon, nutmeg, and orange zest.

3. Cook over medium heat for about 6 minutes, stirring occasionally.

4. Add the cornstarch mixture, bring to a boil, and cook for 2 minutes more, while stirring in a figure-eight pattern. You will have to stir vigorously as it thickens.

5. Remove from the heat. Turn the filling into a bowl and let cool completely. It takes about 40 minutes to chill in my fridge.

Piecrust Cookies

It is quite easy to pre-bake cookie cutter cutouts made with pie dough, place them on a baked open-top fruit pie or custard pie, use them in Pie Deconstructed (page 304), or enjoy them as little piecrust cookies.

Varies depending on your leftover dough

½ recipe Roll-Out Dough (1 disc of dough; see Roll-Out Dough recipes, pages 38–58)

1 egg white

2 teaspoons water

Sugar: sparkling, granulated, or demerara

Ice Cream (Master Recipe: Ice Cream, page 300) for serving

1. Cut out shapes, letters, or numbers using cookie cutters, or free hand with a sharp knife on a cutting mat.

2. Place the cutouts in the fridge until you have made all the designs you will need and are ready to bake them. If you have made the decorations directly on a counter surface, use a cake lifter to lift and place the designs on a sheet pan covered with parchment or a sheet pan liner.

3. Preheat the oven to 400°F (205°C).

4. In a small bowl, place the egg white and water and beat with a fork. Brush the shapes with the egg white wash and sprinkle with the sugar of your choice.

5. Bake for 10 to 12 minutes. Your oven baking time may be different from mine, so be sure to look at about 8 minutes into the oven to see they have baked to a nice golden brown color. If they are very small shapes, it may take only 6 to 8 minutes.

6. Remove from the oven. Carefully slide the parchment paper off the hot sheet pan and onto a flat surface; let cool.

7. Serve with Ice Cream as piecrust cookies or use in Pie Deconstructed (page 304).

How to Make Fruit Powder

This is an easy way to add a splash of color to creations like Peach Packets (page 138) and other dough tops.

A small bag of freeze-dried raspberries, blueberries, or other colorful fruit

1. In a blender or food processor, place the freeze-dried fruit.

2. Process until very fine.

3. Screen out any larger pieces through a sieve strainer. For raspberries, discard the seeds and keep the powder.

4. Store in lidded glass jars until needed.

Candied Citrus Rounds

These candied citrus rounds aren't hard to make at all and they bring such a special touch to a pie. Be sure to get organic citrus and you'll want slices that are no thicker than ⅛ inch (3 mm). Be sure to save the citrus syrup to sweeten and flavor whipping cream or a pie filling, and it is great in ice tea, too. Shake off any extra sugar and store in a small mason jar. When sugar is called for in a recipe, add some extra flavor with your flavored sugar.

Ice

1 to 2 oranges or other citrus sliced into ⅛-inch- (3 mm) thin rounds, seeds removed and ends cut

2 cups (400 g) granulated sugar, plus extra for sprinkling, if desired

1. Fill a big bowl with ice water and set aside.

2. Fill a medium saucepan with water. Turn up the heat and bring to a boil.

3. Add the sliced citrus rounds and boil for 1 minute. Remove the citrus slices and place them in the bowl of ice water. When they are cool, drain off the water.

4. In a large skillet, place the sugar and 2 cups of water, and bring to a boil. Stir occasionally until the sugar dissolves.

5. Turn down the heat to medium-low, add the citrus slices in a single later, and let simmer for 45 to 60 minutes, turning every 15 minutes or so.

6. When the rounds are approaching translucence, remove and place on a rack to dry for at least 1 hour or overnight.

7. Sprinkle over extra sugar if you like.

8. Store any extra candied citrus slices in the fridge in a tightly covered container for up to a month.

Candied Citrus Peels

When making citrus peel, avoid the white pith as much possible as it will give an unwanted bitter taste. My OXO vegetable peeler makes a very thin strip of peel minus the bitter pith. Be sure to get organic citrus. Make with lemons to top a Lemon Chiffon Mousse Pie (page 228), with limes to top a Helen's Key Lime Pie (page 209), or with oranges to top an Orange Spice Carrot Pie (page 277).

2 to 4 lemons, limes, or oranges

7 cups (1.6 L) cold water

3 cups (600 g) granulated sugar

1. Rinse the citrus well. Remove the peel with a vegetable peeler. Avoid the bitter white pith.

2. In a small saucepan, place 2 cups (480 ml) of the cold water and citrus peels. Turn the heat up. As soon as the water comes to a boil, remove the pan and drain off the water.

3. Repeat Step 2 twice more, but the last time let cook for 30 minutes.

4. Remove the peels from the saucepan and set aside.

5. Place 2 cups (400 g) of the sugar in the saucepan and add the remaining 1 cup (240 ml) water. Turn the heat to medium-high and bring to a boil while whisking. When the sugar has dissolved, add the citrus peels, and turn the heat down to medium-low. Simmer the peels until they become translucent. Remove from the heat and carefully remove the peels with a fork or tongs. Set them aside to cool. Save the citrus sugar syrup to use another day.

6. Place the remaining 1 cup (200 g) sugar in a medium bowl and add the cooled citrus peels. Toss with fingers or a fork until the peels are well coated with sugar. Save this extra citrus sugar and use in recipes or to garnish a pie.

7. Remove the peels and shake off as much extra sugar as you can.

8. Store any extra candied peels in the fridge in a tightly covered canning jar for up to a month.

How to Roast Hazelnuts, Pecans, or Walnuts

It's quite easy to roast nuts, but there is one caveat: watch them carefully. If they burn, they will have a most unpleasant taste. I have seen some instructions that call for baking up to 15 minutes at 350°F (175°C). If I left mine in that long, they would burn. Nine minutes is the maximum time in my oven, but every oven is different. I roast a cup or so at a time and place any extra cooled nuts in a glass jar, store in a cool dark place, and use within 4 to 6 weeks. They are a nice treat to sprinkle on pies or a bowl of ice cream.

As many nuts (such as hazelnuts, pecans, or walnuts) as the recipe requires

TO ROAST HAZELNUTS

1. Preheat the oven to 350°F (175°C) and line a small sheet pan with parchment paper, a sheet pan liner, or foil.

2. Evenly spread the hazelnuts on top and place in the preheated oven to bake.

3. Check after 7 minutes. If the skins have become dark, remove them from the oven, and immediately lift the parchment paper, liner, or foil, out of the pan so the hazelnuts will not continue to cook and possibly burn.

4. When the hazelnuts have cooled, there are two ways to remove the skins.

   • Method 1: Take a paper towel and wipe off as many skins as possible.
   • Method 2: Place the nuts in a metal bowl and place a matching bowl inverted over the top. Shake vigorously for a minute or so. Remove the top bowl, and you'll find that most of the skins have fallen off. Shake the bowl a little to allow the skins to fall to the bottom of the bowl, and then lift the hazelnuts out with a slotted spoon so the remaining loosened skins can fall away.

5. Leave whole or chop as needed.

TO ROAST PECANS OR WALNUTS

1. You can easily roast whole nuts such as pecans or walnuts in the oven for 7 to 9 minutes at 350°F (175°C), too. They have no skin to rub off, which makes it easy.

How to Melt Chocolate

You can melt squares of unsweetened baking chocolate in a microwave, or use a double boiler so it won't scorch. Here's how my mom taught me to do it.

As much chocolate as the recipe requires

As much butter as the recipe requires

1. Boil some water.

2. Place squares of baking chocolate in a small bowl.

3. Pour hot water into a saucepan. Set the chocolate-filled bowl in the saucepan and be sure the water is about two-thirds of the way up the sides of the small bowl.

4. Simmer the chocolate on low to medium-low. Be careful to avoid letting any bubbles of boiling water jump into the little bowl or your silky, melted chocolate will form unsightly lumps. Every once in a while check on the softness of the chocolate.

5. If the recipe calls for butter to be added to the chocolate, place it in the little bowl with the chocolate toward the end of the melt. You can probably add it earlier, but that's when my mom added it. You can add vanilla or other extracts at the same time. Remove from the heat.

6. Stir to blend. If you have one of those teeny tiny whisks sitting unused in your gadget drawer, this would be a perfect occasion to use it to blend the chocolate, butter, and extract, but a fork works well, too.

How to Freeze and Refresh Fruit Pies

Freezing an Unbaked Pie

- Make the pie according to the recipe, double wrap unbaked, label, date, and freeze for up to three months.
- Bake the pie frozen, adding about 15 minutes, and sometimes more, to recommended bake time.
- Make sure you see bubbling coming through the vents or lattice, and in the middle.
- Cover loosely with vented foil if the top is getting too brown.

Freezing an Already-Baked Pie

- Make, bake, and cool the pie completely, double wrap, label, date, and freeze for up to four months.
- When ready to serve, place the wrapped baked pie on the counter and defrost at room temperature for about 30 minutes. Unwrap, place in oven preheated to 350°F (175°C), and bake for 30 minutes.
- Cover loosely with vented foil if the top is getting too brown.
- Let sit for 10 minutes or so before serving.

Refreshing a Pie

- A pie with eggs or dairy should always be stored in the fridge.
- Fruit pies can be set on the counter and covered with plastic wrap, a piece of foil, or a pretty tea towel.
- To deter fruit flies, place a mesh food tent over the pie, or place the pie inside a closed microwave or unheated oven.
- Refresh a fruit pie in an oven preheated to 325°F (165°C) for 6 to 10 minutes before serving.

Twenty-Eight Wedding Pies

"I'd be happy to make them," was my reply when I received a phone call from Rose Ann who asked if I would consider making a dozen pies with a *Twin Peaks* theme for her daughter's wedding reception. I am an artisan pie maker, and by that I mean a pie maker who makes one or two pies at a time, so I really had no idea what I had just agreed to do. I haven't had a TV since the mid-1980s and, because I had never seen the TV show *Twin Peaks*, I did not understand the pie culture that surrounds this cult classic. In my pre-bake research, I found out lots of things.

The Double R Diner's cherry pie features prominently in the series, and a well-known line from the show is, "That's a damn fine cherry pie!" From the start, I knew that cherry pies were a must. When the number of replies for the wedding increased, the number of pies did as well . . . to 28. At eight slices per 9-inch (23 cm) pie plate, this would yield approximately 224 slices. Local berries are abundant in the late summer where I live, so I decided to take advantage of this bounty, along with some sweet juicy peaches, and the mandatory cherries.

With the fillings decided, at least in my mind, I turned my attention to what the top of the pies would look like. I wanted to reflect not only the *Twin Peaks* theme, so very important to the bride and groom, but to celebrate their union. What to do? I know that I learn best by seeing how things are done. I contacted pie-top artist extraordinaire, Jessica Leigh Clark-Bojin, for some practical how-to-do-it advice, followed by a trip to her pie-making studio in Vancouver, British Columbia, Canada, for a one-on-one, hands-on practicum. We used dough that I brought with me, and her techniques showed me how to make the *Twin Peaks*–themed tops that I hoped the bride and groom were envisioning. Afterward, with new skills, as well as a new friend, I headed home to Pie Cottage and successfully put into practice what I had learned. The most nerve-racking part of the entire process was transporting the finished 28 pies to the reception site. But with nary a mishap, I handed them over to the catering crew, and then I sat back to enjoy the celebration. If you are thinking that these must be some very good friends, you are absolutely right. Would I do it again? In a word, yes, but only for my son, if and when that day ever comes.

Plan for Multiple Celebration Pies

Organizing, planning, and pre-making components of multiple pies is key for turning what could be an overwhelming one-day task for a home baker into some multi-hour sessions spread out over a few days, or even weeks. Our game plan will give us options along the way for both dough and fillings. Ready? Here we go.

Step 1. Making Fruit Fillings

OPTION 1. ONE MONTH BEFORE: Prep and freeze individual fruit fillings, with the exact amount of already-made filling needed for one pie in each freezer bag. Mark and date the freezer bags. Repeat for as many pies as you will be making. This step is a big time saver when done ahead.

OPTION 2. UP TO ONE WEEK BEFORE: Make stove-top fruit filling for as many pies as you will need and let cool. Store in the fridge until ready to use. This can be done up to a week in advance (see Stove-Top Fruit Filling, page 306).

Step 2. Make Dough Up to One Month Before

OPTION 1. Roll out half of the dough, fill the pie pans, trim, crimp, and freeze unbaked. Place parchment paper between each filled pan. Double wrap the entire stack of filled pie pans with plastic wrap before freezing. Dough can be in the freezer for up to one month.

OPTION 2. If you don't have time to roll out the dough and fill the pans at this time, you can freeze all the dough discs, and then defrost and roll at a later time, as in Step 3.

Step 3. Roll the Dough

A WEEK OR MORE BEFORE: You can skip this step if you have already rolled, formed, and frozen the pie shells as in Step 2: Option 1. If not, defrost half of the dough discs you made in Step 2: Option 2. Roll out a defrosted disc; fill a pie pan with it, trim, and crimp the edges. Repeat with as many pie pans as you need to fill. You can refreeze them unbaked for use when you are ready to add the fruit fillings and bake the pies.

Step 4. Pie Top Designs

TWO DAYS BEFORE: Defrost the remaining dough discs. Roll out, and then cut out shapes for pie top designs and rounds. Set aside in a safe place (see How to Decorate an Open-Faced Pie, opposite).

Step 5. If Using an Unbaked Frozen Fruit Filling

ONE DAY BEFORE: It's almost the big day and you should be feeling pretty relaxed since all the preparation is done. All we'll do today is bake the pies and let them cool.

- Remove the dough-filled pie pans out of the freezer, unwrap, and set on the counter.
- Partially defrost the frozen fruit fillings.
- Place one semi-defrosted filling in each. You'll see some frozen fruit crystals. Take a wooden spoon and smoosh the semi-frozen filling down a bit to fill the pans as evenly as you can.
- Place sheet pans in the oven while you preheat to 400°F (205°C). Then set the filled pie pans on preheated sheet pans and bake for 45 to 60 minutes until you see steady

bubbling. You may have do the baking in stages depending on how large your oven is and how many ovens you have.

- Remove the finished pies from the oven and let cool completely.

Step 6. On the Day of the Event

This final step, where we top the pie with our baked designs, is the easiest yet.

- Place the already-baked pie tops and designs on top of the cooled filling in the already baked open-faced pies.
- Pack the pies in individual bakery boxes, load them up, and carefully transport them to the event venue.

How to Decorate an Open-Faced Pie

When making 28 pies for a wedding, I pre-baked open-faced fruit pies, and then decorated them with separate round pre-baked pie tops that were personalized with the stencil and cinnamon technique (see Detailed Directions for Marquees, page 320). The tops take only 10 to 12 minutes to bake. After they cool, you'll have a perfectly round and flat top to place on the baked pie. They just have to be finished off with optional pre-baked personalized marquee designs.

Once you have all of your special Marquee Cut Outs baked and ready to go, it's time to place them on top of the cooled pies.

1. Place the baked and cooled pie on the counter.

2. With a cake lifter, carefully center and place a decorated and baked pie top round directly on top of the cooled filling. Hopefully, you made these discs slightly smaller than the filled pie pan so they fit in easily. If not, place it on top of the filling or crimped rim as best you can.

3. If adding a marquee or other shape design on top, spread a teaspoon or two of lemon curd on the center back of a marquees with a small spoon and place it carefully in the center of the decorated round top. Alternatively, you can place the lemon curd on top of the baked round top, and then set the baked marquee on top of it, wiggling it a bit so that it glues itself in place. Both ways work.

4. Repeat with each pie.

5. Take a deep breath and admire your beautiful work.

Some Last Words

If creating a pie with a decorated top is more than you have time for, serve the pies open faced, topped with Whipped Cream (see Master Recipe: Whipped Cream, page 182), served with store-bought or homemade Ice Cream (see Master Recipe: Ice Cream, page 300), or with Custard Sauce (page 118).

Detailed Directions for Marquees

Before you begin, place a sheet of parchment paper on a sheet pan and set aside.

Step 1. Roll and Cut the Dough

A. On a flat surface, roll out a disc of pie dough.

B. Flour the fondant mold design you would like to use. I used one in the shape of a strand of small pearls to be used as marquee lights. Cut a very thin strip of dough the length of the design and place it in the mold. Gently push the dough down with your fingers. Wipe off the extra with the pad of your thumb so that the top of the dough is level with the top of the mold.

C. Using the marquee cookie cutter (or other cookie cutter of your choice), carefully cut out as many shapes as needed for your pie tops. If your hand is steady and you are creative, you could also do this freehand with a sharp knife, or small-scale precision knife, with the dough on a plastic cutting mat. I prefer the cookie cutter, as I will get the same exact shape each time. With the pastry brush, remove any extra flour.

Step 2. Place the Stencil, Apply the Egg Wash, and Add Cinnamon

A. Place the cutout shape on top of the parchment-covered sheet pan. Center the stencil on top of the marquee design.

B. Pour a tablespoon or so of egg whites into a small bowl. Using a silicone brush, apply the egg white on top of the stencil. Try not to slop it on, but do apply enough so that it can cover each of the stencil openings. With your fingertips, press down on the stencil to get the best seal you can.

C. Apply some cinnamon on top.

1. Roll and cut the dough.

2. Place stencil, paint, and add cinnamon.

3. Pat down cinnamon and remove excess.

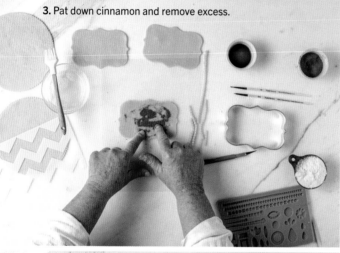

4. Remove stencil and tidy up.

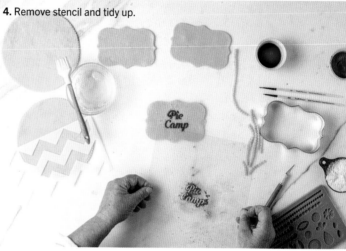

5. Add the marquee lights.

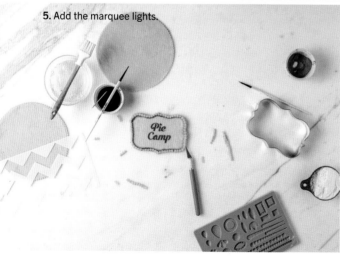

6. Bake, cool, and place on pie.

Step 3. Pat Down the Cinnamon and Remove Excess

A. Pat down the cinnamon carefully with your fingertips. Wipe the extra cinnamon off to the side of the stencil with your fingertips, taking care not to get the cinnamon on top of the dough outside the range of the stencil.

Step 4. Remove the Stencil and Tidy Up

A. Carefully remove the stencil (there will be some extra cinnamon on top) lifting it straight up. Go slowly. If it sticks in any area, tug very gently until the stencil releases.

B. Use the small-scale precision knife to tidy up the cinnamon design as needed. For the blank space in letters like A, O, and P, use the knife to carefully push aside the cinnamon inside of the letter so that the blank space remains. Place in the fridge and repeat with as many marquees as needed.

Step 5. Add the Marquee Lights

A. Paint a bit of egg white on the edge of the marquee. Carefully pull the dough strip out of the fondant mold, using the tip of the precision knife if needed, and lay it on top of the edge you have just painted with egg white. Lightly secure it in place with your fingertips.

B. Repeat Steps 9 and 10 until the strips completely encircle the marquee as one connected strand of marquee lights. Lightly paint the top of the dough strips with egg white.

C. Pour several teaspoons of vanilla into a small bowl. Place a small amount of food coloring on a wooden cocktail fork stick and place it inside the bowl with the vanilla, but don't mix it in.

D. Dip the paintbrush into the area of the vanilla where the food coloring is and brush around the inside edge of the marquee light dough strip. When baked, this added touch will define the detail of the design of marquee lights that otherwise would bake out when the dough puffs up.

E. If you have made the decoration directly on a counter surface, use a cake lifter to remove them and place on a parchment-covered baking pan. Place the decorated marquee in the fridge. Repeat the entire process until you have all your cutouts decorated

Step 6. Bake, Cool, and Place on Pie

A. Place the marquees in an oven, preheated to 400°F (205°C) and bake for 10 to 12 minutes. Your oven baking time may be different than mine, so be sure to look at about 8 minutes into the bake to get an idea of how things are moving along. You might bake one test marquee before committing to placing all of them in the oven. Remove them from the oven. Carefully slide the parchment paper with the baked designs off the hot sheet pan and onto a flat surface. Let cool.

B. Depending on your design, you might either place the baked and cooled marquee directly on top of your already baked and cooled pie filling, or you might set it aside to add as one of the components needed in the final design.

C. When placing a pre-baked design on top of an already baked pie with a full top crust, I spread a teaspoon or two of lemon curd on the center back of a marquee, and place it carefully in the center of the decorated round top. Alternatively, you can place the lemon curd on top of the baked round top, and then set the baked marquis on top of it, wiggling it a bit so that it glues itself in place. Both ways work.

AN EASY VARIATION

Decorate and bake serving-size pie-shaped wedges. After they cool, arrange them on top of an already baked open-faced pie. Leave a slight bit of space between each wedge. Cut the pieces using the space between the wedges as your guide.

NOTES:

- It's fine to carefully wrap and freeze undecorated, unbaked cutout shapes in a sturdy box. Defrost and decorate them just before baking.

- Make some extra shapes in case of breakage and taste testing.

- Before baking, add a sprinkling of sugar to the shapes. Avoid getting any sugar on lettering that may be in the design.

- These baked-up shapes make nice little pie dough cookies, too (see Piecrust Cookies, page 308).

Afterword

The Apple Doesn't Drop Too Far from the Tree

I am an unplanned love child, born between my birth mother's two marriages. A few months before she gave birth to me, she traveled from Ohio to Montecito, California, where she had some family, and she stayed there until I arrived. At the hospital she requested that she not see me, hold me, or be told whether I was a boy or a girl. She gave me up for adoption, returned to her life, and a few months later remarried, telling no one about what had happened except her new husband. She had three more children—the youngest of whom is my sister, Helen. At the ages of 66 and 58, we met for the first time.

For many years, decades in fact, I searched for my birth family, but I always hit dead ends. In 1978, before I was to marry wuzband #1, I wanted to find out if there might be any health issues in my family of origin that could affect my decision to have children or not. My real mom, and by real I mean the one who walked me in the middle of the night when I was teething, bandaged my skinned knees, and sent me to school with endless brown bag lunches, selflessly offered to help by placing phone calls to our pediatrician, who, she said, had known my birth family, and to the lawyer and long-time family friend who had handled the adoption. Unfortunately, both were less than helpful. The doctor hung up on my mom, and the lawyer said that he had burned all his files when he became a superior court judge.

A few years later, I sent a letter to the State of California asking for any non-identifying information from the file that contained my original birth certificate, especially any information which was health related. Not long after, an envelope arrived and, when I opened it, I found a single piece of paper packed with information that my mother had provided to her case manager. Names were not included, of course, but I learned that my mother had been 23, my father

27, and that both had been born in Ohio. It also included:

PHYSICAL DESCRIPTIONS:

Mother: Exceptionally attractive, well and expensively dressed. Fair coloring, blue eyes, blond hair, clear, fair complexion. Poised, self-assured, relatively high intelligence.

Father (according to her): About 6 feet tall, medium build, brown eyes, brown hair, olive complexion, nice looking, brilliant but moody.

OCCUPATION:

Mother: Had been a nurse's aide and group supervisor in a children's home.

Father: Worked in advertising at a television station.

SPECIAL INTERESTS:

Mother: Very good in languages and liked to write but had not published.

Father: Not given.

HEALTH:

Mother: Good health, knows of no mental or physical disorders in family. Maternal aunt has hay fever allergies.

Father: In good health, and she thinks all relatives healthy with no serious or adverse history.

RELIGION:

Mother: Protestant.

Father: Jewish.

During the busy years of raising my own young family, the project was pushed to the back burner. But in the mid-1990s, a volunteer searcher, who aided members of birth trian-gles, was able to locate an address for my birth mother. I sent a card with the words, "We haven't been in touch since . . . [and I gave my birth date]. I would love to hear from you." My request went unanswered for weeks, so I decided to place the call. This was years before easy access to computers and the internet, so I first dialed 411 directory assistance. Within seconds I had a number. My hand was trembling as I dialed, and a few rings later I heard a cheery voice on the other end say, "Hel-Lo." It was her, my mother, the woman who had given birth to me. I would love to say that it was an easy conversation and that she had been looking for me, too, but that's not how it went. Yes, my card had been received, but she had put it away in a drawer.

"What is it that you want?"

The tone in her voice had turned cool now, and I knew she could hang up on me at any moment.

I asked for any information about her and my family of origin that she would be willing to share. I was ready with pen in hand, and I still have the notes I scribbled down with her responses. She told me of the very difficult time it had been in her life, and one that she had tried to place behind her. She told me I had an older half-brother from her first marriage, and there were three children that came, after me, from her second marriage. She asked if I had any children, and I told her of her grandchildren, Sara (15) and Duncan (8). I sensed her reluctance to talk much longer, and I asked if we might chat again after we had had some time to process what had just transpired between us. She agreed, we set a date, said goodbye. A few days later, an envelope arrived with pictures and names, of her children—my four half sibs—and one of her.

Now, 23 years after that phone call, and a year and a half after my birth mother's passing, I was meeting my sister, Helen, who was my mother's youngest daughter and named for her. Coincidentally, Helen was the name of my adoptive mother, too. My sister and I had connected by social media messaging the night before I was to speak in New York City on a book tour. She lives on an island in the Caribbean and has two daughters, both of whom live in the City.

"Would it be okay if my daughters came to the book event?"

Would it? Absolutely. The next night we met. One had studied opera, as had I; and the other lived just two blocks away from where I had on the Upper West Side when I attended music school. We smiled and chatted through the entire evening, and we took selfies with our phones. Soon after, I heard from my sister Helen. We kept in touch over the months, getting to know each other by sharing snippets of our lives. We made a plan to meet in person when both of us would be in New York, which happened just before the photo shoot for this book.

On the day we met, we hugged, not once but twice. We sat down and began to talk, slowly at first, gauging what was appropriate, and feeling how it was to be in the presence of the sister you hadn't known you had. We searched out each other's face, and compared our hair, fine and easily tangled; our eyes, bright blue like our mother's; our choice of blouses that day, flowing in patterns of blue. We talked of our children and, of course, our mother, Helen, who, I learned, loved to cook, bake, tend her vegetable and flower gardens, and read voraciously. All things I love to do, too. Most of all, I wanted to know if our mother was a happy person, and when I asked, my sister immediately took my hand and answered, "Yes, Mom was a very happy person."

We took a cab ride uptown to the apart-

ment of my niece, whom I had met just months earlier, and we continued to share stories of family, and where and how we live. Then we spent the afternoon baking together, for as life would provide yet another coincidence, my sister Helen is a pastry chef. She had for a time even worked in a Santa Barbara bakery that I used to go to and buy an occasional treat. The world is small, is it not? Using her recipe, we made an apple crisp pie, my niece photo documenting the occasion. By the time it had cooled enough to slice, my other niece arrived, and the four of us were getting along with the ease one feels when knowing others for a lifetime. We laughed at the same jokes, shared the same facial expressions and mannerisms, while we ate bite after delicious bite of the still warm pie we had made together.

The next day, all four of us piled into a car and headed to the town, just an hour away, where my sister had grown up. She showed me parks, the school, and each of the houses she had lived in as a girl. As we stopped by each one, I asked her two questions.

"Which was your room?" and "Was it a happy time?"

"Yes," she said. "It was a very happy time."

As our day came to a close, we drove to the cemetery where our mother is buried. Hand in hand, with tears flowing down our faces, we walked to her grave marker. In silence, we each laid a flower on it. Then, Helen introduced me to Mom, and Mom to me. I listened as she told her that if she had been able to meet me, she knows she would have loved me, and I believe I would have loved her, too. For even though we were not to meet in this life, she is in our faces, our eyes, and our love of family, gardens, books, and baking. Because, you see, the apple, it really doesn't drop too far from the tree.

Helen's Apple Crisp Pie

Makes one 9-inch (23 cm)
deep-dish pie

I am grateful to have met my birth sister, Helen, and to have had the wonderful opportunity to make pie with her. As we rolled, baked, and ate this simple and delicious pie, we also created a sweet memory—the first of many that we have now shared. But this pie will always have my heart. Helen says this apple crisp pie is "good at any temperature and particularly delicious the next morning for breakfast."

½ recipe Roll-Out Dough (see Roll-Out Dough recipes, pages 38–58)

6 medium apples, preferably Granny Smith or Honeycrisp, but any tangy apple will do

3 tablespoons cornstarch

⅔ cup (135 g) granulated sugar

2 teaspoon fresh-squeezed lemon juice

½ teaspoon ground cinnamon

¼ teaspoon freshly ground nutmeg

CRISP TOPPING

½ cup (70 g) flour

½ cup (100 g) brown sugar

8 tablespoons (1 stick; 112 g) very cold or frozen butter, cut in small cubes (sugar cube size)

¾ cup (70 g) old-fashioned rolled oats

1 teaspoon cinnamon

1. Preheat the oven to 375°F (190°C).

2. Make and roll out the pie dough. Gently place the dough in a chilled pie pan and crimp the edges about ½ inch above the pie pan to keep all the juices inside when baking (see How to Crimp, Flute, and Edge the Crust, page 59). Set aside or refrigerate if it's a hot day.

3. Peel, core, and slice the apples into nice thick slices.

4. Combine the apples with the cornstarch, sugar, lemon juice, ½ teaspoon cinnamon, and nutmeg, and mix until everything is evenly distributed.

5. Pour the filling into the crust, mounding it fairly high in the middle.

6. For the crisp topping: Combine the flour, brown sugar, butter, rolled oats, and cinnamon in a bowl.

7. Cut in the cold butter with your fingers, a cutting utensil, or the paddle of a stand mixer (which my sister says is faster and easier) until you have a nice crumbly texture.

8. Sprinkle the topping over the apples. Scoop up whatever falls off and find a way to get it back onto the pie. Press the crisp topping lightly if needed to keep any pieces from falling off.

9. Place the pie on a baking sheet.

10. Bake for 10 minutes.

11. Lower the heat to 325°F (165°C) and bake 30 to 40 minutes longer until the crumble is golden brown and there is some juice bubbling through it in a few places. If the juice isn't bubbling out, it's not done yet, so bake longer. Cool to your desired temperature: hot, warm, or cool.

12. Serve with love, always.

Resources

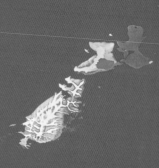

Bibliography

I had the good fortune to have a pie-making grandmother to show me how to make pie, but I continue to learn from bakers and cooks, both home and professional, and from authors who have written about baking. In the pages just before the bibliography of *French Provincial Cooking*, Elizabeth David writes, "There are people who hold that cookery books are unnecessary." Whether slender spiral-bound church cookbooks that I find at yard sales and thrift stores, the volumes that accompany me home from the stacks at my local branch of the North Olympic Library System (a big thank you to Benjamin Franklin, who, in 1731, founded the first free lending library in Philadelphia), and baking and cooking books that find their way onto my shelves, even if it is one small tidbit, there is always something I learn from them.

Like my dear friend, Leigh Olson, who champions the home cook at The Heritage Cookbook Project (theheritagecookbookproject.com), when I am holding a box of well-worn and stained 3-by-5-inch index cards with handwritten recipes, I am holding a family history, for as Leigh says, "Every recipe has a story to tell." So does every pie. You can find a detailed bibliography at artofthepie.com/bibliography.

Sources

All-Purpose Flour, Gluten-Free Flours, Nutmeals, and Other Baking Products

BOB'S RED MILL
www.bobsredmill.com

KING ARTHUR
www.kingarthurflour.com

Butter

KERRYGOLD
www.kerrygoldusa.com

Vegan Substitute for Butter

EARTH BALANCE VEGAN BUTTERY STICK
www.earthbalancenatural.com

Fresh Rendered Leaf Lard

BICHELMEYER MEATS
704 Cheyenne Avenue
Kansas City, Kansas 66105
913-342-5945

DIETRICH'S MEATS AND COUNTRY STORE
www.dietrichsmeats.com

FANNIE AND FLO
www.fannieandflo.net

WAGSHAL'S
4845 Massachusetts Ave NW
Washington DC 20016
202-363-5698

Spices

PENZEY'S
www.penzeys.com

Rolling Pins

FLETCHERS MILL
www.fletchersmill.com

Pie Pans, Plates, and Dishes

Ceramic

EMILE HENRY
www.emilehenryusa.com

LE CREUSET
www.lecreuset.com

STAUB PIE PANS
www.staub.fr

Glass

OXO
www.oxo.com

Pie Basket

Peterboro Basket Company
www.peterborobasket.com

Culinary Equipment and Tools

SUR LA TABLE
www.surlatable.com

WILLIAMS SONOMA
www.williams-sonoma.com

Knives and Cookware

ZWILLING
www.zwilling.com

Made at Pie
Pie Camp Made a
Made at Pie Camp Made
Pie Camp Made at Pie Camp
Made at Pie Camp Made at Pie
Pie Camp Made at Pie Camp Made
Made at Pie Camp Made at Pie Camp
Pie Camp Made at Pie Camp Made at Pie
Made at Pie Camp Made at Pie Camp
Camp Made at Pie Camp Made at Pie Camp
ade at Pie Camp Made at Pie Camp Made at
mp Made at Pie Camp Made at Pie Camp
t Pie Camp Made at Pie Camp Made at Pie
de at Pie Camp Made at Pie Camp Made
mp Made at Pie Camp Made at Pie Cam
Pie Camp Made at Pie Camp Made at
e at Pie Camp Made at Pie Camp
Made at Pie Camp Made at
mp Made at Pie Camp
Pie Camp Made at
de at Pie Cam
Made

Acknowledgments

To bring a book to life is a tremendous team effort, and I am so very grateful to all who have joined "Team Pie" to create Pie Camp.

My deepest gratitude to my agent, Joy Tutela, and my editor, Ann Treistman. My thanks to the entire team at The Countryman Press and W. W. Norton, including Nicholas Teodoro, Jessica Gilo, Will Scarlett, Isabel McCarthy, Diane Durrett, and Jessica Murphy. To the photo team of Andrew Scrivani, Soo-Jeong Kang, and Iah Pinkney, and to book designer, Nick Caruso, for making all three of my books so beautiful.

Thank you to tasters, testers, and teachers, Leigh Olson, Angel Lucas, Catherine Gewertz, Patty Jennings, Teresa Palzkill, Cathy Grossman, Oriana Murray, Debi Davis Koenig, Jane Evans Bonacci, Jenni Field, Mary Alice Boulter, Joe Fisk, Sandra Vahsholtz, Margaret Wilcox, Olivia Vito, Annie Challenger, Cheryl and Philip Young, Marilyn Perkins, Karen Bishop, Patricia Keeney, Sue-Ellen Kraft, Joe Lavin, and my Knitwit Sisters in Port Angeles.

A special thank you to Jessica Leigh Clark-Bojin for sending Pie Camp stencils (multiple times), to chocolate expert Simran Sethi, and as always to Judy Amster-Burton for reading the early manuscript.

To Cindy Ericksen, for your friendship, good humor, calming presence, assistance at Pie Camps, and, along with your husband Paul, for endless tasting and critiquing of pies for this book.

To my son Duncan, for leading Pie Day Camps, testing and tasting, installing new ovens at Pie Cottage, and being the kind and amazing man you are. You will always be the apple of my eye.

To all the pie makers who came before me, those who are here now, and those who are yet to come.

And, finally, to my beautiful sister Helen.

Index